"*I'm blown away at how engaging your writing is, both style and substance. This seems like a really important perspective the church needs to hear, so thank you for being vulnerable and lending your voice to it. It was very well written and a needed message that resonated deeply with me but I've not heard articulated elsewhere very often. Great read, thank you for pouring your heart into this!*" – Scott Monk

"*You might think that an entire book on Job is a lot of pages to devote to asking the age-old question of why? Alanna doesn't shy away from the hard parts of the story. She doesn't sugar coat any of Job's struggles or her own. Instead, she leans into them. In the end, why seems to matter so much less than we thought it did. Instead, it is more of a book about who God really is.*

- *This book is a tender companion to anyone who is wounded or suffering.*
- *These words teach us how to sit beside instead of offering advice.*
- *These words tell a compelling story, but mostly they point to a bigger one.*
- *These words offer no platitudes or action steps, but instead extend truth and compassion.*
- *They do not provide a way out, instead they offer a partner on your way through.*
- *These words do not try to be a shelter in a storm, instead they point us to the beauty in the midst of the storm itself and a promise that you are not alone in the middle of it.*

This book describes a God who is so much bigger and richer than the one we might think we want. It is something I am still reckoning with. It is a beautiful reckoning, some would even call it a re-enchantment."

– Michelle Hurst

"*These are really good and very applicable truths for everyone. I think it's well-written and speaks truth in a compassionate way that will help others put words to their feelings and thoughts.*" – Sonja Lovell

MODERN DAY JOB

Reconciling Disenchantment with God

Alanna Matcek

ISBN 9798991406901 (Paperback)
ISBN 9798991406918 (eBook)
ISBN 9798991406925 (Audiobook)
ISBN 9798991406932 (Hardcover)

Library of Congress Control Number: 2024918507

In memory of you, Dad

TABLE OF CONTENTS

TABLE OF CONTENTS

Introduction: A Letter to the Reader   p.xi

Introduction:
A Letter To You

It's not supposed to fall apart, is it? Life. It's supposed to be this thing that you plan and build and are guaranteed success in when you do it right. That's the story I believed growing up. So, I tried really hard to make it happen, even sacrificing my own needs and happiness at times after making mistakes as if it were in my power to remedy them. Somehow "getting back on the right track" was going to right the ship and ensure my future life would be good.

I thought the first thing I'd ever publish would be something much less weighty. Something *not* birthed out of grieving. I suppose I should have expected this because life has made me good at sitting with people in the trenches. It feels a lot more like home than most other places. What I didn't anticipate was sitting in my own trench resonating with Job.

Looking back, I cannot tell you where it all went wrong. The truth is I'm not sure it ever did. Life isn't supposed to be a fairytale, but then no one tells you that. They read you stories like Cinderella before you've even left the womb. Hindsight being 20/20, I realize now that happily ever after wasn't something I was set up to achieve. Not because my circumstances precluded it but because fairytales are guaranteed to stunt your growth. I didn't know that until I was 41 years old and found myself in the places where I was certain hope could never grow. You just don't know what the wilderness can provide until you're in it.

If you are reading this book, maybe you are there. Maybe you, like me, discovered that the God you've always known isn't the same God you see after that loss. If so, I want you to know that you are not alone. My prayer is that your soul will thrive in the dry places, that springs of Life will quench the parched pieces of your heart, and that your eyes will adjust to finding their way to the Door of Hope in the Valley of your Trouble.

―――――――――――――

"Therefore I am now going to allure her;
I will lead her into the wilderness
and speak tenderly to her.
There I will give her back her vineyards,
and will make the Valley of Achor (Trouble) a door of hope.
There she will respond as in the days of her youth,
as in the day she came up out of Egypt."
~ Hosea 2:15

―――――――――――――

While in the very middle of writing this book, I found myself resonating once more with Job, this time on a deeper level. At the time, I didn't fully understand what was going on. In looking back now, I do. Life never resolves but then we don't want to believe that. We hope for a life that makes sense to us by the end of it. Only that kind of plateau isn't guaranteed. Rather, our destiny is one of wrestling. Like Jacob, if we hold on long enough, we'll find it comes with a blessing *and* a limp.

My husband and I were talking with a friend the other night and he asked why I thought Jesus kept the holes in His hands after He died and was resurrected. I said, "Because it is by His wounds that we are healed." I've found that wounding is essential to the human condition of healing. None of us ever want to *need* healing, but once we've been wounded, we develop an odd gratitude for it because it means, if someone else has been through it too, there just might be hope for curing our ailment.

The longer I live, the more I realize that the story of Job isn't a once and done thing. It sounds like it on the surface, but when you start putting yourself in Job's shoes, you realize that not all suffering is limited to the immediate. Some of it lasts a lifetime even if joy accompanies you. Some pains come back around time and time again. Whether they are at our own hands or just life itself isn't the point. Escaping pain isn't our destiny and that's what we have to reconcile with.

When I wrote the first half of this book, it was on the heels of some very significant events that occurred literally one after the other. I say in chapter one that it felt like they were connected even though none had any link to the next. By the time I began writing, it felt like that season of grief had passed. There were so many shifts in perspective throughout the course of living it and, after a long season of continued upheaval, it felt like I had finally landed.

I didn't anticipate that seasons like that could come around again, at least not with that measure of severity. Yet, that's the thing I think we gloss right over at the end of the story of Job. We act like it's a fairytale that resolves so beautifully, however, that's not really the case. Once you've experienced loss of that magnitude, you realize nothing escapes its grasp. Loss permeates everything. I've come to believe that, should you choose to take Job's approach, you learn to hold the rest of life with a deeper appreciation and a looser grip. It's an odd place of surrender that gives you joy in greater measure right inside the full awareness that you can lose so much at any given moment.

There has to be a place for this. A sustenance for that experience. For me, it's required reconciling the God I believed Him to be with the God He really is. I think there is an element of this that was also true of Job. Our understanding is so limited, but what if that is the thing that we most need? Instead of more knowledge, what if we need more dependency? It doesn't mean God won't expand our awareness. He did that clearly with Job and, as the second half of this book shows, He did the same thing with me. I think He does that with all of us if we allow it, but the pathway almost always involves suffering.

Suffering is often why we get disenchanted. That's not the God in whom we want to believe, but it is the God we need. As you read, I imagine you'll find so many places that you too resonate with Job. His life is a difficult one to tackle and it isn't his life that I set out to grasp or explain. I doubt that is even possible. My hope instead is that we all can find pieces of ourselves in Job's story because, like him, it is to trouble that we also are born. It is how we reconcile this that determines our approach. Like Job, we may start in one spot, move to another, and land in an entirely different one by the end as we navigate deep emotions, battle spiritual forces, and endure pain and misunderstanding in our efforts to reconcile what we knew of God with what He chooses to (and not to) reveal.

I have not arrived at some place that wraps life up in a bow like the fairytales we read. Not life this side of the grave anyway. In fact, quite the opposite. I've found that grief, pain, and suffering will always accompany me. There is no formula for escaping these. There also isn't one for embracing them either. Rather, like every person's story of faith, whether in the halls of scripture or the halls of our homes, we wrestle our way through over and over. Things we've put to rest come back round again. Things we thought we'd never put down find their way to permanent shelves.

It is with much grace that I think we have to hold our lives because, as Job and others around him discovered, there is just so much we don't know and cannot control. Yet, it is still to these things we are called. Life beckons us with a persistence we cannot resist while Death hunts us down with an intense fierceness. My hope is that we develop the perseverance and integrity required to sit in between these while we traverse life on earth, each of us as Modern Day Jobs.

~ Alanna

PART ONE

PART ONE

Chapter One:
Trouble

---

*"Yet man is born to trouble as surely as
sparks fly upward."*

~Job 5:7

L ive long enough and, at some point, you're bound to feel like Job. We all have our own versions of tragedy, don't we? The rips in our dreams, tears in our souls, shattering of foundations we spent years of our lives building upon. Sometimes they come in quiet and slow, rising like a low tide does until it's swallowed most of you whole. Others bulldoze through like a tornado, in and out in moments, leaving behind a wreckage trail that can take a lifetime to rebuild. The suddenness with which tragedy may appear will steal your breath away while the endless lingering of it creates a persistent anguish that fills your days.

The worst of mine occurred in a time continuum like dominoes falling, one after the other with no end in sight, each somehow touching the next as if they were related. I felt lost in space, with no anchor on which to hold, and afraid that everything I knew to be true had been exchanged for this black hole, a vacuum where my formerly solid future was taken. If you've ever experienced one, you know that the devastation left behind after a severe hurricane is often indescribable. Sometimes life is the same way.

Growing up, I thought it was my job to avoid trouble. I believed that if I just did enough, understood enough, and performed well enough, then I could prevent the inevitable. The weight of the world felt like my responsibility and I understood trouble to be something I either caused or created, not an event that every person who ever breathes on this earth is guaranteed to endure.

I didn't know that, even if it were possible to get everything right, your whole world could still fall apart and trouble become your constant companion. So, it felt devastating when, after I finally did attempt to right the ship and began pressing into wholeness, turning my tide for good, all my efforts were seemingly met with one disaster after another. The God who was supposed to love me, protect me, and ensure my safe-enough passage through this world wasn't doing that and I felt left hung out to dry, disillusioned by a reality with which I wasn't equipped to cope.

It seems so many of us can spend entire lifetimes chasing impossible pots of gold at the end of unreachable rainbows. The things we want to be true often aren't and the things we wish weren't can become our truest realities. As a child, I learned to carry around with me this nagging sense that perfection was possible and it was my duty to ensure nothing got messed up. Recently, I started calling that place "The Land of Should" - where everything is how we believe it ought to be and nothing is as it shouldn't. We can get stuck there if we choose, fighting so hard against reality, as if there were another option when really it's just a scene we dreamed.

It's taken me years to understand why Job had the perspective he did. It's because The Land of Should *wasn't* a dream he dreamed. It was real. He understood something only our souls can see. Ecclesiastes 3:11 (CJB) tells us that, "He has made everything suited to its time; also, he has given human beings an awareness of eternity; but in such a way that they can't fully comprehend, from beginning to end, the things God does." We are finite beings, limited by time and space, yet our hearts, minds, and souls know and long for another way.

We will never escape Eden. It is the imprint of our origin, the beginning of every person's story. When we long for The Land of Should, we are really longing for Eden, for eternity, for the way and location that is stamped on our very souls. The place where things are as they were always intended to be and where God is exactly how we need.

I didn't see it coming – my life's entire implosion. Then again, who ever really does? Looking back now, it seems like a quick movie scene where a building is demolished in one fell swoop. At the time, it crept in more like a rising tide that slowly swelled into a tsunami only to be followed by years of ebb and flow. I'm not sure I've ever seen it fully recede and it might never do so. That is just the nature of some tragedies. Maybe you've experienced the same. Whatever the situation you now find or have found yourself in, just know - you are not alone. Trouble finds us all.

When my dad died and my husband left, they happened in such close succession that I found my last name to be something that stung and somehow suspended me in space. My name didn't belong anywhere because the two men whose names had shaped who I'd become were gone. I wasn't fully ready to change my last name when I got married again and it took me a while to adjust. It's funny how things like that affect you once you have a choice you understand the meaning of.

I know now what a name represents, what you bring to it, how it precedes you as you live. There are so many ways when you marry into a family that you either become like them or you stand out as the one who is different than everyone else. I often tend to fall into the latter category and, looking back, I suppose that's been true of my life since day one. Last names aren't always things you grow into, sometimes they grow into you.

You can bet that when tragedy strikes, as it always does, someone will inevitably say, "Pain will make you better or it will make you bitter." Often Job and his wife are compared as the two sides of that coin. The unspoken truth is – we all understand Job's wife. We get her comment, "Curse God and die." She wasn't just being bitter. She was broken, hurting, lonely, her whole life ripped apart all at once too. Although the focus was on Job, her identity was no less under assault than his own and both of them stripped of the ability to find solace in the other one. That's the thing about life – it doesn't happen in a vacuum. The fallout doesn't just affect us or even our household. It affects so many people and circumstances around us. Sometimes you look around and witness devastation with effects like a nuclear bomb, extending for miles beyond what the eye can see.

At the time it all imploded, I didn't want to curse God, but I certainly wanted to control Him. I wanted Him to be the God I'd conjured up over several decades, the One who protected me the way I felt I needed protecting, who ushered in a particular kind of compassion, who wouldn't make me traverse the wilderness alone. I didn't perceive myself as being a stubborn Israelite. Despite my aversion to the word "deserve," if I was being honest, I wanted a world where what I believed I deserved was what I got.

I needed a God who didn't designate desolate places as His meeting spot with grieving souls.

Overwhelmed by the loss He'd allowed and, like a genie I could place my wishes upon, I wanted Him to fix it all, to make the pain bearable and the circumstances less awful. Waking up day after day to the same devastating scene that sometimes got significantly worse before showing any sign of improvement at all felt impossible. It's funny how in the worst situations, we turn to the people who've also been in the worst situations and make their words our own. I did that on repeat with Job, for the first time aware of how one could wish to the very depths of their soul not simply to die but to have never even lived at all.

For months after my dad died, maybe more than a year really, I couldn't bear to listen to songs that in any way represented death, much less death turned to life. Once I could finally bear to return, I stood in church for nearly two years straight with tears streaming down my face, begging the God I wanted Him to be to make it all not true, to change the words to almost every song that was sung. I clung to my version of compassion like a lifeboat all the while railing against Him and what He'd allowed in my life as Job had. Finding myself disillusioned with my understanding of who I had believed Him to be, I struggled to see the heart of a God who loved me.

Disappointment is often used to describe our relationship with God, but in instances of deep pain, disappointment alone just doesn't quite cover it. I looked up the word disenchantment the other day. It is defined as "a feeling of disappointment about someone or something you previously respected or admired."[1] That fits better. Where disappointment leaves you feeling like it doesn't express the depth of your experience, like maybe a glimmer of hope still exists, disenchantment goes right to the core of identity and what feels like irredeemable loss.

It is the same reason we hear so many people discussing parent wounds, holes left where the roles their fathers and mothers were supposed to play in their lives were empty, or worse – destructive. As humans, we create these images and expectations of who people should be, so when we find them to be less than that,

4

particularly in significant roles, we are not merely disappointed.

Instead, we feel a deep sense of abiding loss that affects our very core. We no longer believe safety is possible and think that perhaps our sense of belonging and understanding of not only ourselves, but of them, is gone. So, it's no surprise then when life comes calling and God answers with a resounding, "I'll allow it," that we often feel shocked or leveled, and a deep desire to escape comes over us.

The Garden of Eden was a place of safety, security, provision, and connection. It is where we humans were fully known, loved, and understood, where disconnection did not exist. When circumstances bring nothing but trouble, especially upon the heels of us doing the very things we believe or perhaps know are loving, honoring to God, or exemplify mercy and justice, it can feel soul crushing. Over time, that weight gives way to an undercurrent of abandonment.

We know things like that don't happen in Eden and we believe a God who loves people enough to die for them doesn't allow it. So, we don't know what to do when He does. We ask ourselves, "What now?" Reconciling these seemingly different people - who we believed Him to be and who it now appears He is - feels impossible.

If you have ever experienced trauma or walked with someone coping with trauma, you know what I mean. Receiving the shocking news that their spouse has been cheating on them for years can send them into a tailspin that some people never recover from. Burying a child? There are no words. So many tragedies not only alter our perception of the other person or God, but also ourselves and everything that held together our understanding of how to operate in the world.

When my world fell apart, I was wholly unprepared for God to allow everything I knew of myself, my world, and my identity to be torn apart. Nothing was untouched and I didn't want to have to sift through the burnt pieces to determine which ones to keep. It seemed incredibly unfair to expect my children to do it too, especially while their family was splitting at every seam. The injustice that accompanies tragedy is overwhelming at times and we grapple to find even one thread of hope at the end of our ropes. God seems distant at best, unreal or cruel at worst. A God who loves us would most certainly never allow these to be our realities, right?

Job clearly felt the tension between reality and belief just as we do. Until then, he was a man of faith, praying over even the unintentional sins that his children *might* have committed. To imagine that the One he trusted most would allow all this was a gut punch unlike any other.

> **Maybe you've been there or are there now. The place
> where Disenchantment defines your days, where you
> think maybe this whole God thing is just not good
> enough to be true.**

I've had to wrestle with those questions too. What kind of God would allow me to see Him as not good? What kind of God allows people claiming to represent Him to be unkind, even brutal, to harm more than they heal, to serve up judgment and condemnation in doses we hope God Himself wouldn't swallow? What type of Heavenly Father would ever allow my life to be demolished and then send me to wander in desolate places, seemingly alone, with no sense of direction or hope that I'd ever escape?

When Job's life fell like dominoes, one immediate blow after the other, he uttered over and over how he wished he'd never been born. He cursed the ground, the day of his birth, and ever having experienced life at all. No amount of empathy can prepare you for living the actual reality of indescribable pain and loss.

On my worst days, I spent hour after hour on the bathroom floor, my tears and soul-wrenching sobs pouring across the cold tiles as I watched everything I once knew to be true slip away into the cracks. I understand now why Job's friends came and, upon seeing him and the demolition of his life, sat in complete silence for an entire week before any of them dared to speak. There are some griefs so deep that no words of comfort or solace can relieve.

Throughout his railing and deep anguish, Job begged God for an audience. He just wanted to *know*. Don't we all? We want to *know*. *Why* is this happening, what has caused it, what can be done, when will it end, *what now*? For heaven's sake, *where* is mercy? *What is going on?* Over and over we beg for answers and shout demands into a black sky, often receiving only silence in response.

We don't know it, but when tragedy strikes, we want the same thing as Job. He wanted to know that God was still on the throne, that even though his own identity was unrecognizable in the context of all he'd ever known, God's hadn't changed at all. He needed to know that his identity wasn't gone right along with his life's implosion. Job needed to experience that trusting the One he had for all these years wasn't a waste and that, even in the not knowing, his identity rested on the name of the One who held everything in place.

God never told Job why as far as we know. He didn't pull back the curtains of time and show Job how Satan was working overtime on him. He didn't reveal the annals of history to come and how many billions of people would analyze his life. He simply showed Job Himself and said,

You trusted Me before and you need to trust me now. What I have done and will do from beginning to end is eternal. You are finite. That sense in your soul, that longing for The Land of Should, for a return to Eden, is well placed. But, you are going to have to trust that although things are exactly as they Shouldn't Be, while you are here on cursed ground without a way of escape, I have not changed.

God makes no promises to erase our loss or to undo our pain. He doesn't even say He will ease it. Instead, He promises that He will be enough for it all. Honestly, at the time, it doesn't feel like it – and often not for years, or maybe even a lifetime after. He doesn't *feel* like enough. Because enough has always been defined as having something more than just God. That's the nature of humanity and life on earth. God wasn't enough in the Garden of Eden and He isn't enough now - that's the lie Satan sold Eve, the one Adam swallowed, and the one we all wrestle with every day, whether we believe it or not. The truth is the God we believed Him to be, the one we stand in the aftermath of our life's destruction disenchanted with, that God was never going to be enough. Not for this reality.

In *The Lion, The Witch, and The Wardrobe*, the children arrive in Narnia and are told about Aslan, the great lion who is both ferocious and gentle all at once. Susan asks Mr. Beaver, "Is he – quite safe? I shall feel rather nervous about meeting a lion." Mr.

Beaver replies, "Safe? Who said anything about safe? 'Course he isn't safe. But he's good. He's the King, I tell you."[2]

And that's just it, isn't it? We desperately believe we need a God who is safe. One we understand. One who controls the world in such a way that we feel continually loved, cared for, where our sensibilities aren't unduly challenged, and our lives feel at peace – or at least like the possibility is always on the horizon.

We want a God that comforts us in our troubles, but never allows the trials to be too severe. Maybe for our enemies, but not for us. We want a God who doesn't endure long with injustice, who rights wrongs and swiftly so, and who would never for one second call out much less punish anything we might consider sin because He is altogether too busy forgiving us. He understands that "we know not what we do" and we are only human after all.

If we are honest, every single one of us wants some version of God made in *our* image, not His.

So, what do we do when we come face to face with the real one? The God who allows terrible tragedy, who gives Satan freedom to open fire on our lives with assault weapons no human could ever devise? Reconciling our fabricated understanding of God with the actual reality of Him is an incredible challenge many of us choose not to face.

Darkness is easier. Loving everyone and ignoring sin will straight up win you accolades on this planet. Why choose to face any version of God other than the one that is safe? Because reality affords us no other option if we are to ever find our way back to Eden. That's why. It's the only place to fully know and be known, to see God face to face with nothing to distort the view. It's the place where shame disappears and true love abounds.

Your soul, my soul, every soul that has ever graced this planet is bound to it. We are born with hearts of flesh and souls immortal. This world was created for perfection but is coded – temporarily – for desolation and destruction. This universe is a hard place where we need a God who isn't safe.

Only a God who is good but also quite dangerous can be trusted with the injustices making headline news and knocking down our doors every day. No God who is safe enough will ever allow our children to die, our homes to be taken, our identities ripped apart, and still have the courage or ability to redeem our days. That takes a bravery that only a certain kind of soul will undertake.

It's literally the story of Jesus. He left everything good, connective, whole, and safe and came to a place dirty, scarred, full of people without faith, or in His own words upon seeing us, "they were harassed and helpless, like sheep without a shepherd." *That* is the effect of sin upon a world destined for glory. We can't start at the end and work backwards. We must start at the beginning and work forward. When you realize that everything *starts* with glory, goodness, and beauty, then you realize the incredible tragedy it is for that to be marred, broken, and tainted.

It's only a redemption story because Eden is where it began.

So, of course our hearts grieve and our souls feel emptied when we realize the truth of where we have come to be and the kind of God we actually have versus the One we imagined we needed. Of course we feel disenchanted. The only God we've ever conceived of is gone and no longer good enough to our mind's eye, and we are left with nothing with which to console ourselves. We don't want a God who allows tragedies because we want the God of Eden who stays inside the Garden gates where everything is always good. Who we need is Emmanuel - God with us - the One who bears our burdens, carries our sorrows, and is deeply acquainted with our grief in a sin-soaked world.

What we often mistake as the truth is really the same lie Satan has been telling us since the dawn of time - "I know who God *really* is, and He's holding out on you, so you cannot trust Him." What he didn't mention is that because God *is* exactly who Satan knows He is, he understands God is not safe but is in fact very, very good. He knows that God created a world of safety, goodness, and provision where He placed us to enjoy it. He understands Eden and the significance of not being in it. He also knows that that same God, in His goodness, doesn't force us to love Him or choose Him, but gives us the option to know what He knows - to experience not only the good we were designed to eternally enjoy, but also the evil that Satan himself is trying to dole out at every moment.

God doesn't withhold knowledge or opportunity and He doesn't force His agenda on us. Rather, as a result of His goodness, He leaves the choice with us all the while warning us that we aren't prepared to handle the choice of being like Him without Him.   Just as we cannot send our 5 year olds out into the world to handle it alone - they are simply not equipped and never will be in their 5 year old state - we cannot be sent into a place other than Eden without a God whose heart is good but most definitely not safe. You cannot do battle in a safe zone, friends. Earth is not safe and we are wholly unprepared for this fact. We were built after all for Eden.

Only a God who has created a world where we don't know shame, don't experience pain, don't endure disconnection or suffering, can guide us through a world where all of these things are our daily realities. Only He can navigate the minefields of a world where Satan is prince and we are sought to be his subjects. When Paul said that "our struggle is not against flesh and blood, but against evil spiritual forces in the heavens" (Eph. 6:12) he meant that with all seriousness. It really is. Satan doesn't care about you or me or any other person he's ever met. He cares only that he gets one up on God and if he gets to sacrifice one of us to make that happen, well, that's just the cherry on top. It was his agenda all along - destroy everything God treasures most.

We always think it is about us, but the truth is the battle started before the dawn of time and has always been about Satan getting his licks in on God. We are simply casualties of his war upon the heavens. Thus, it comes as quite a shock to the system when we realize that the God we've conjured up cannot live only in Eden. He, like us, has to leave. It's the only way to still have us. That is the God we need. The One who won't simply heal or even prevent our wounds but will allow them because He understands that they are necessary and part of life in this place. The only God we can trust is One who allows grief and suffering to be the way in which He overcomes the curse we all face. The God who leaves Eden to pursue us.

Satan's agenda is rather short-sighted. He may be hell bent, but he's focused primarily on temporary destruction and loss because it's all he's got. He doesn't hold the keys to eternal salvation. God is in the business of redemption, creation, and restoration, and eternally so. Although He longs for us not to partner with Satan in the destruction of our lives, taking good God-given desires in the exact opposite directions of His design for us, He also is unwilling to leave us in that place and let Satan have the last word. That's why He works for our good in *all* things, even absolute destruction and desolation. It's why, when we left Eden, He did too.

And so, we find ourselves disenchanted, in a place where things are not at all as they should be, with a God from Eden that isn't enough for the hard realities around us. We find ourselves in need of a God no longer only in Eden, but the God of Heaven and Earth. Reconciling ourselves to that is the journey.

Chapter Two:
The Way Through

"There are better things ahead than any we leave behind."

~ C.S. Lewis[3]

Exponential courage is required to believe in a God who allows absolute tragedy but somehow has a heart that is good. Eden is the only place where life really makes sense to us. Life outside the Garden? Not so much. It's the reason we laugh about people saying world peace is their ultimate dream while at once secretly desiring the same thing. What wouldn't any of us give up right now to have it?

Oprah Winfrey once said, "I know for sure what we dwell on is who we become."[4] Scripture says the same. If you focus on disappointment, you will spend your days becoming a person disenchanted with God, perhaps not believing in Him at all. The things you once knew to be true will fade to black and you'll believe that your former understanding of hope, in any form you can really swallow, is gone. When that type of disillusionment sets in, it starts to feel like there is no other option but to soothe your soul by doing God's job yourself. So, you set out to right the wrongs, heal the hurts, and make the world a better place.

The alternative is anger, a hostile resignation that leaves a bitter taste in your mouth for God and what He's allowed. Your days are spent missing out on goodness because you are clinging to injustice. Even if you recognize there is no remedy, no justice that will undo it all, you nevertheless stubbornly dig in your heels and demand understanding for your plight. I have to wonder if that isn't one reason

Job demanded over and over for an audience with God.

When your life has been leveled and you have nowhere else to go because everything, quite literally, is gone, who else is there to turn to? No one has the power of God. Only He has the power to undo what has been done. No human can bring your children back to life, restore your fortune, heal your physical body, and guarantee you anything but a wretched existence for all of your days. Only God can. The reality though is that is not what we want.

If we are really honest, we don't want redemption. What we want is to never have needed it at all.

The truth of my own story is that I didn't want God to bring goodness out of the tragedy in my life. Quite frankly, living through that process was a nightmare in so many ways. Making it through looks good on paper but enduring it is brutal. What I really wanted was to never need the goodness or restoration that life after tragedy can bring. I'd rather it have gone right the first time and people to have done what they were supposed to so that this kind of suffering and anguish could have been avoided by us all. Instead, I was left with broken dreams, absent hope, and a God that seemed to care about anything but my soul.

Alcoholics Anonymous offers a 12-step program, the first of which we all are destined to wrestle with in some form or another if we are to ever move the dial past disenchantment. Theirs says, "We admitted we were powerless over alcohol – that our lives had become unmanageable."[5] If we are honest, we need to admit the same thing – just about life itself, not alcohol. Each of us longs for fulfillment at a soul level, but that only comes through the willingness to allow God to be who He really is. It's embracing acceptance. Acceptance not only of our world's condition and our soul's needs, but also God's true identity. He is good, but He is not safe. He allows tragedy. He redeems the grave. He blesses His enemy and He makes war on all that would destroy the beauty of what He's created. He allows a path we would never, ever choose.

Job wasn't living a sin-filled life. He wasn't destroying his neighbor or climbing the ladder of success at his family's expense. As far as we can tell, he was respected, well-known, loving, faithful, reverent, and wise. He lived a good life and sought to honor God at levels that most of us don't. Yet, his life was the one destroyed and put on display. That just sits wrong, doesn't it? If he'd been a terrible person, we could reconcile ourselves to the fact that he suffered so much, even if the punishment seemed a bit too much for the crime. That wasn't the case though. It makes us uncomfortable that we can do it all right and still experience trouble.

We are painfully aware of our powerlessness over the world, the unmanageable pieces of our days. It's a difficult thing to exist in a world where such terrible transgressions have been committed and not be able to rectify all the wrongs, isn't it? How many of us wouldn't jump at the first chance we were given to abolish so much of history? Slavery, communism, genocide, hate, racism, rape, and on and on and on. We get so disheartened by trying to do good in a place that seems to absorb life like the grave. We don't realize it, but *that* is the knowledge of good and evil. It's not just knowing what the world is like without evil, but knowing precisely how it is when evil reigns. Knowledge isn't a mere intellectual exercise. It is an immersive experience.

It took me years to begin to understand why God answered Job the way He did. If you read the discourse between the two of them once God finally pulls the curtain back just enough to answer Job, His response is intense and seems like He's ignoring Job's plight. He details His authority, His practices, His vast knowledge and understanding with broad strokes, specific detail, and a mighty strength. It all seems wholly unrelated to what Job was experiencing. That's because He was speaking not as the God walking with Job in the safety of the Garden of Eden, but as the God of Heaven and Earth dealing with Job's plight outside of Eden's gates in a world warring for his very soul.

The truth is that life outside the Garden *is* a war zone, so rather than trying to recreate what He's already done, God's focus is on preventing us from being taken as eternal prisoner. He knows what it means, the chains and bonds to which we will be held. He knows the suffering we will endure, so He does what any good parent would do in the face of no other choice. He allows us the pain of war while rescuing us from its permanent effects. We may not be able to change our children's circumstances all the time, but we can often mitigate their damage.

Children inherently know and accept what we find to be so

hard as adults. Just today, my 8 year old stepson found himself in a situation where he was being bullied. His response to the bully wasn't one of wanting a Dad who was safe. Instead, he told the bully that his Dad was big and assured this kid that his Dad would not be safe in the face of such attacks. That's the kind of God we want too. One whose heart is good but whose being is dangerous. A God who doesn't take injustice lightly, who may not do things the way we think should be done, but who nevertheless has the ability to traverse this world the way it is. The problem is reconciling that God with the one we conjured up when we were dreaming of living in Eden. We want His goodness without needing His protection and safety.

Disillusionment is a tool that will either lead us away from God or straight into His arms. It takes immense guts for someone who has been hurt - by the church, by manmade systems that don't represent the heart of God, by people who most certainly aren't Jesus and don't look a bit like Him despite what they *say* - to return to a place where they could be hurt again. I don't condone returning to abusive homes, toxic relationships, or people determined to walk on you. That's never healthy. I do, however, believe that redemption can be found in the same locations where pain was birthed. You don't have to return to your family of origin to find love and belonging in another family you join. You aren't required to go back to the same church that broke you in order to find the incredible richness that walking in connection with others at a different church can afford. You aren't obligated to adhere to the same ideologies, principles, or mindsets that cost you dearly in order to embrace still having ideologies, principles, and mindsets.

The truth is that when our lives are falling apart, all we want is for God to put the pieces back together like Humpty Dumpty again, don't we? We don't want to be changed. We don't want to know His greater plan. We don't care if our character will be improved or our faith more solid or our future better. We just want the pain to stop. We want today to be like yesterday, not tomorrow. *Yet, the only way to embrace tomorrow is by living through today.* That's the one day we never want to live through when we're sitting in the ash heaps of our lives. The problem is - God doesn't do things the way we want.

We love to quote the verses about God's ways and thoughts

being higher than our own. They are, but it's hard to believe that's true when you look at the world today. It's hard to own that when it seems like a good God wouldn't allow this type of catastrophe to touch His creation. He wouldn't choose people to represent Him whose hearts aren't good, actions worse, and responses anything but like Jesus. I don't know about you, but I can get pretty wrapped up in simply *feeling* better. I imagine Job would have gladly taken up feeling better had it been offered. If you look around, you'll see that so many of our social justice missions, as wonderful and vitally necessary as they are, center their focus on helping people to *feel* better rather than to truly *be* better.

The difference between disenchantment and faith is satisfaction. We don't look for contentment much though, do we? It's human nature to seek new things, new experiences, and to never let ourselves settle into one thing or place for too long. We crave instant gratification, all of us, in one way or another. Sometimes it's for good reason. However, if the mission is for our lives to actually improve, then at some point, we have to be willing to let improvement do its work to satisfy our hearts and fulfill our needs.

We often confuse the desire to *feel better* with the need to be made whole. God doesn't always answer that desire. Sometimes His response is to give us more of Himself in a way that seems harsh, unkind, or irrelevant to our predicament. What Job saw after God spoke was that His heart was for Job, not against him. He saw a God whose heart was holding all things together while Job's world was falling apart. A safe God cannot handle both. For me, living in the space between disenchantment and satisfaction meant I had to stop looking to my circumstances for contentment. I'm not going to lie to you and wrap all this up in a pretty bow like I've conquered discontent. I haven't. I'm as fully human today as I was then. What I have learned is how to navigate it.

One of the worst parts of enduring tragedy is knowing everything doesn't resolve. If you've ever experienced severe anxiety, you know – that feeling that you just *have* to get it handled *right now,* that you *need* to talk, to work it out, to *do* something to fix it *immediately.* Tragedy though will stop you right in your tracks. Some things just *can't* be worked out.

When they carried my dad out of the house in a black bag, I didn't think I would keep breathing. Time kept going but my understanding of it stopped as if the clock itself had turned off. Nothing was worse than experiencing the full reality of him being gone. There was no future reality that could ever replace right now, nothing to look forward to where life with him would come back around.

I'm as certain as I'm breathing right now that he is in heaven. I have absolutely no doubt I will see him again one day. But the only way that happens? My dad had to die and, one day, my kids have to go through what I did. They will experience my body being carried out. And *that* is the tension in which we live, isn't it? We just don't get to escape it. This world is not our forever home no matter how much we try to make it so.

If this is where you find yourself wrestling right now, I get it. I understand where you are at. Where hope is lost and life feels anything but bearable. I'm not here to sell you a tale, distract you with platitudes, or pretend that life isn't what we both know and experience for certain. If you are in the trenches, that's not what you need to hear.

The Valley of the Shadow of Death isn't where we sing for joy or tell jokes to ease the ache. It's not where you're going to pull yourself up by your bootstraps and bulldoze through the pain until it disappears. This is where you bring the truth, where you shed light on the darkest places. Where you show up with all your pain, all your doubts, all your fear. It's where your disenchantment with how things are and who God is fills the air. It's the place that the unspoken feels more true than all else you hear and you wonder if perhaps you'd been getting it wrong believing in God for all these years.

Let me tell you something, friends. Job wanted to *know*. He wanted an audience with the Most High and he did not relent until God appeared. Your circumstances are going to shout at you to let God just fade right into the background. You will have days when Jesus is the last name on earth you want to hear. The plight of this world and your own soul will cause you to question whether living was ever worth it at all. When that day comes – and it will – know this: it matters. All this you are suffering, everything you have endured, there is a place for it, a plot you didn't write but are experiencing, and everything that has led you here and everything that will carry you forward – it matters. My encouragement to you is – don't give up. Not yet.

I know you don't think you can. What I'm asking isn't a mustering through or soldiering on though. It's a waiting. It's an active space of rest where you see it through a little longer, let it resonate a little deeper, and ask the questions you haven't yet. Like Job, you *insist* on finding out who God Himself really is. Wait until it is with *Him* that you have had an audience.

> Don't let your pain be the only thing that informs you
> and this world your only lens through which you see
> Him.

Where you are drenched in sorrow, where your spirit aches with dread, where your heart feels heavy and you are certain this is the end, make one thing your mission: Don't go out without knowing. Don't leave faith in the dust or God in the rearview mirror. Reconcile your disenchantment. Rest in the very hardest places. I know it feels impossible. I know what I'm asking may be the most insane thing you've ever heard. I get it. I've been there. I can't promise you a specific outcome with certain details intact.

All I can say is this: the journey is worthy of making, even if it doesn't have the initial desired result. The wilderness has a way of changing what we desire most. It reshapes our heart's longings and fills them with what we most need. Friends, that is the essence of disenchantment – it's letting go of the God we wanted, the one we admired and enchanted ourselves with, and embracing Him for the God He really is.

Chapter Three:
Character on Trial

"True character is revealed in the choices a human being makes under pressure. The greater the pressure, the deeper the revelation, the truer the choice to the character's essential nature."

~ Robert McKee[6]

I have both a friend and a son who are push through no matter what guys. They'd rather get everything completely wrong and have to rise from the ashes twice than they would sit still with awfulness for even a moment. Maybe you're different. Maybe you don't rush headlong into battle or bulldoze your way through life. Perhaps you aren't the kick and scream, dig in your heels type. Maybe you're the one with a quiet ache, the stoic who still believed in God when you had no reason left, certain He wasn't going to let it end the way it did. In the aftermath, you sat on that bench for a while, certain in your soul that another chapter was coming around the bend. Maybe you are the one who realized in your disappointment that no one was coming and no story continuation would be written, so you let your belief, your trust, your hope in Him fade. Turning away, shoulders hunched, heart aching, you walked quietly into the distance alone.

Job sat for heaven only knows how long in a place of turmoil, physical ailment, and suffering. His days in that space are not numbered for us. All we know is that they occurred and one day down the road they ended. The space that lingers between those two is where we often find ourselves. It is the place where discomfort calls us to lean in, to be vulnerable, to say with honesty how much we hate it all. When we don't rail, don't spit venom at the sky, or kick and scream against God, we can wake up instead to a quiet disillusionment where no words seem to fit. We linger in the place between not understanding and what comes next. I wonder what would happen if we recognized that it is in that very place that God leans in close. He too wants to know. "What will he choose? Does she know how much I love her? Will Satan win the heart of this one?" I wonder how He can bear to watch. It must be a torturous existence to see the creation You have made covered in sores and wounds, with gaping holes in their soul that You cannot immediately mend.

Part of knowing God as the one of Heaven and Earth is understanding how true He will always be to His character. He cannot lie, cannot cheat, cannot shift things to seem a little different. He is unable to manipulate or remove our right to choose. Forever, He will be our staunchest advocate – even to the gates of hell. While Satan will literally break down our door and barge in with a relentless deluge of reasons why God is not for us and we need to choose him instead, God will remain silently on the porch, waiting for an invitation to come in. He has every intention of cleaning up the mess, righting the wrongs, restoring the broken, and healing the hurting places. It's just that He wants to do it *with us*. He knows it is the only way we will heal.

What Job didn't know is that *God* pointed him out to Satan. After his customary romp around the earth, Satan had come to God looking to cause trouble. He didn't come alone. He came with the audience of God's leading angels while they were reporting in to the throne. God could have waited until they left before He spoke, but He didn't. Instead, with an audience of heaven, hell, and earth before Him, God steered Satan in the direction of Job.

> "The LORD said to Satan, 'Have you considered my servant, Job? There is no one on earth like him; he is blameless and upright, a man who fears God and shuns evil.'" (Job 1:8)

At first it seems pretty awesome – God's endorsement. It is glowing – "*no one on earth like Job.*" Yet, when the full reality of their conversation sets in, and Satan focuses his entire attention and resources on Job, it seems so unfair, doesn't it? I'm sure everyone watching agreed. I imagine that when Satan told God he couldn't get to

Job because of His protection and God granted him access, every angel, demon, and living creature immediately whipped their eyes in Job's direction, zooming in on a story that would come to occupy the annals of time forever.

There was a reason for leaving Eden. Yes, sin was the crux. But I believe there was another one – an undercurrent that was the effect of sin. I'm convinced it was that we could never fully know, understand, or appreciate God for all He really is if we'd just stayed in Eden. Yes, we would have known goodness, glory, and perfect communion nonstop had we stayed forever in the Garden. It was what He intended. But in Eden, we never would have known what it meant to join God in the cost of being true. We didn't need to.

There is something we don't understand about the undercurrent of God intending for good what Satan uses to destroy us. Sin itself, our circumstances, trials, things that will inevitably level us – they are quite often terrible. God *isn't* saying those things are inherently good when He says He's working for us. He never wanted us to experience those in the first place. What He means is, "*I am going to use inevitable tragedy for good in your life if you let me. Where Satan brings unavoidable destruction, death, and pain, I will bring redemption, healing, and life abundantly.*"

Before Satan became who he is now, he was Lucifer – the most beautiful angel of all. Created by God and at His side for what seems to be a good while. The angels knew that if they weren't answering to God, they were to Lucifer. Only God knew betrayal was coming. Only He knew that He would have to be true to Himself, casting Lucifer out of the heavens, granting the angels a chance to choose their master. I'm sure it was a painful day when it dawned.

Character always comes at a price.

Yet, we never expect to have to pay the cost, do we? The price character is tagged with is something we intend to capitalize on, not owe. But paying for something is the only way you ever really know its worth to you.

Job had set his life up and I get it because I did too. I knew the places I had gone wrong and, just like Job, I prayed God would forgive my children for things neither they nor I realized they might do against Him also. I begged in earnest that God would save my marriage, my father, my family, my job, my home. I asked Him time and time again to make good on His promises. I wasn't perfect but I was being faithful, walking true, and sacrificing myself for His good over and over again.

Although I didn't expect that He'd just be a genie in a bottle who gave me whatever I requested, I did expect that my efforts would garner me at least some type of reward. Some piece of good in the here and now to cling to. The sacrifices I had made were not small and I knew that, even where I had gotten it all wrong, He could redeem. So, I begged Him to do so. I followed hard after His heart and took to Him my tears and aches. I asked Him to give me whatever it took to make life as I knew it work.

I don't fancy myself Job, the most righteous person on the planet. I don't believe God stood in heaven when Satan showed up and called me out by name like He did Job. He most certainly could not say of my life that I was the only one with that level of integrity on earth as He had Job. I am, however, entirely certain that when Satan came to God seeking permission to destroy all that I held close, God answered the same way. He granted allowances for destruction, knowing it was my character on the line, not my comfort.

We deceive ourselves into believing that our comfort is God's main concern, don't we? So, when that is ripped from us, we start to doubt His love. One by one, God allowed every single one of the things I listed - and more - to fall like dominoes in my life. Each direction I turned after the one before failed me disappeared like the ground beneath me. It was a season filled with quicksand, sinkholes, and neverending earthquakes.

Although I thought I'd already learned that comfort was never going to fulfill me, I didn't expect that the God of Heaven and Earth would grant Satan authority to wreak havoc on my life or my family's lives. So, when it happened, I didn't understand that it wasn't because I was getting it all wrong or because God wanted to teach me a lesson. Where Satan meant for it to destroy me, God allowed it because He believed in me.

Even the quietest stoics among us have a breaking point. All of us have a piece of our souls that shatter in silence where, once we feel that deep, abiding ache for long enough, we set the towel down in defeat and simply walk away with our heads to the ground. I have to wonder if God doesn't sob, if His soul isn't wrenched to its very depths when that happens. Because the thing is - He knows.

He knows how much we need Him. He knows how exposed we are alone. He knows from His own personal walks across the dirt of this earth just how lonely, desolate, and painful traversing this world can be. There is nothing His heart desires more than to bring us home, to restore Eden.

But friends, this isn't that part of the story. The one where we return home. The one where Eden is rebuilt and our lives are restored. This is the part where He remains true to Himself – and to us – and allows Satan the opportunity to destroy everything that ever made us believe in Him at all. He allows our faith to be tested, not just so Satan will know where we stand or even so we will know what we are made of. He allows it so we will know Him as _He_ really is.

I've said since I was a little girl, "I just want God with skin on." And every time it's felt like God has failed me, I've gone in search of that. I've recreated God in man's own image more times than I can count. I've fallen so incredibly in love with the God in mankind that I've forgotten at times that God Himself existed at all. It must be a painful thing for Him to gently pry our fingers back, pricking open wound after wound, leaving trails of blood from the spikes where we had created a version of Him that we wanted so very much, clinging to it no matter how much it hurt us.

It must be grievous to watch us take the most beautiful desires and opportunities He has placed in our hearts – where we can meet Him most – and run straight in the opposite direction. I cannot fathom the pain it causes to see not only your own dreams fall apart, but the dreams of the ones you created to dream with you. His heart must break over and over again when He has to say in a near whisper, "Child, this is not who I am and this is not what I have created you for."

Granting freedom is perhaps the most painful cost a parent will ever pay. It is so much easier when they are little and cannot choose for themselves how they will live or what they will do. Those days are short and come rapidly to an end. Over the years, but in what seems like an instant, they are off making their own choices or experiencing the results of other people's choices over them.

It is a difficult thing to spend year after year planting values, seeds of hope, faith, and wisdom, and nurturing the soil in which their young hearts and minds grow only to one day have to let it all go. To let them decide for themselves, allowing them to throw stones against all that you taught them was worthwhile and true should they choose to do so. To let your child make their own way in the world, knowing there are still days when what they need most is you (all the while not forcing yourself on them), is one of the hardest things a parent will ever do.

Not all children are born into homes where their parents are creating a version of Eden for them. All too many are born into places of tragedy and pain, arriving in homes seeping with disillusionment, laced with hate, their value shoved onto a shelf in the basement, abandoned and alone. Children in these situations don't arrive necessarily believing that God is watching over them, ensuring they will have a good life. They're already experiencing the opposite of what we call good.

Instead, they believe that if God really was the God of Eden, of true goodness, He would come rescue them from life as they know it. No matter how we start and no matter where we end up, we all still wrestle with the same thing. We want a God with skin on who makes the pains of this life go away, who rids us of the difficulties of being human. We want this world to be enough and His promises to be true right now in ways they can only be when the final Day of Redemption comes.

———

Friend, God will never take away your choice. Your choice of how to see Him, how to see yourself, whether to believe all of this is a hoax or the one true reality. When Satan asks for and is granted permission to demolish beautiful things in your life, God will always afford you the opportunity to choose whether you trust that He is who He says He is and that He believes in you.

The song says, "*His eye is on the sparrow and I know He watches me.*"7 If that is the case, then there isn't a day of your life, not a hair on your head, or a moment of your story that escapes His glance. When the rest of heaven looked away, when Satan gave up and left God to restore Job's days, God's face remained steadfast in its place.

His eye is on you. He takes notice of your days. When you think all is lost, when the absolute worst of your days come calling and knock you the farthest down you have ever been, that is when His breath is closest. It is when He longs to show you that the heart He had for you in Eden is the same one that beats for you now. That how He showed Himself to be good there, He will show Himself to be strong and redemptive now.

The key is in the willingness to wait.

It's the place we most want *not* to be. It's where tragedy and faith collide. It takes more faith to believe that God can restore or redeem something than it does to believe He can create nothing out of thin air. We are bent to destruction and we believe that, even if it is restored, it will never be good enough. That good enough only exists when nothing ever gets marred in the first place. We don't want to trust that leaving Eden, that God removing His hedge of protection over our lives will actually be the place that our faith has the greatest opportunity to grow. Redemption is painful and not what we would ever choose. We want it done right the first time.

So, what if this is right? What if this *is* the first time? What if this was the plan all along? Not for our destruction but for our belief? What if we needed to believe not just in God and His goodness, but in ourselves and our ability to join Him in something way more purposeful than a perfect experience in the Garden of Eden? What if the only way for us to truly know and be known was to leave Eden and enter this place that all too often feels like hell? I am convinced that whenever Satan zeroes in on our lives, determined to destroy us, God does likewise, determined to thwart not his plans but his purposes in those.

Arlington Cemetery will forever be hallowed ground in my life. Burying someone there on Memorial Day, listening to Amazing Grace on bagpipes, watching the flag be folded and handed over in grief, hearing shot after shot ring out – it stays with you for all of your days. I can't even watch a similar pretend scene on a tv show or movie without it bringing me to tears. The value we place on the lives of soldiers who willingly go into battle for strangers they don't even know, with ideals and principles they're barely old enough at enlistment to fully understand, is enormous. It should be. Nothing really brings the worth of something to light quite like life and death. So, what if this is it? The crucible. The place we find out, not whether God is good or not, but whether we *want* Him - and whether *He* really wants *us*.

It's impossible to know something's value unless you can lose it.

You either pay the price for it or it has no worth at all. What we experienced but would never have known we understood in Eden is just that - God's value and our own. We never would have understood the worthiness of living in perfect harmony, God's goodness abounding at every turn, if we hadn't experienced the depth of evil and all its effects.

It would have been impossible to appreciate a God willing to battle in the spiritual and physical realms for our very beings if we had remained in a place protected from it all. We wouldn't understand the value of being chosen nor of choosing if the depth of that cost never presented itself.

I'm not suggesting God required sin and shame in order for us to know Him. I don't believe His intent was ever this. It couldn't be because His goal in creating us was to be *with us* – *always*. Life outside of Eden, where death and destruction are the name of the game, that was never His way. That is Satan. That is evil manifested in every possible direction. God could've made it go away, yes. He could've been a dictator who directed all traffic and ensured us lives of ease. But to do so would've required that He be untrue to His character, that He remove the possibility of grief. What we don't understand is that while our own will tear every piece of our hearts and souls to shreds, His is deeper.

He didn't lose one child, one life, one 100 year span. He didn't suffer for a century and then it ended. The assault on His heart, His creation, His beloved treasured people (which is *all* of us, whether or not we believe in Him) – it began thousands of years ago and still has not ended. He doesn't watch one child be crippled or lost without escape. He sees billions. Every day. The assault on life isn't limited to people either – it is His entire creation right down to the ground beneath our feet.

What we have to understand is our God is not a God who withholds. In planting the tree with the fruit of the knowledge of good and evil in the Garden of Eden, He left it up to us – how much we wanted to know - of Him, of Satan, of ourselves. The experiences were never required. We could've gone on in constant harmony for eternity. In fact, He tried to make that our reality by giving us the command *not* to eat the fruit. He never wanted us to experience this. He never wanted it for Himself. However, because He is good, because He is not safe, because He is the fullness of all there is, He never withholds the choice.

He will always grant us the ability - to know good *and* evil, joy *and* sorrow, pain *and* healing. Although we never *had* to leave Eden in order to experience God's fullness, He created a path for us in case we did. He knew what could exist inside its hedges and what could not. So, He made a way – a way for us to find our way back home should we ever choose to eat of the fruit and truly know what all of us do now.

The beauty is this: If we were going, He was going with us. If we were going to know, He wanted us to know Him outside the Garden too. The knowledge of evil wasn't the only thing we hadn't experienced while in Eden – it was also the goodness that comes from experiencing God on a different level. Life post-shame. That is the heart of a God who channels His goodness as the undertow of tragedy, the One of whom we can join with the saints of history to say, *"What you intended against me for evil, God intended for good."* (Genesis 50:20, BSB)

That's just not how it *feels*. Our hearts and lives were created for Eden, for safety, for light places where love abounds. It sounds glorious, doesn't it, to be in constant communion, no worries to disturb us, no griefs to pain us, no losses to level or trouble us, and no stressors to keep us awake? It's the kind of gloriousness I dream of daily. The only reason I do though is because I don't live in Eden, and I never have, not even for one day. I appreciate its value because I've experienced life outside its gates.

I know now what it means to have a God who is willing to champion me in the face of the most brutal enemy that exists. Can I be honest though? I don't like it. Not for one single second. My heart screams in deep pain every time I'm hit with another sting from the grave. I still beg God to take it away. My humanity never ceases to paralyze me somewhere along the way. I have to force myself to return to the same place, to *teach* my eyes to see – to *learn* to walk by faith.

No one tells you, but the sun doesn't shine once you leave Eden. It's pretty dark. There's a lot of smoke and haze. Acrid smells, shouts of pain, a lot of destruction through which you daily weave your way. It's no picnic. There is little to no light for your path. That's why we need a God who makes a way. Who creates streams in the desert, provides manna in the wilderness, and who promises this isn't our resting place. We need a God who sees what we can't, who won't try to make earth a safe haven but rather comes Himself to be our shelter, our light, our fortress, our shield. He enters into the destruction and desolation and offers the one thing we need most. It was never Eden. It never will be.

It's Him. It's always been Him.

Chapter Four:
When Hope Takes a Back Seat

"Hope is the last thing ever lost."
~Italian Proverb[8]

Hope feels like a fickle thing, doesn't it? Always coming and going. We try desperately to put it in the driver's seat, to make our dreams come true, our hopes realized in the present day. When you read the story of Job, he started out the same way, with prayers that God forgive his children even for times when "they know not what they do." Yet, in the aftermath of the days of his disaster, Job doesn't seem to spend a lot of time envisioning hope on the horizon, waiting for that positive turn of events. If you've ever experienced a true measure of the depth of pain and loss that Job did, you know why. When life leaves you sitting in devastation like a tornado, hope feels like it vaporized with the wind.

Hope is the last thing you have the ability to hold onto
because it is the very thing you've lost most.

There came a time in my own story when I sat in my therapist's office, my voice straining just to whisper, tears streaming down my face. I told her, *"I can't do it anymore. I'm not going to try to hope. All of mine is gone. I am going to just let all of you who still have your hope intact carry it around for me. I don't have the strength."* Maybe you can't imagine even uttering those words. Maybe setting down hope seems absurd to you. For me, there was a great weight lifted when I let hope go. It no longer summoned me, sapping my strength. Hope is a heavy thing to carry when you are mired in grief.

One of the things they teach you time and again in counselor training programs is to help people envision hope on the horizon. They tell you people need something to live for. The problem is that sometimes tomorrow looks too much like today, so living for tomorrow doesn't always work. There were days when all I did was crawl my way through. I didn't summon courage and couldn't conjure up hope. So, I just allowed myself to be. All too often I had no energy to do anything else. If you've been there, you know. For the first time ever, like Job, life had sapped me of the ability to do all else.

Brené Brown encourages us that the path to rising strong is allowing yourself to sit in discomfort.[9] She's right, yet the hardest thing to do when life gets discouraging is to simply be. I've found it's also in allowing yourself to have days where hope not only does not abound, but where a shred of it doesn't even exist on the horizon. I think we've told ourselves for maybe centuries now that hope is our bread and butter, that hope is what will keep us going in times of trouble. Over and over again we're told, *"Don't give up hope!"* Although that's not terrible advice, sometimes hope can be a necessity while not being a priority. Sometimes it's okay to leave hope up to someone else to carry while we prioritize our own mental, emotional, and physical health. People don't say that enough, but it's true. It's okay to choose healing for yourself.

I doubt when Job went through all he did that he thought for one second that he was choosing himself. Yet, that's nevertheless the story I see. He didn't have hope and he didn't have anyone on whom to hold. So, he simply didn't. He laid his hope and his body down. He wept, scraped his sores, cried out to the God of the sky, and didn't seek solace in his friends or his wife. Job didn't have the bandwidth to hold onto hope and that is a depth of grief I now wholly understand. When hope gets too heavy, where do you go?

I was reading recently about the time Jesus was talking with His disciples when things were getting intense in ministry and people had started turning away. Many of His followers had begun to count the cost and concluded it was a higher one than they wanted to pay. So, Jesus asked His disciples, *"What about you, do you want to leave too?"* Peter replied with perhaps the best answer ever given. He said, *"Lord, to whom shall we go? You [alone] have the words of eternal life [you are our only hope]."* (John 6:68, AMP)

I love this. Sometimes when you find yourself in that place, the one of desperation, of loss unending, of pain indescribable, there is nowhere to go. You can't escape and there isn't a circumstantial change that will make it all go away. Sometimes someone else just simply has to be there, holding onto hope for you because you have none.

The price of following Jesus is exchanging the hope of this world for identity in Him.

There is a reason He calls us to "take up your cross and follow me." (Matthew 16:24, CEV) The only path through this world is one that involves suffering. He knew that. It's why He came. Not so we wouldn't suffer, but so we wouldn't do it alone or in futility. For the longest time, I didn't accept that deal. I wasn't okay with a God who allowed so much suffering, at least not in my own life. I'd rarely, if ever, asked why but I begged Him on repeat to make it stop. He didn't. That's not the story He came to offer. Hope in the currency of heaven doesn't look like hope here on earth.

My dad died never having let go. His eyes were so trained on seeing God's goodness in the land of the living that he refused to let go of what was possible. If there was one thing I could change about his death without stopping him from dying, that would be it. I wish my dad would have seen that death here is possible, that even though God *could* choose at any moment to rescue us from our circumstances, sometimes He doesn't. We have to prepare ourselves for that fact. When my dad was dying, he never said goodbye. Instead of letting go, he lived like he'd never have to. It is hard to be left with the repercussions reverberating around you of a goodbye never spoken. Although it hurts still, I wonder now if hope for him had to be on the impossible, on a God who could do all things, so that he could endure long and suffer much.

Somewhere along the way I sold myself a version of hope not so different than my father's. I believed the lie that most everything gone wrong was not only somehow my fault but also able to be fixed – by me. Somehow I turned all the bad into good or at least believed I could if I just worked hard enough, sacrificed enough, and did all the things to the best of my ability. Excellence has been my middle name since I was born. So, I clung to a version of hope in which everything worked out. All the wrongs righted, all the bad made good, and all the struggles ending on a positive note. Like my dad, I wanted it all to work out just as I'd conceived.

When we sell ourselves a specific kind of reality, we disable our ability to see God for who He really is. Hope isn't really hope if it's something we can control. I didn't believe that truth. I'd designed a life plan, not only for me, but for my family too. I was working the plan and the plan was working. Or so I told myself. Plans have to have contingency strategies if they are going to be successful and those contingencies are best based in reality. Otherwise, you will find yourself in unexpected territory with no way through. That's where I landed. I had assured myself that the God I knew would never allow the things my life came to hold and that hope was a known variable. I couldn't have been more wrong.

I f you've ever been at the end of your rope, you know what it means to hold on. There is something about clinging to those last threads of what you know that have a desperation unlike any other. I think it might be when we are strongest – just before we let go. I've rarely come across anyone who has given up hope on purpose. Most of us don't. It's the last thing we surrender.

Job's initial response to tragedy was blessing God for giving and taking away, praising Him for the opportunities to have loved and lost at all. I get that. The shock hasn't set in yet, the weariness of days hasn't lingered long or much, the suffering of a body in pain hasn't riddled you hour after hour, excruciating minute after minute. The deepest of grief is still yet to come. So, hope at that point remains possible. Our view of it might have shifted, but we haven't yet let it go. Thus, we hold on.

I don't know exactly when Job exchanged hope for the wish of simply never having known at all, but that moment came for him as it does for all of us mired in the deepest of griefs. There comes a time where you don't simply wish it would end, you wish it had never begun in the first place. You realize that knowing all the joy you did, that the opportunity God gave you to have loved at all has become so excruciating in the aftermath of loss, that to never have known at all would be better. Maybe you've been there. Maybe you are there now. If so, then you, like me, understand this truth: Hope is the interwoven thread in our identity that, like our veins, carries life to everything; therefore, losing it is like losing literal pieces of ourselves.

I recall putting down my hope. I recall being unable to carry it anymore. Hope was a heavy rock, a burdensome weight that my grief could no longer bear. In order to walk the wilderness I found myself in, I had to set it down. This wasn't a season for finding the Promised Land. It was a season of letting go. I didn't know I'd been enslaved in Egypt. I didn't know I was on a journey home. I had no idea that I'd already been living in exile for years on end, that the God I needed to know wasn't interested in me recreating Eden, but in me allowing Him to not only hold but to *be* my hope.

The wilderness is a harsh place. It's full of extreme weather patterns, flash floods, desert cacti, wild animals, and desperation. It's not somewhere people intentionally go to build a home. It's an exile from the places where we create homes. So, when you find yourself there, you cannot help but ask where you went wrong, what this means now, how to get out, and if you ever will. Stay long enough and you'll start to believe in mirages and hightail it towards an oasis you were certain you saw but doesn't exist. You'll chase fantasies and suffer heat stroke. After a while, you will pray for death.

For a little while, Job fancied telling God how it was, how he didn't deserve all this, how it made absolutely no sense at all. He envisioned having a conversation where he let God know He'd gotten it all wrong, where what was happening was not what he deserved. We all want a God who is going to be gentle and kind to us in response to the massive fallouts of our days. We want Him to usher in comfort, soothing our aches. We don't want a God who seems to harshly respond to our tragedy with a terse, "Trust me."

We want God to see us, to return to us our hope. We want intangibles to become tangible and the end to be in sight. To us, that is hope. To God, it is not. When He tells us to walk by faith, not sight, He means that. He means, like a parent determined to save their child in a warzone, "Be quiet. Hold my hand. Don't ask what's happening. There isn't time for that right now. Just *trust me*. I'm making a way for us to get home."

The wilderness is land where provision is scarce and food doesn't grow. No one plants a garden in the middle of the wilderness and expects it to survive. It won't. The reason the Israelites made it for 40 years in such a desolate place was because God provided. He didn't let their shoes wear out, their clothes need replacement, their bellies starve, or their bodies break. That's what the wilderness will do to you without Him.

Without Him as your hope, you have none.

That's what I didn't understand. I wanted *this* world's hope. The kind I could grasp and navigate and control. I wanted, and I imagine Job did at some point too, a hope with skin on, a tangible value that I could use to develop and work a plan. I wanted an Eden of sorts right in the middle of desolation. God knows this and still removes our hope. Not because He is cruel or mean, but because He intended all along to replace it with something better. Himself.

He knows that if we have access to the Tree of Life in a place damaged by death and decay, we will bind ourselves forever to this place, trying in eternal vain to bring a version of heaven to a place chained to hell. So, in His wisdom and grace, He takes away that hope and replaces it with what we need most. **God is the Eden we've always needed most.** He is the Person that embodies our only living hope. The kind found on this earth was never meant to be the end goal. God's presence, Him walking with us, His identity as Emmanuel – *that* is what made Eden home.

Chapter Five:
Knowing

"Love at first sight is the most common eye disease."
~The Joker[10]

I'm sure you've gathered by now that mine wasn't the story I wanted. I didn't know Job, but after reading his story, I wouldn't choose it either. No version of tragedy fits, does it? I don't want it - not for him, for you, or for me. Redemption, even in its best form, still sounds to my ears like a song gone wrong, like notes that were never intended to be played at once. Although I'm learning to tune into the underlying harmony, it's still a skill I'm working to hone.

When my ex-husband moved out, one of my friends who'd walked the same journey before me said, "Don't leave the spaces empty. Fill them up. Closets, drawers, shelves, counters - wherever he left a hole, put something in its place." It turned out to be one of the best pieces of advice I received. We don't really prepare ourselves for the holes that tragedies leave behind. We spend so much energy on not ever having them at all that we are unprepared for what to do when they come.

I sat tonight in the same room with a woman and her husband and I saw her story in my own. She's many days behind where I was, still in the place where she doesn't know. She feels in her soul but doesn't yet see with her eyes the writing on the wall. She is still in love with the idea of them, their family, of it all going right instead of feeling so wrong. She believes God will save it - that their destiny is her version of their salvation.

I get it. I've been there, in The Land of Should, clinging desperately to my definition of hope. Her husband? He almost seems to know what she doesn't. I hope I'm wrong. My heart wants desperately for her to be correct, for her version of a story they're still writing to be what comes true. Yet, I cannot help but think, "If it all falls apart, what will she do with the holes?" Even moreso, will she be able to accept the ones that she herself created?

Right now, she's trying to prevent them from coming, going in every direction including the wrong ones to stop disaster on the horizon. They're already sinkholes imploding from the bottom up, but she's trying in desperation to cover them. She's looking for dirt to fill them up, a God who will bolster, a marriage that doesn't require so much change in them both. It's a difficult place to be – the one just before it all goes to hell. I wonder how the narrative would change if we were willing to trade in our versions of hope for the truth of knowing.

What I wish I would have prayed back then when I was in her shoes, knowing what I do now, is for God to prepare me for what I didn't know. I wish, instead of shortchanging myself and remaining a doormat of sorts, I'd asked Him to replace my hope with a truth that would bolster me through the inevitable storms to come. As I said before, trouble finds us all. The problem is that we spend so many of our days praying it won't and trying to prevent disaster from ever striking. What if we spent more of them on knowing it will?

When disaster began falling like dominoes across my life, I wasn't looking to bless God for it like Job initially did. Where Job's first response upon surveying the demolition of his life was, "The Lord gives and the Lord takes away. Blessed be the name of the Lord," mine was camping out in a space full of questions, not understanding, begging God to tell me why He was allowing this to be my story. I was certain it wasn't supposed to be this way. I told Him, "God, this is where You are supposed to show up in all your redeeming glory!" So, I didn't know what to do when the ways in which I wanted Him to, He didn't.

The holes that disaster left in Job's life weren't filled with new people and new circumstances as if those erased the massive losses he'd endured. His next set of children didn't replace his first nor his new life his old one. The gaping wounds left from Satan's attack weren't replaced by more of the same temporary things in which to hope. They were filled by God Himself, holes occupied with new perspectives, new insights, and a faith much deeper than all that with which Job began. That's where we have to start if we are ever going to be able to let go of our version of hope and replace it with the truth of knowing. We have to begin with the holes.

Knowing for me meant putting things in cupboards and drawers where I knew my husband's things would never be again. It meant acquainting myself in the day to day with a life I'd never again lead. I had to accept my Dad's voice would never again be on the other end of the phone line and that I'd never set foot back in this particular house I'd called home. I was forced to find new employment, not once but twice, due to my offices being closed and employers changing career paths. It meant accepting the holes existed. That was both painful and healing. For the first time, I got to choose. I got to choose knowing and owning a truth I hadn't ever embraced, allowing that to redefine the spaces the holes had left in my life.

The word hope implies that we are lacking something, that what we want or need is still around the bend. We are looking forward, not backwards, and we need that next thing in order for it to be fulfilled. Hope really only does you good if you know something is going to go wrong or that your resources will be inadequate. Imagine for just a moment if we actually *expected* trouble, if we anticipated lack, if we knew disaster was coming and foresaw the fallout - how different would our response to it be?

When we are attacked, we are immensely grateful when someone comes to our aid. If we see disaster on the horizon and someone helps us pick up the pieces, we say, "Thank you. I'm so glad I didn't have to do it without you." When we are in an accident and a stranger stops to help or we have a flat tire or are need of some money and someone steps up, we express our gratitude. The very countries who battle alongside us in times of war or offer us safe havens of peace, we label as our allies.

Friends, we have a God who shows up for us outside the Garden of Eden in the battlefield for our very souls and lives. He is the most powerful friend and ally we could ever conjure up. There is no superhero ever imagined who is more brave, loving, strong, persistent, or capable than our God. So, why don't we see our plight and thank Him for showing up? For coming to our rescue? Why do we get so angry, so disheartened, so frustrated or desperate that we'd rather walk alone than deal with Him at all?

For me, it was because of the holes. His help wasn't the kind I wanted. I never wanted to *need* help at all. I never wanted it to go wrong. That's really the crux of it for us all. We don't want the holes. We don't want to know. We want to have an intellectual understanding of good and evil, but not an immersive experience. Knowing acquaints us in intimate ways not only with God but with pain. There is so much pain in knowing things, isn't there? Knowing means understanding that pain is unavoidable, that destruction *will* come, and that we won't by ourselves ever be enough. Knowing is the reason why, when we should be expressing appreciation for God's help and presence, we instead fault Him for letting us ever need Him at all.

I don't envy my friends their future horizon. I know what that type of tragedy holds and it is the kind of painful you don't just get right back up from. It changes you - usually for the rest of your life. I learned something critical during my own journey through the same wilderness they're walking into. Leaning into a place, especially a hard one, will change your view and strengthen your soul more than any escape will ever allow. When you stop trying to escape, stop insisting on your version of hope fulfilled, you learn how to navigate the place where you find yourself. It's an acceptance of the holes - a giving up of your kind of hope and exchanging it for God's, just like He had to do with us.

Job started with that perspective when he praised God for both gifts and loss at once. *That* is the key to reconciling disenchantment. Even though my circumstances began taking turns towards the better and I began seeing occasional glimmers of light at the end of the tunnel, it took me much longer after disaster to believe that God's heart for me could be trusted. Even longer for me to pick hope back up. I'd settled past anger into disenchantment where I just couldn't reconcile the God I believed in before with the God I was experiencing now. The holes tragedy had left in my world were gaping wide open and all too real.

If this is where you find yourself today, I get where you're at. I understand the lack of faith. It's almost absurd to conceive of, isn't it? Can I give you some grace for this place where you find yourself? Faith isn't something to summon up and this isn't the time to get your courage and hope pumped. When tragedy strikes, that's when we need to give ourselves permission to step off the field and to take a seat on the bench. It's okay to take time, a long while if necessary, in order to really heal.

Knowing is an owning for yourself of God's response to our plight outside of the gates of Eden. God knows. He understands how much His protection affords us and what it means when it's gone. When Satan came to God, he was asked if he'd considered Job. Satan's response?

> *"Of course I've considered Job, but what's the point,*
> *God? You've got this man so protected, so hedged up,*
> *what can I possibly do to him? Attacking Job is a waste*
> *of my time."*

God's response is a painful one. I imagine Satan had a moment of shock and disbelief when God granted him access to His beloved. He removed the protective hedge around Job and Satan went after his life with a vengeance unlike many others recorded.

Friends, if we think that Satan isn't talking to God about us, asking for permission to touch our personal lives, we couldn't be more wrong. He has a plan for each of us, one he does not hesitate to execute. He loves creating holes and making us feel lack. When it happens, we experience the intensity of evil breathing down our necks and the absence of God's protection around us. Stepping outside of Eden is a full immersion into space where the primary intention is to ruin everything we were made for. That's why we cry, scream, and rail against the Garden gates, begging to be let back in. We all know it because eternity was set in our hearts by God Himself: Eden is where we were intended to live. It is the place for which we were created and the only place we really want to be.

Knowing isn't just our experience. God knows too. He understands that to be Himself, a God *with* us, He has to pay the price right alongside us. If we think it is easy for God to be Himself when His creation is writhing in pain, we are very mistaken. When we bleed, so does He. Where pain rips our hearts to pieces, it likewise grieves Him deeply. If we believe for one second that it is easy allowing His protective hedges to be removed from our lives, resulting in our pain and suffering, then we don't understand His heart for us at all.

God isn't in the business of destruction. He did not create our trouble, but He did allow it. I know that doesn't feel okay. I know it seems so opposite to the nature of what we interpret as loving. But that is the point of all this then, isn't it? Understanding who He *really* is, not who we've made Him out to be. Over and over in the Old Testament, God called His people to lay down their idols, to set aside anything that would turn their hearts away from Him. He didn't do it because He was just a jealous, angry God who wanted all the glory. He said it because He understood the power of knowing.

Knowing good and evil is an experience, not an intellectual assent.

God knew that the moment we ate that fruit, our hearts would be bent. He understood the desires He placed within us and the directions Satan would tempt us to take them. That's why He urges us time and time again, "Look at me. Pray without ceasing. Devote yourselves, your lives, your hearts, your families to this understanding. If you don't, you're going to miss it. Tragedy will come and sweep everything you love away and, if you don't understand who I really am, you will think it's because I abandoned you. You will lose your faith. Whatever you do, even if you have to die for it, cling to nothing else like you cling to Me. Knowing me, who I really am, will keep you safe when absolutely everything else fails."

Trouble is guaranteed. Jesus Himself said it: "*In this world, you will have trouble.*" (John 16:35) One day you will find yourself, like my friend and me, in a place of tragedy. There will be holes left, wounds gaping, situations un-remedied. It will hurt and ache. It may break your life wide open. Not all of it is guaranteed to heal this side of the grave. That too is part of knowing. Accepting that where trouble is, lack appears, and that holes create space. It's left empty so something else can take its place.

What we so desperately want to shake our fists at and make not true is nevertheless our only saving grace. God did not cause our trouble. He's the one who joined us in it. When all hope was lost, He showed up. When everything went wrong, He made streams in a desert, sustained us in a brutal wilderness, and brought us water where there was none.

What Satan meant for evil, God will repurpose for good. It is who He is. I know that's not the story we want and it's certainly not how it feels during its existence. Look at Job. This place you are, the story you are experiencing? It's not new. It's one we all in our own ways face. Where you are, where you will be, is where we all find ourselves, in a land where we were never intended to live. Our parched souls and dry mouths are aching for different knowledge. We long for living water in a place where the effects of sin no longer exist.

If we are to ever know the hope that comes from trouble, we have to reconcile ourselves to experiencing it. We have to make peace with the holes. Satan tempts and badgers us to fill them with him instead of Jesus, to make this temporary world our eternal salvation. God longs for us to choose to let Him occupy the space. It is only in the place of our greatest disaster that we can find something permanent with which to fill our empty spaces - a hope worthy of endurance and a Person willing to occupy our battlefields. The One who fights alongside us, infusing us with a hope deep and sufficient enough to sustain us in a fallen world. As Paul wrote,

> "For we are *saved* by *hope*: but **hope that is *seen* is not hope**... all these things that I once thought very worthwhile – now I've thrown them all away so that I can put my trust and hope in Christ alone." [11]

So, the question remains: if trouble is inevitable, what do we do with pain it creates?

Chapter Six:
Pain

"The cure for pain is in the pain."

~ Rumi[12]

One of the first pains beckoning on the horizon of my life's impending disaster arrived at night in the form of baby scorpions. Shortly after moving into the home we'd just built in 2016, I was awakened by multiple sharp, stinging pains that burned like hellfire. Screaming in pain, I jumped from the bed terrified of what was happening. My then husband leapt out of bed with me, throwing back the covers to see what was going on. I don't know if you've ever been to Texas, but there are plenty of scorpions. I'd seen a red one up close but never realized there are also semi-translucent ones, almost invisible to the naked eye against certain backdrops. My vision already requires glasses, so add to that the darkness of night, being awakened from a dead sleep, and pain, and I was anything but coherent and capable of correctly identifying the creatures attacking me.

My husband located and killed two baby scorpions, only identifiable because their translucence stood in stark contrast to the color of our sheets. I couldn't go back to sleep. Not only was I in pain, but I was now petrified of more crawling into bed with me. They easily blended into the color of the carpet so I couldn't see them even with the lights on. Most importantly, they had found their way not only into our home, but specifically into my side of the bed in the middle of the night.

Over the course of the next 12 hours, I felt increasingly worse. If you know anything about scorpion stings, you know that the initial pain often increases over time as do all the other symptoms such as swelling, nausea, and feelings similar to receiving an adrenaline or steroid shot. Although children are usually the ones to experience inconsolable crying, I had my own episode of it. The worst of it took about 24 hours to subside.

About a week later, I was at my counselor's office when the topic of the scorpion stings came up. She said the strangest thing in response to my story. She looked me right in the eye and said, "Alanna, I think the scorpions are God's way of telling you that you aren't in control of things." That statement shook me because I thought, "What kind of God is going to use scorpions to tell me that? There are better ways. Surely she is wrong." I dismissed her idea. She wasn't wrong though and I had absolutely no idea then just how right my life to come would prove her to be.

C.S. Lewis once wrote,

> *"Pain insists upon being attended to. God whispers to us*
> *in our pleasures, speaks in our consciences, but shouts*
> *in our pains. It is his megaphone to rouse a deaf world."*[13]

Job's entire life stopped and re-centered itself around one thing: pain. Until I started writing this, I hadn't really considered it, but the book of Job is 42 chapters long. It's the 6th longest book out of the entire 66 books in the Bible. Yet only a few brief paragraphs are spent telling us readers about Job's life before and after devastation. 41 entire chapters are spent on pain, some of them quite long. It's like God knew that we would spend more time on our pain as humans than we would on all our other emotions combined.

Whether we like it or not, pain is the background noise to which we tune our lives, isn't it? It is the factor that shapes our worldview unlike any other. No one gets to opt out. No one has the ability to choose a pain-free existence. Even people with damaged pain receptors know what loss feels like. Jim Morrison is quoted saying, "Pain is meant to wake us up. People try to hide their pain. But they're wrong. Pain is something to carry, like a radio."[14] Pain is intended to tell us something and not just that things are going wrong. Pain is also the sound God uses to teach us to hear His voice.

We cannot conceive of a God who can allow destruction and devastation and somehow bring about goodness in such a terrible, tragic place. Pain shouts at us that it isn't true. Yet the reality is that the goodness of a God who allows pain is also the goodness of a God who knows there is no other option. The existence of pain from God's perspective is unlike the one we have on earth. Here, pain is used as a tool of control, a weapon of assault on our senses. Interrogators employ torture as a method to get information while terrorists brutalize or starve people into giving up their loyalties.

**In the currency of heaven, however, pain is God's
invitation to draw us close to Him.**

Our problem with pain is the same as our problem with trouble. We want a God who, if He were really sovereign, would absolve our lives of pain and dispel the world of trouble. We want Him to restore Eden right here, right now. Pain to us feels like evidence that He isn't really on the throne, that He isn't really sovereign. We know that if we were God, we would do things differently, things that made more earthly sense. We wouldn't allow suffering of monumental proportions. We wouldn't tolerate injustice. We would make social justice our mission and the world our platform. If we are being honest with ourselves, God falls short of our expectations, doesn't He?

A s a highly sensitive empath, I not only feel my pain but I often experience yours too. Your feelings, your life, whatever you are going through that you think I don't understand? I probably do. You and I so often become one and the same. It may sound crazy, but ask any empath and they'll tell you. It's hard-wired into us. I've hated this part of living since I was a child, the one where I seem to experience double the pain. No matter where we go, we can never escape the sound pain causes that reverberates through our days, riding the waves across the globe, traversing through our lives with an unending ache. No matter who is suffering, I cannot seem to help but somehow feel their pain.

When I was raising kids, I had a rule: "No Bodies." Ask any of my kids what my number one rule was when they were growing up and "no bodies" is the first thing every one of them will tell you. It had benefits for them and brought peace to our household, but it was birthed out of a need in me to escape enduring more pain. I couldn't bear to watch one of them hurt the other, especially physically, so I made a rule not to allow any kind of physical altercations that could cause that type of pain or lead to hate. Although I've never regretted making that rule and I'm certain I'll carry it over with my grandchildren too, I understand so much more now what the real meaning for me was behind it.

Pain isn't something we are wired to endure. Our bodies are designed to tell us we have pain so that we can stop what is causing it. Inflammation rises up to hold parts of us still so they can heal before we move on. Pain reminds us the injury still exists and forces us to move slower. Ask anyone with chronic pain and they will tell you that it is a miserable existence, to have the nerves flaring up and cells firing nonstop.

When I got sick in 2015, sicker than I have ever been in my life, the doctor prescribed me a medicine that was black boxed by the FDA. I didn't have a clue what it was going to do to me. After a single dose, I could feel my kidneys. Literally feel them. Although I tend to have a pretty high pain tolerance, my body ached in ways and places I didn't know was possible. Every nerve ending felt like it was on fire and nothing I did brought relief. The fallout of taking that medicine was months long. Sickness had already leveled me, but the "cure" almost killed me.

Sometimes God's ways of entering our pain feel like that remedy. We think what isn't making us stronger just might kill us afterall. Satan is already on the warpath for our lives and souls, but he doesn't stop. Why would he? Pain is the weapon he uses to make us believe God has left us alone. The more pain he can cause, the less likely we are to trust God. Sometimes I think we underestimate our enemy. He's had thousands of years with the human race, but we each walk in as babies with no experience at all. He acquaints us with pain as soon as possible, knowing if he can get us to believe God isn't good, the battle for our heart is likely won.

I don't think we understand what it meant when God sent His Son to live here with us. He stepped out of an eternity where there was no suffering, no pain, no dirt including His own, and came to a place riddled with it all. He did it because He knew there was no other choice. Staying in Eden meant leaving us. That was the exact opposite of His goal. He didn't create us so He could leave us behind. He isn't a God who avoids suffering. He is the One who enters in, who embraces what He did not cause because eternal suffering for Him is not having us at all. I don't think we realize just how very much we are loved.

Satan, however, does. So, he assaults the thing God loves most. Us. He is a no holds barred kind of devil who doesn't give up. His vision may be short-sighted but it absolutely works. We are short-sighted creatures ourselves, created with needs we cannot alone meet – needs for sustenance and for peace. God is a God of order, so wherever Satan can create chaos, he does. His hope is that chaos will prevent us from experiencing God's peace. That's why Paul tells us where to fix our thoughts.

God knows we are going to suffer. He knows we live in a land saturated with chaos. Satan, as temporary prince of earth, is the king of causing confusion and suffering. Although we cannot experience the full effects of it in the here and now, God will always be the living antidote to all that ails us. That's why He sent us Jesus, the Prince of Peace and King of Kings.

Pain has marked my days in ways nothing else ever will. It's brought my priorities to light with details that no amount of organizing and troubleshooting ever could. Pain forces us to hone in on what matters most. When Job was sitting in the worst of his days, pain was his never-ending companion. He couldn't find one spot of his existence that had been left untouched. What is so hard to reconcile is that God doesn't promise to make the effects of pain and suffering go away.

Philippians 4:7 tells us that, when we turn our fears and requests over to God, "the peace of God, which transcends all understanding, will guard your hearts and your minds in Christ Jesus." It doesn't say He will erase our trouble or eliminate our pain. It says His peace will be our guard, our fortress, our place of rest in times of tribulation. What we have to reconcile ourselves to is that, if God is to be where we are, He too has to step out of the Garden and face the gates of hell on earth. If He cannot spare us, He likewise will not spare Himself. So, He acquaints Himself with *our* reality. He exchanges *His* reality for our own.

This is what Isaiah meant when he wrote,

Who believes what we've heard and seen? Who would have thought GOD's saving power would look like this? The servant grew up before God – a scrawny seedling, a scrubby plant in a parched field. There was nothing attractive about him, nothing to cause us to take a second look. He was looked down on and passed over, a man who suffered, who knew pain firsthand. One look at him and people turned away. We looked down on him, thought he was scum. But the fact is, it was our pains he carried – our disfigurements, all the things wrong with us. We thought he brought it on himself, that God was punishing him for his own failures. But it was our sins that did that to him, that ripped and tore and crushed him – our sins! He took the punishment, and that made us whole. Through his bruises we get healed."

(Isaiah 53:1-5, MSG)

It is the only way. It always was. Him *with* us. I know I've said it 100 times already, but there is no other option, friends. He is our only hope. He hasn't abandoned us, but He also cannot erase the path to being with us. Pain isn't optional. It is the way to where we are. It's the only road that leads us all back to Eden.

Sometimes I've looked at the people around me and several seem to have lived quite the charmed life. Their days are not marked with the pain mine have been. They don't seem bothered or oppressed by a struggling existence. I don't grasp life in a world where a Pollyanna mentality makes sense. What I've learned is that their day comes too. They either get intimately acquainted with pain and loss because it roars through their lives, leaving unexpected devastation in its wake, or they get up day after day to face a world groaning and writhing in pain, the effects of which they are forced to deal with, like it or not. One way or the other, we will always be invited into pain. It is always the only way to really know Jesus face to face.

When my life shattered into pieces, I had an idea of how pain was supposed to go. We all construct our own versions of how to navigate suffering, don't we? I'd unknowingly assigned the people around me roles and tried to ensure they fulfilled those. It was still having my needs met in a way I could control where I knew for certain I wouldn't be left hung out to dry. Yet, that's not where I found hope. So many of those people I was sure would be by my side for the long haul ended up being people I had to leave by the wayside. Some had already walked away.

It's not that they were uncaring. It's that they just didn't know. They didn't have a faith grounded in the lasting kind of hope, the one that embraces pain as a lifestyle and endures long and much. Theirs wasn't a God without skin on that they simply had to trust. My life gave me no other option. I was either going to follow an unknown God into a battle zone mostly not of my own making or I was going to be left trying to figure this out entirely on my own.

We really don't realize that's the root of it all. It always comes back to choice. We like to think that Adam and Eve made the decision once for us all, but the truth is it's always in front of us. Every single time Satan holds up our lives for examination he reminds us, "God isn't someone you can trust. He is withholding good. You won't find what you're looking for in Him. You need more and *you* have to be the one to go get it." So, we do. We choose. Over and over and over again.

Our lives are rent with the neverending question, "Will I trust God? Do I believe He is who He says He is? Or do I want the knowledge of evil *and* good?" Every single one of us eats the fruit. Every single one of us chooses. To believe we never would is to believe that we are, as Lucifer said, God. It is to take on His attributes, believing we are capable, without having His power, authority, or goodness. It is to assign ourselves a character we don't actually embody.

None of us wants to believe that's true. Ask any parent. We believe that when our baby takes its first breath of oxygen outside the womb, they are pure, innocent, and perfect. The world has not yet spoiled them and we believe that if they are just kept in this safe, bubbled space, they will become who we tell ourselves they are down deep inside – good. But it isn't true. Children aren't born good. They are born, like adults, with a nature tethered to sin. They have to be taught to value good. Just like us, they have to learn that evil isn't good and that the knowledge of it won't bring us good apart from God.

***Only God can make the knowledge of good** and *evil something worth knowing.*

Satan intends for it to devastate us, to chain us forever to shame. Only a God who has Himself stepped out of heaven to join us here on earth will ensure that suffering has a purpose and pain has a place. Where Satan knows we will fall like lightning, God knows our pain is the only way of escape. It is the greatest crucible of faith. He never wanted us to need Him in this way because He knew what it would cost. Not only Him, but us. As a parent you know that it is a million times easier for you to endure pain than to watch your children suffer through one minute of it. Pain was never His intent. Us knowing evil, not just good, was also something He never wanted. *He* didn't make the choice. It wasn't His to make. It's always been ours and we all have made it.

Pain is one of the most disorienting experiences in life. It can render us completely helpless and leave us with no hope at all. Pain is the crucible that defines more about us than perhaps any other experience and mine had changed me. Job too lived that. Aside from Jesus, Job may have been able to speak to pain better than anyone else who has lived on this planet. Pain shapes how we see not only ourselves and the world, but also how or *if* we value God at all. God doesn't come here to wreck your world, immerse you in pain, and teach you a life lesson. You aren't getting it all wrong and just deserve unending tragedy as a result. Although there is merit to the wages of sin being death, that's not the whole storyline here.

Jesus was completely sinless yet suffered much. Job, the most righteous man on earth, was doing exactly what God told him. He was honorable, respectful, a man worthy of following. Even Satan knew that God's hand was on him, protecting him, hedging his life in a form of seen hope. However, somewhere along the way, life *is* guaranteed to fall apart and pain *is* promised to show up. It is in that place where we have to do business with the phrase echoed throughout scripture and the walls of history, "What you meant for evil, God meant for good."

When we are going through it, we find ourselves just like I did on that fateful night of being attacked by baby scorpions in my sleep. We awaken to a pain we can't stop, the source not always immediately identifiable, and effects that radiate for a long while. Our covers are thrown back, lives exposed, and safety no longer a guaranteed option. We will do whatever it takes to just simply make the pain stop. Sometimes nothing works. So, then what? What happens when all hope feels lost, when trouble is unending, and pain fills our days?

That is when we get to make the most important choice. It's when we decide what God's truth really means to us. We can recreate Him in our own image and carry on, believing in a God that works things out how we want, or we can keep wandering in the wilderness, allowing Him to prepare us – trusting that the Promised Land exists and that this wilderness we are traversing day after day isn't our permanent destiny. Trust is the hardest piece. It is the one where we either accept truth as it really is or we create our own version of it. Nothing you decide will ever be more important. What we don't realize when it's happening is that pain is also the standard by which our depth of life is measured. Avoiding pain only serves us while things are easy. One day, though, life will come calling and we have to choose – how deep do you really want your life to be?

You may want pain to remain at bay, but what you're choosing is joy in equal measure.

If your grief is brief, so your satisfaction will be. There is something about being willing to let life run deep that breaks your heart wide open to a truth none of us want to embrace. It is the beauty and hardship of being human. We are always at once too much and never enough for this world. Eden is where our hearts were born and where our souls continually return to. As our original destiny, we long for The Land of Should - a day when things are as they should be, when restoration and grace rule the day, and our lives are at peace.

Pain – well, it's the way home.

Chapter Seven:
The Driver Named Trust

———

"To fly, we have to have resistance."
~Maya Lin[15]

What I didn't realize about loss going into it is how much it is like facing a fear and overcoming it. I am terrified of heights. Last year, we were invited to a college football game. The stadium here is quite high. Although I'd worked in that stadium for years as a teenager, it had been so many years since I'd been inside that I didn't realize how they'd built up the new walkways and surrounding. A little over 100,000 people attend these games, so I was just walking with the crowd, talking with someone as we made our way up one flight of stairs or outdoor escalator after another. All of a sudden, we got to a certain height and the only space between me and the next landing was an escalator suspended multiple stories in the air.

I have never in my life started crying because I was afraid of heights. I usually just look at them and go, "Yeah, no. Not for me." Then, I back away. Not this time. It was so sudden and unexpected, with me having been so engrossed in conversation and unaware of my surroundings, that when I looked up and realized just where I was, immediate panic ensued. I started crying, almost hyperventilating, and scared my own self with the suddenness of my response. I wasn't sure I could go on and watch the game. All I wanted to do was get to a safe place, away from the risk of heights and falling. Somewhere concrete that I could hold onto and understand.

Fortunately, whoever created this stadium had the sense to put a set of concrete stairs right in the center where you don't feel suspended in space as you climb up. As we took the stairs, I couldn't seem to catch my breath for a bit. I was afraid of my own fear. My panic was so sudden and my reaction so unexpected and intense that I felt like I was two people inside my own body at once for a few minutes, one of them observing and trying to calm down the other one who was losing her mind. We finally made it to the stands and it was better, but not much. They were very high up. There were things around us to ground my vision so, as long as I didn't lean too far forward or walk in certain spots, I was okay.

Life can feel that way. It can lull you into stability, distract you with engagement, then out of the blue show you things for what they really are and take your breath away. When Job and his friends were sitting in the ash heap of his life, Job's companions began to draw conclusions and make assertions, lodging arguments against Job that he *must* have made a mistake. Surely all of this was somehow Job's fault. This kind of disaster doesn't just happen. It certainly doesn't happen to good people who are right with God they contended.

It's the same storyline we all believe. Good begets good and the karma bus only comes for the deservedly evil ones. We cannot fathom unwarranted disaster being poured out on us, much less on someone who's the picture of a man after God's own heart, the most righteous person we know. We can't wrap our brains around it. The pull of life in Eden is strong and never leaves us. So, we go looking in the wrong place for understanding – this world - and try to ensure a fate that our actions guarantee us to earn.

———————

Before my understanding of life as I knew it shattered and circumstances happened one after the other out of my control, I handed small things over to God. I didn't spend a lot of time on the big stuff because I wasn't prepared to let those go. I kept telling myself as we all do that the God I understood Him to be wasn't going to let that happen – "surely not to me." We had a system worked out, God and me. I'd do the things and He'd ensure my safety. That might not have been the deal God offered, but it was the one I'd signed Him up for. Like Job's friends, I wanted a life and a God that I could understand. I wanted a system I could work and situations I could, to a degree, ensure the results from so that any pain or loss that *did* come might be stretching but was still manageable.

One of the most quoted verses from Job is found in chapter 13 verse 15. Job's friends are laying it out for him telling him he *must* have done something, even if it's something he doesn't realize, and assuring him that if he'd just confess and beg God for forgiveness, his suffering plight would come to an end. Job is angry by this point after listening to their nonsense because he now understands something they have yet to grasp. Job realized – *there isn't anything I did that caused this. I am living injustice. I am suffering for reasons unknown. Even if I had committed the worst of sins as my friends allege I may have, it would not have resulted in this. No, this tragedy is something else altogether and not one bit of it is my doing.*

We all find ourselves there, don't we? Situations out of control, unwarranted disaster, lives ripped apart for absolutely no understandable reason. My husband was three months shy of turning 14 when it happened to his family. On the way to his great-grandmother's funeral, their vehicle carrying almost the entire family was hit. He remembers it like it was yesterday. The crunch of metal, the glass shattering, the haze and pain that followed, the air filled with the sounds of his little brother crying. He recalls his other little brother's injuries, both of his grandparents and his mother with life-threatening wounds, and him at 13 years old trying to find a way to help everyone but being unable to do so.

That alone would have been enough to stay with him for the rest of his days. There are some sounds, some experiences, some awakenings to reality that never leave you no matter how long you live. But, for him, that was just the beginning. His mother died the next day and his grandfather the month after. They never made it to his great-grandmother's funeral. Each of the people in the accident had some form of injury, some minor, others not so much. As for my husband, where his body was left unscathed, his heart was permanently torn open.

The truth is we are all going to find our days inexplicably torn apart at some point. We are *going* to suffer and endure pains not of our own doing. Some of them are the result of other people's choices and some of them, well, they are just part of living in a world that is cursed. We all wake up at some point to a reality we can't keep breathing in. It may even hit us unexpectedly, with a force that scares our own selves, and we won't know where to take it. We'll just look around in desperation for a concrete stairwell where we can sit down to stabilize ourselves for a moment.

When Job's friends initially witnessed the disaster that was his life, they sat with him in silence for 7 days. Grief of that magnitude is something none of us has real words to speak to when we first witness what it means. But as time drags on and minutes turn to hours and hours to days and days to weeks, we stop being able to just sit in the grief anymore and we start trying to make sense of things. We don't care any longer what the truth really is, we just need it to not be that injustice happens to the just and tragedy unspeakable can come at any moment upon anyone. We need our reality to stop being so awful. So, we narrate another storyline and conjure up a containable version of hope.

Friends, can I gently say this? We need a God without skin on. We do, all of us. We are living in a world that cannot sustain hope. Everything we put our trust in at some point fails us. It's the nature of this place. It's bent to destruction, death, and decay. Nothing is permanent. None of it is guaranteed. If we are going to make it through here, with an enemy that will absolutely use goodness as a weapon against us, we need a God who is bigger than the narrative of our earthly trust.

Job knew that. He saw what his friends didn't. He was living it. He didn't ever claim perfection, but he did know that his *heart* was right before God. He knew that he spoke from a clear conscience. That's why he understood what none of his friends could. He knew that there had to be more going on than he could possibly grasp. So, his response to all their assaults on his character and calls for him to repent was,

"Though he slay me, yet I will trust in Him."
(Job 13:15, KJV)

This line wasn't spoken on day one. If you read Job, you'll see that by the time these words are uttered, Job's life has become a disaster for everyone not only to reel in horror while watching, but by then was so tragic that he'd become the person the town mocked. Even young people who hadn't lived long enough to develop characters of their own were making fun of Job in the streets and gloating over a good man fallen. They assumed he was prideful, that his power and influence were stripped from him at God's hands because Job was, at heart, haughty. All of them, every single one, couldn't have been more wrong.

That's really where we find ourselves, isn't it? When push comes to shove, when we have to stand our ground, when we have to choose in the worst of the worst situations where to place our trust, do we really know where we can stand? Only Job knew his own heart, his own interactions with God, his prayers for his children, and his deep value upon being like God in ways that were kind, just, and loving.

What his friends and neighbors and wife didn't know is that Satan had just used all of that goodness as a weapon to destroy Job. Satan wasn't just interested in taking away all that Job had, his business operations, his home, his kids, his workers, his livelihood, or his health. **Satan wanted to take his *value* in the eyes of every person around him.** He wanted Job to feel like nothing, like less than nothing, and to give in to the humiliation and claim defeat. He wanted Job to turn his back on God and say, "I *knew* you would turn on me. You are not at all who I believed you to be. You are *not* good. I can't trust you."

What Satan wasn't banking on is the same question we have to wrestle with for ourselves if we are going to make it through life outside Eden's gates: Who am I really trusting in anyway? Before my life imploded, I held everything close. I tried to keep the ends from fraying and shored up the boat. Certain that if I did everything well enough, there wouldn't come a time when I'd be called upon to give the things I loved most up, I kept making plans and living out my days. Trust was a word my counselor and I discussed, but it wasn't a lifestyle I pursued. Life had taught me trust was dangerous, so I found it much safer to keep things in a nest, or at least the tree, that I could nurture and take care of.

God isn't interested in us living small. You could look at Job's life prior to its destruction and say he was living anything but small. He was one of the most powerful, influential, well-known men in the entire region. His capacity to help people was immense, and his wisdom respected. People wanted not only to be around Job, they wanted to *be* Job. To say the least, his life was already big before it came to a screeching halt.

Here is the rub that it took me years to embrace: Your life isn't about you. In fact, your life may be so much about something else that you don't even see it during a single one of your days. The mattering may be found on the other side of your grave in the lives and studies of people who come after you. Job's life was huge for a man of his day. What he did and said mattered. He was living big, but that's the thing about God. His ways are higher than our ways, His thoughts greater than our thoughts. What He sees goes past our 100-year stage on into centuries and millenniums and eternity.

Where Job's life got the attention of many people around him those days, the destruction of it has gotten the attention of *billions* ever since. Tens if not hundreds of billions of people have heard the story of Job, studied his life, looked for God, and found solace in Job's pain. Where he could have made a difference in the lives of the people he touched in his day, God saw that as living smaller than necessary. So, when Satan was given free rein to assault Job's days, God showed up and said, "I'm going to show you what living big really means."

Your pain has a purpose. It's beyond what you can see. So, here's the crux of it: If you are not willing to let trust inform your pain, you are going to miss where it's going. You won't see the heart of the one who loves you. You will miss the place where your vindication doesn't come from your lips, but His. You won't see the fruit of joining Him outside of Eden. **Trust is a weapon that extinguishes the effects of our enemy's toolbox.**

Before my days were filled with constant sorrow, I lived in a way that was manageable. I hedged my bets and trusted God with things I still had some control over. I wasn't prepared for Satan to take all the good things – truly good, wonderful things I was doing and had worked for, a good father who was perhaps the very best man and closest to Job I've ever known – and destroy them. I wasn't ready to trust God to handle them, much less me in the aftermath of that tragedy.

Since then, I've stopped doing that as much. I've learned to embrace the loss. Risk is no longer frightening in the same way it once was. I don't hedge my bets as much anymore. I'm unafraid now of going all in at times. I believe in boundaries, but not with Jesus. I don't redirect God's choices. I may beg and plead for Him to take action a certain way, I may ask that He grant certain requests, I may even feel terrified about the potential outcomes, but when I ask, I do so now with open hands, willing to let Him have His way. I know Satan hasn't given up on me. He will find another vulnerability and he will press it.

The difference now is two-fold: 1) I am unafraid of living in a way I never have been. Whatever it costs me, it costs. I can't spend my time trying to preserve a future I never had control of anyway. 2) I know the God who is driving and I've handed over the steering wheel. I choose to trust. Here's what we don't really understand about trust, about the place we prevent ourselves from going: Trust isn't knowing. It's embracing *not* knowing.

It's refusing to assign God a position and demanding that He fill it. It's saying, "All I know is this – my eggs are going in your basket and I'm relying on you to protect my investment. I don't know what that will look like. I may have an idea in my head, but I am trusting that your character is going to be worthy of my hope." As humans, we are always going to rely on something. Whether it be our own understanding, circumstances we control or at least maneuver, or another person we know, in one way or another we are all placing our trust somewhere and it is absolutely driving where we go and how we see the road.

When Job said, "Though he slay me, yet I will trust in Him," he wasn't saying that he was hoping God would work out his circumstances. He wasn't asking God to show up and right the wrongs and fix all the pain. He was saying, *"God, I have absolutely NO idea what is happening here. None of this makes sense. There isn't a reason I can conceive of. You and I both know that, even on my very worst day, I couldn't have done enough to cause this. I can't see the why so all I've got is you. I am trusting that YOU are exactly who I believe you to be. That your character is bigger than what my circumstances are telling me. That goodness comes in ways I can't see and that you will make beauty out of this ash heap."*

Job refused to give up his integrity because his integrity was never based on himself. It was always based on God's character being bigger than everything else. Job wasn't righteous in his own right. He pursued God, yes. He lived sacrificially, yes. He served well and loved much. He ensured justice and walked humbly with His God as Micah 6:8 says. All these great and wonderful things though *did not* create his righteousness. Not one bit of that mattered outside of this one vital part: Job trusted God. We don't understand just how valuable our trust is.

Job didn't try to recreate God in his own image. He didn't ask God to make sense. He didn't demand that God mete out justice or follow a certain path so that the human race could justify themselves before Him. He just said, "Look. I'm not enough. My kids aren't enough. We are all of us doing the very best we can. To the degree we are failing you somewhere, please forgive us. Aside from that, my life is in your hands. Their lives are in your hands. You are the person, the place where my trust lies because You are the only source of goodness to be had. You are the definition of truth on which my entire life is built. So, whether you hand me tragedy or blessing, I will trust you."

"Though he slay me,
yet I will trust in Him."

This is how: It's knowing that character, goodness, honor, worth, respect, all the things lovely and beautiful and promising *cannot* be found outside of the One who is the living representation of them. It is the absolute reliance in the very worst of your days upon the character of a person without skin on. It is taking your hands off the steering wheel, looking out into the terrifying space you find yourself, and saying,

> *"I'm not going to try to explain this away. I'm not running for the concrete stairwell. I am terrified to my very core, but I'm just going to wait for You to show up. I believe You will because I believe, with a faith that defies all logic, that You are good where everything else is not. I believe that there is no possibility of even finding goodness outside of You. I am choosing to trust that, if it weren't for your good character and trustworthy name, I would be left here in dust and ashes for the rest of my days with the world mocking my misplaced faith. Yet, I know that even if I don't see the results I want in this day, in my present reality, that even after my breath in this body is extinguished, Your goodness will carry on and my trust and utter reliance upon that will be rewarded."*

Joining God in redemption is a story I never wanted. I doubt it was one Job wanted. I imagine if we were talking right now, you'd tell me it wasn't one you wanted. We rarely want the storylines we are handed. We always want the speaking parts, not the ones where we sit on stage as the donkey, the one everyone makes fun of, the example of what appears to be a tale of everything gone wrong.

We don't want to be Mary, having trusted God with our lives, only to find ourselves pregnant and the man we are to marry looking to get rid of us. To birth God's son, to raise Him up, to come to understand who God is and what He's doing only to watch this person we love more than anything be crucified, our lives made laughingstocks of, our souls ripped open and our pain on display for the whole world to see.

One of my very favorite Christmas songs is *Mary, Did You Know*. Ceelo Green and Pentatonix each sing versions that bring tears to my eyes every time I hear them. Because that is what faith is. That is what trust requires. It is not a known thing. **It is in the not knowing where we find our freedom.** It is in the letting go, falling backwards, risking safety, surrendering understanding, and yielding control that we find the ability to say, like Job,

"Though he slay me, *yet* I will trust in Him."
(emphasis mine)

Chapter Eight:
The Wilderness Isn't Home

―――――――

"Not all those who wander are lost."

~J.R.R. Tolkien[16]

I once put the quote above on the hood of my Jeep with a compass rose in the center. It reminded me every time I saw it that there was purpose in wherever I found myself. It seems imperative to remind us all that wandering is inevitable, but it's not the same as being lost. The seasons where you find yourself in the wilderness hold meaning and it's important not to forget that when hope isn't clearly displayed on the horizon. For me, disaster wasn't so long ago, but it's been long enough that I no longer feel weighed down by it like I did at the time it was happening. When you're in the throes of it, the goal is usually just survival.

It seemed important to pause here to share my current reality. Today, I'm in a place of healing. My dad's death will have been 4 years ago now in just a couple short months. The ache doesn't sting the way it did in 2019 and I'm not in the middle of divorce, death, job changes, home loss, and kids leaving home all at once like I was then. The worst of the chaos is over and I'm in a season of rebuilding now. I find myself on the other end of the story of Job.

That said, I also realize that, for as much I now know and can open my heart and arms to the journey I'm on, I feel in equal measure that there is so much I'm still figuring out. Plenty of things that are still wrong or unresolved. Although this book has an ending, it's not one where everything gets wrapped up in a bow. It can't because my journey, like all of ours, is still ongoing. The calling for Eden is still deep within my soul and my heart longs for freedom in a way words cannot really define. I want to fly and to be settled. It's an odd place in the middle calling for wings and roots at once.

As a young empty nester, having grown kids has taught me more about presence in ways I couldn't have understood while they were at home. I'm learning to lean into circumstances differently and I wonder if Job did the same. His life was torn apart but later redeemed. He had to do it twice. No one tells you this, but redemption is a difficult place to be. It's where you've moved past the art of just surviving by putting one foot in front of the other to actually jumping, skipping, and running. You begin pursuing living again and it's a peculiar space to embody after the fallout of immense change and loss.

I share this with you because it's important to know that this journey isn't one of arriving. It is the experience of becoming. None of us has arrived and we never will – at least not on this side of the grave. The story is always evolving. Every day is like another episode in a series that ends with the phrase "to be continued." Although I'm healing, my whole world isn't settled. I still struggle with so many of the very things I'm writing about because the truth is that this *is* the human condition and these situations *are* our earthly battles. That doesn't go away. It was very pronounced during the season of my life's bottom falling out, but the day to day reality of living in a world at war with itself remains an ever present constant in which I find myself.

Today, I find myself wrestling with boundaries and identity. Like you, my life holds so many unknowns. I said earlier that I didn't know at first how to handle my new last name, but the truth is deeper than that. I don't always know how to handle this life I have chosen. In so many ways, I'm still reorienting myself. I've jumped the gun in areas, on occasion out of desperation, but mostly as a result of exhaustion. That's taken a toll in unanticipated ways. One of the things this long season has taught me is the strong don't survive by being the strongest. The strong just usually keep going longer than everyone else. It's easy to believe that we who are labeled "strong" have some superpower that equips us to "man up" or "cowboy on" when the reality couldn't be more off. We don't know what we are doing any more than anyone else does. It's just that we usually keep going.

I'm finding myself in a place where continuing to just keep going is unhealthy. I need to take a pause. To regroup, to re-found my principles and boundaries. What no one tells you is that the wilderness is a bit disorienting. The Israelites wandered in circles. For 40 years, they just wound round and round and round. You have to wonder – why did it take so long? Surely *someone* would have gotten fed up and gone in search of a way out. As humans, I think we accustom ourselves to our surroundings. We get acclimated to "the way things are" so we stop looking for anything else. We got lost while we were running and, now that we aren't in survival mode anymore, we aren't super interested in it returning. Can I remind us all of something?

The wilderness isn't our home.

This place we find ourselves isn't what we were made for. When the Israelites escaped Egypt and landed in the wilderness, that wasn't their final destination. But there is a reason they got stuck there. There is an explanation for why so many people lived their entire lives in that wilderness, never knowing any other place as home. They lost sight of continuing on.

As tempting as it may be to make my peace with my circumstances and surroundings, I don't want to make a home in the wilderness. I don't want to give up even if exhaustion beckons me. Instead, I want to learn the value of the pause, of waiting on God to reveal Himself and how His identity impacts my own. I currently find myself on the way back round a circle I've seen before again, but this time there are glimpses of the Promised Land on the horizon. Whether I make it there isn't up to anyone else but me. As William Ernest Henley once wrote, "I am the master of my fate; I am the captain of my soul."[17] In other words, I get to choose whether or not I make it to my destination.

When disaster struck and it began to seem as if an endless lingering in that place was his permanent doom, Job refused to give up. He didn't make peace with his surroundings. He never stopped looking. His eyes and heart were pointed to heaven and his insistence upon an audience with the Most High was a vision on which he never loosened his grip. It is so tempting when we get weary to just give up. Life is hard and circumstances can level you in ways you have no control over. I think many of the Israelites did that. Wandering day after day, week after week, year after year until one decade became two, three, and four – I think they were beyond weary. Their souls were longing for new water, their hearts no longer set on the horizon. So many of them made that wilderness their permanent abode.

Wherever you are on that journey through the wilderness, I want to remind you that you don't have to make a place for yourself there. The wilderness is not where people go to establish themselves. It's a place for wandering, for finding God and yourself. It's where relationship and identity are established, where trust is implemented, where boundaries hem you in long enough that you learn to choose them for yourself. Just because you wander does not mean you are lost. We can't lose sight of that.

So often the Bible seems to indicate that the purpose of the wilderness is bound up in our identity and our relationship with the Creator. It seems to be the place where we come face to face with the harsh reality that we are needy creatures and that without someone or something to sustain us, we cannot entirely make it on our own. We may survive, but we won't live well and we certainly won't be sure of who we are. I don't know about you, but choosing myself the way that God chooses me might be the hardest thing I've ever done.

At this very minute, I am wrestling hard with that reality. It requires standing for things I don't want to and allowing others to live with the consequences of their decisions because their decisions are hurting me. It's the outer edge of the wilderness, but it's still a desert nevertheless. I haven't crossed into the Promised Land. I'm in the middle of some really hard decisions these days, decisions about directions my life will take. They carry a weight that I'm still learning how to hold.

I recognize now the incredible impact my decisions have on people around me, but I seem to ignore that when it comes to my own value. Somehow, I sell myself short and give in to the pull of immediate, temporal comfort instead of long-term fulfillment and gain. Job's eyes were so fixed on God for so long that even loss beyond comprehension couldn't wrench them away. I don't think I've ever loved Him that well.

Job had to choose God for himself. His wife turned against him. His friends turned against him. His neighbors, city, and even strangers who didn't know him looked at him mocking. That said, Job didn't turn to God because he had nowhere else to go. He turned to Him because that's where he was already looking. I don't know about you, but I'm not that kind of faithful. I all too easily forget. If I'm honest, I don't run that hard towards my goals. I don't pursue them like I'm on fire. I chase them when it's challenging, but I stop when it costs me everything. I don't wait well. Like Job understood, I'm learning that faithfulness requires discipline. It requires an intensity that I wasn't really prepared to engage with.

I used to believe being faithful meant not screwing up. It was a perfection of sorts where I got things right and lived the life Jesus modeled. Being faithful actually means being true, loyal, and steadfast. It's a touchstone of sorts, the experience of coming back to God, no matter in what condition we find ourselves, over and over again. It's the refusal, despite our failures and lack, to give up on the life God has for us. Sometimes it means simply waiting and trusting that, if you stay long enough, God will reveal Himself – as He really is, not as we imagined Him to be.

Tuning our hearts and training our eyes for that kind of vision is life changing. I watched my dad do it. I am convinced that that and nothing else is what enabled him to endure the excruciating journey through pancreatic cancer and, prior to that, his life which was anything but easy. He was able because he'd set his heart, his mind, his vision in one direction and pursued it without ceasing. Even in death, he waited with expectation.

———

I sat with a friend yesterday who never ceases to say hard things to me. He is a mirror to me through my own wanderings. After listening to the spaces where I'm still sitting, he questioned, *"So, why are you not moving? Why are you settling? What is holding you in place?"* After a while of considering, I answered that it was me, it was a piece of my identity with which I am wrestling. He understood but still challenged me, *"Don't wrestle so long that you waste this time you keep saying you've discovered is so precious. If you really believe what you are saying, then your life is going to show its evidence."*

Job's life *was* the evidence. The destruction, the fallout, the complete devastation? *That* was evidence that his heart was in the right place. His responses through and after everything went down only reaffirmed its value. Tragedy isn't the only place we will find meaning. So much of it hinges on our willingness to expectantly wait and keep pursuing that which our souls long for. This is why it is so important that we don't make the wilderness our home. I know how incredibly tempting it is. I've been there repeatedly and not much else sounded better than giving in. It's taken years for me to realize it's mostly a matter of perspective.

Cooperating with the truth of life outside Eden is an incredibly difficult space. I don't always occupy it well. I tend to get bogged down in the constant struggle of it and decide it'd just be better to make a home here than it would be to keep traveling through it. I start looking for ways to sustain life in the barrenness instead of demanding of myself that I do whatever it takes to make it to the Promised Land.

Sometimes you find yourself wandering because you left Egypt and escaped the slavery of exile. Sometimes you find yourself in it because you actually listened to God and were doing things His way. What we have to reconcile ourselves to is the fact that we aren't going to make it through this life in an easy fashion no matter what path we choose. The question is whether or not in the process we are really going to encounter the God of truth or settle for the one of our own making.

Both like and unlike Job, I all too often have fixed my eyes on my circumstances instead of the One who holds my hand. I look out in fear, terrified at what I see, afraid that I won't matter again, that I will be left in this horrific state by myself, and I forget all about my destination. I run for immediate shelter instead of long term safety and I hurt myself time and time again.

Maybe you've been here also. Maybe you feel like Job and know you didn't bring this on yourself. Maybe you're sitting in a place of resentment and bitterness, knowing you didn't deserve this. Or maybe you see your mistakes and think you did. Maybe, like Job's friends, you think God is holding something over your head, waiting for you to repent, and it's just too heavy. Maybe you feel beyond forgiveness. Or maybe, like the Israelites, you've made your peace with slavery and, compared to life in the wilderness, Egypt just doesn't seem all that bad.

No matter to which of these or something else we relate, one thing remains true: We were made for more. This isn't it. Eden occupies our hearts for a reason. Our job isn't to recreate it here or to settle for a lesser home. I think the hardest part of this journey is reconciling ourselves to the fact that it's necessary.

Reconciling disenchantment with God is also accepting that being disenchanted is essential to really knowing Him.

As I've said before, that isn't what I ever wanted. If it meant going through this, I'd prefer to sign off. That's my humanity talking. My heart though? Well, it longs to be seen and known and loved. I don't want this journey to have been pointless, and the only way it won't be is for me to accept that disenchantment with the God I believed Him to be is an absolute necessity. Like you, I don't want that to be true. I don't like embracing heartache. I want Eden here today. I don't want to need redeeming grace – not for me or for you. I don't enjoy experiencing lack or living in a battlefield. I want the God I've conjured Him to be to be the God He really is. I want Him to be a bit more of a genie who grants me a wish or two. I don't relish the process of reconciling what I thought with what reality proves itself to be. Some pieces of this journey are simply excruciating and I lose sight of so much while trying to navigate them.

When God left Eden with us, I imagine pulling the veil up between being fully known and seeing through a glass dimly must have been incredibly painful for Him. I know that, as a parent, I've hated nothing more than when my kids miss my heart for them. I've shed many tears as a mother when my heart was in the right place, my actions necessary, but their understanding of me and what I was doing was the exact opposite of reality. It's so hard to be unknown, to feel that emptiness in between. That's why God kept pursuing us. It's why He left Eden. It's why He's here now, sitting with us as we reconcile our disenchantment with who we thought Him to be.

I don't know about you, but I need a God who stays. One who stands behind the veil and doesn't move even though I can't see what He sees. I need to know that I can keep coming back, asking questions, railing against the veil in between what I see and what I believe. I need a God who lets me experience things I don't understand so that I will find the real Him that I seek. Our circumstances being reconciled doesn't really matter, yet that's where we settle, making homes in the wilderness, seeking the restoration of our circumstances more than we seek knowing God Himself.

I don't know what the journey looks like from here. I'm still traveling, but I am learning something integral: disenchantment isn't bad. It actually holds the key to understanding. It's where mystery and fear meld together, where exhaustion lays its head down, where Providence shows up, and where we can rest our souls while asking incredibly hard questions. That is where I find myself. Seeing a little, unsure of exactly where I'm going, but certain that the God I once knew is thankfully no longer only in Eden.

He is *with* me. He Himself is the Eden I most need and it is Himself that He brings wherever I go. The wilderness, the mountaintop, the Valley of the Shadow of Death. Everywhere I find myself, He is present. God's goal isn't to stop my wandering. It is to remind me that, despite all my wandering, *I am not lost*. Neither is He. The wilderness is not my home. Rather, it is in the wandering through the most desolate of places that we begin reconciling our disenchantment with who we thought God to be.

The wilderness is the place where we start to find
ourselves and the God we've always wanted to know.

Chapter Nine:
Longing

"Longing is the agony of the nearness of the distant."
~Martin Heidegger[18]

I was writing a friend today and we share some similar struggles. In reading the same book, we both seized upon the same concept – feeling like our expectations are too much, that we ourselves feel at once like too much and not enough. She's embarking on a day that tends to be painful on an annual basis. Having been in those exact shoes, I relate so much to where she finds herself, so I wrote this in response,

> *"It's so hard to hold space with gratitude for what's been without allowing the longing for what could be to run away with us. Somehow expectation is the great chasm between. And I suppose that's the purpose of faith. Knowing our "cannots" are Jesus' invitations to bring healing in the spaces between without deciding for Him what the outcome should be. Holding the definition of hope loosely but clinging to the One who makes it a reality in any form it comes. ... May it be [a day] where truth is the doorway to ashes made beautiful."*

I have no idea where you find yourself. It could be on the floor pouring your heart and soul out. Maybe it's in the throes of anger, resentment, or worse – regret. Maybe you are in a place where it feels like hope will never win out and what has been will always come back to pass. I don't know and I won't fill this space with platitudes. Instead, I'd rather invite us both to a place where being real is held with tenderness and truth bound up in one. Where the harshness of unchanging realities can linger with the desires that break our hearts when left unmet.

There is a verse in Proverbs that says, *"Hope deferred makes the heart sick, but a longing fulfilled is a tree of life."* (Prov. 13:12) I think we all struggle with its truth. A thousand times over we hope for things only to find hope itself dashed into little pieces. We want the tree of life, the fulfillment that it brings, right here right now. When you're in the throes of deep grief, fulfillment doesn't look the same as it does when you're charging towards your goals. In moments of anger or a world that makes us hard, fulfillment itself lingers with a taste that's bitter and desire grown cold.

In moments like where Job found himself, fulfillment meant only one thing. Seeing God – the one allowing all this tragedy. Not in a positive, healing, happy way. Job wasn't looking for comfort. He was frustrated, exhausted, weary, a bit angry, deeply grieved, and certainly overwhelmed. He wanted a talk – to hash it out with God. To get answers to what was going on. Fulfillment for Job entailed having an audience with the Most High Himself.

So many of us wrestle with the "enoughness" of a God we can't see or physically engage. We are temporal creatures, driven by earthly pleasures and necessities, so it just doesn't seem so terrible for us to ask Him to fulfill a hope of ours or to not allow tragedy to wreck our worlds. Even the strongest of us have a fragility that we'd rather not have to encounter. Longing makes us acutely aware of our insufficiencies, limitations, and lack. Having to rely on someone else for just about anything is seen as a sign of weakness and we'd rather it be a luxury we opt to possess.

Job was stripped of all things that could fill him up. What I find so interesting is that where Satan thought that would be the end of Job, the thing that crippled him, God saw it as an opportunity for Job to truly know himself. Satan had already said in essence, "Listen, God. You've got Your boy Job so covered up, surrounded, provided for, and privileged that he has no reason *not* to trust You and think the absolute best of all You offer. What does he lack?" God's response wasn't to defend Job, which is the approach I think all of us would take. Instead, He offers Job up and says, "Don't kill him, but go find out for yourself."

God enters into our lack knowing that every single time, if we live long enough, we are *going* to find ourselves feeling that tension of hope deferred, longing for a tree of life to sustain us. Eden didn't just hold the Tree of the Knowledge of Good and Evil. It also held the Tree of Life – the one that nourished Eve and Adam. It was the fulfillment of need and longing to which they returned time and time again whenever they wanted.

> **What our souls seem to know but our minds seem to lack is
> the understanding that life in a sin-soaked world is
> *supposed* to make our hearts sick.**

Longings *are* going to be unfulfilled. Hopes *will* be deferred. We *are* going to be sick about it. Sometimes so much so that we don't want to keep going. Or, if we do, we are angry and harsh, and our hatred of a world gone wrong gets spewed in every direction, its recipients deserving or not. Longing hits everyone a little bit differently, but our first response is rarely compassion for others or ourselves.

Have you ever found yourself waiting so long for hope to be realized that you give up on waiting and just start trying to make it happen? Some people call that controlling or anxious. I call it pain. The reality is that we all come here with Eden set in our hearts. God Himself put eternity within us so it's no wonder we desire perfection. We long for beauty realized and hope fulfilled. We want to eat from that Tree of Life and experience all the goodness its fruit offers. When that doesn't happen, we feel pain. This isn't the life we were made to sustain and our hearts know it.

The problem with pain is that we aren't much for waiting. We get antsy when time runs long or expectation robs our joy in the here and now. I know from personal experience how easy it is to give up or give in. How easy it is to walk away or develop my own action plan. If my energy is low, I'm more likely to give in. The day to day becomes unbearable and I just don't think I can summon up what it takes to face another one of the same. If I'm motivated by anger, hardship, or righting the wrongs, I am likely to jump the gun, forget considering a wise course of action, and skip right past the teamwork phase and instead tell God exactly how it is. Either way, I'm just looking for a way through or out – to fulfill that longing in one way or another myself.

If we are going to hold space for our longings and be tender with our hopes and needs, then we have to reconcile ourselves to the fact that the goal is not that we figure out how to make this earth more like heaven. If that was what God wanted for us, if that was really what was *best*, He wouldn't have ever shut the gates to Eden. It'd be right there in the middle of us, with its fruit available for the taking. It's not though and we have to ask ourselves why.

I think it's the same reason that Job came to realize. He had livestock, influence, family, business, power, and possessions in great abundance. He knew what it meant to live well. He even knew what it meant to be socially just, to help the poor, to lift up the needy, to advocate for righteousness for the mistreated and downtrodden. He was himself living grace and mercy to people in need of it. He wasn't living in lack and he was bridging the gap of it in the lives of those around him.

Yet, when he found himself lacking, he didn't ask for everything back. He didn't even ask for justice, for revenge, for something to assuage the unfairness of it all. Instead, when facing tragedy, Job asked to *know*. To have a reason for his suffering. He wanted a purpose for his pain and a longing that superseded anything temporal this world had to offer him. He didn't merely want escape from the mess but a God who joined him in it.

We don't have the ability to restore this world alone and it's remarkable that we continue trying. We didn't create it yet we consistently attempt time and time again to tame it. Interestingly, when God situated Adam and Eve over the earth, He never situated them over each other. He set them up in a place of cooperation *with* each other. Even when sin came on the scene, He never said, your job is to conquer one another. Rather, *God* made the first sacrifice knowing that even then, before all of humanity came to be and it was just the three of them, Adam and Eve couldn't save themselves. They needed God. Sin One and they were already down for the count. They couldn't even handle the basics without being in need and acutely aware of their lack.

God is a way-maker, but the way doesn't come at our hands. We don't get to design the outcomes and yet we continue to try. We strive and strive and strive for longings fulfilled and rail against God when our hope is deferred. **We fail to recognize that a sin-soaked world is delaying His longing fulfilled too.** We are all in this boat together. Even now, when we buy something and it breaks or malfunctions, what do we do? Redesign it ourselves? Not usually. Some may try, but most of us call up the manufacturer and say, "Hey, your equipment isn't working like it was designed. What do I do now?"

The thing is that none of us were there during creation. None of us know every single in and out of our own design. We don't have full understanding of the intents and purposes for things, the reasons behind why specific situations were set up the way they are by God. That's one of the very things God points out to Job during their eventual conversation. He asks Job time and time again, "Were you there when...? Did you see why...? Do you understand the inner workings of...? Can you even grasp the methodology behind...?"

This is why, despite Job's immense grief and intense pain, he is able to stand in awe of God and go, "I will be silent. I have nothing more I can say. You are so much more than I ever expected or imagined. I will be quiet." God's goal wasn't to get Job to shut up and stop complaining. His purpose was to let Job know that, if I've got all this under control, I've got your situation handled too. There is no chance I haven't witnessed all you're enduring and there is no way I'm not privy to why it's occurring. I've made plans and created things beyond your comprehension, things that will straight up terrify you, things that you couldn't possibly manage even if you created the most powerful machine ever known to mankind. So, if you want an audience with me, brace yourself because the God you imagined me to be isn't even close to the God I actually am.

Friends, *that* is the kind of God we need. One who understands the sickness of a heart whose hope is still lingering, whose fulfillment of longing has been deferred. We need a God who aches as we ache but who also reveals Himself as able. Sure, He could right all the wrongs and mete out justice beyond our comprehension. He could do things we can't even imagine in the here and now. But, oh the loss that would be to us all. We'd miss out on knowing Him and ourselves.

We'd lose the right to choose and the choice would be made for us. Lives in numbers that stagger beyond our imagination would be lost in ways we aren't prepared for the fall out of, and we'd find ourselves right back where we are now – disenchanted with the God we thought He was instead of the God He actually is. Only then, there'd be no hope of reconciling ourselves to that or to Him. That loss? Well, it's unspeakable.

God is *present* in our sickness, our heartache of a world gone wrong, a longing unfulfilled. He designed us. He knows that for which we were all created. He sees the effects of sin's curse on creation better than any of us could ever acquaint ourselves with. So, it is with a heart of compassion, a hope that He defers Himself, that He lets us experience longing. We need to understand that reconciling ourselves to disenchantment with the God we thought Him to be is also the freedom of connecting ourselves with the heart of the God who knows the people He created us as originally. There is a purpose in embracing hope deferred and longings unfulfilled.

It draws us to the heart of Jesus.

He knows this world wasn't intended to turn on itself. He knows that men were never supposed to conquer and kill one another. God understands fully that what man represents His heart to be and what His heart actually is are all too often lightyears apart. So, longing is itself that thing that drives us to know Him, to understand the design behind all that He created. Seeing a world cursed, experiencing a sickened heart at the deferment of our hope, longing for fulfillment is what should be driving us *to* God, not away from Him.

It is in this very place of deep lack and honest assessment that we align ourselves with a God who has limitless resources and hitch our wagon to the One who has a plan to restore everything. We can't do it ourselves. No social justice mission is going to be a success forever because everything we do here is limited in time and scope, and no mission can escape the curse of a world that is driven to destroy itself.

That is the wall against which we will beat our heads time and time and time again. So, if we want restoration, if we want answers, if we want to *know*, then like Job, we can't get mired in the here and now – we *have* to insist on an audience with the Almighty Himself. We *must* insist on knowing and in doing so, hold space for our longings, to carry hopes deferred with gentleness for the expectation in the ways and time that they will be fulfilled.

God made us a promise: "As the rain and the snow come down from heaven, and do not return to it without watering the earth and making it bud and flourish, so that it yields seed for the sower and bread for the eater, so is my word that goes out from my mouth: It will not return to me empty, but it will accomplish what I desire and achieve the purpose for which I sent it." (Isaiah 55:10-11)

Here's the rub: Like my friend and me, *we don't get to decide what that looks like.* We cannot choose the outcome. We cannot assign God a specific result. He is not a genie and we are not granted wishes. So, how do we hold longing with the tenderness required for us to sit in places that deferred hope makes our hearts sick and not give in or give up? I think it's what Job clung to and what I wrote to my friend,

"I suppose that's the purpose of faith. Knowing our "cannots" are Jesus' invitations to bring healing in the spaces between without deciding for Him what the outcome should be. Holding the definition of hope loosely but clinging to the One who makes it a reality in any form it comes. ... May it be ... where truth is the doorway to ashes made beautiful."

Chapter Ten:
Faith and The Injustice of It All

"I guess the only time most people think about injustice is when it happens to them."

~Charles Bukowski[19]

For several years now, injustice has felt the tagline marking my days. Maybe you've felt the same way. Sometimes situations and people hurt us in ways that cut deep and stay long. For me, it's taken a good while to realize that the relentless assault on my sense of justice was really an assault on my identity. The places my heart aches most, where I feel the rage of injustice burning in my soul, those are ones where I'm using my voice as a catalyst for growth, where who I am matters most.

I don't know if any of us start out bearing injustice well. My guess is that Job had lived a while by the time his world imploded, so he'd probably learned the art of losing well. He'd probably been the personal recipient of unfair treatment more times than he could count and thus developed the wisdom of responding appropriately. There is an element of Job's initial response to loss that tells us he was a man of maturity. He knew his priorities and tragedy wasn't going to create an immediate division from those.

I don't know about you, but I find one of the hardest things about enduring injustice is maintaining focus. I can get so caught up in the emotions of a moment that I forget the point behind engaging in it. It becomes more about my experience being validated than it ever was about my message being heard at all. Being heard and acknowledged makes us feel as if our viewpoint holds value, so not experiencing that is a deep blow.

I think Job felt that. Once the reality set in and the injustice was made clear to him, Job began a constant discourse of needing an audience with God. He pled nonstop to make his case before the courtroom of heaven, all the while acknowledging that doing so probably wouldn't make a difference. Job seemed to understand at once that his condition was hopeless yet his argument worthy so he was willing to risk it. I get that. I've tried the same on repeat in these unjust situations I've encountered in recent years. Like Job, I've also recognized that it's a lesson in futility.

Growing up, I never understood Jesus' comments about not throwing our pearls before swine. It seemed a bit harsh, comparing people to pigs. It took years for me to realize that Jesus wasn't putting a label on others, but rather issuing a boundary call to us. What He meant was we can't put things that are valuable to us in the mud where they will be devalued and trampled upon by those who don't value them like we do. That may be one of the hardest action steps of injustice. Bearing it well requires maturity.

Choosing not to have the conversation, choosing to walk away without explaining, choosing to honor the fact that you're stamped with God's image and the person in front of you doesn't see it. Instead of fighting for the value they refuse to acknowledge, you choose to exit the situation. You choose mercy, not for them, but for your own aching soul.

All of us can relate somehow. When life stings, when unexpected grief boils up, when circumstances the size of meteors crater into the sides of our worlds, we feel it. The injustice of carrying around pain that isn't fair, that so often isn't even our own doing. It's here that we get frustrated with God. It's here that we understand people are human and maybe they make terrible choices that we ourselves wouldn't make, but what we can't wrap our minds around is a God who allows it.

He permits injustice and there isn't one of us who doesn't feel the unfairness of His election. I think it's important to pause and consider that for a moment. The allowance of injustice is God's election, not our doing. All we can do is either cooperate and trust Him or rage against the machine and try to fix what we believe He isn't doing. There really isn't an in between. Letting life happen to us is still living in unbelief – it's surrendering to a world undone as if trust was never even an option at all.

We live in a society where input equals output, so we expect that doing good means receiving the same. So, why did Job receive the opposite? Instead of blessing and greatness his entire life long, Job was shoved into the spotlight of being the poster child for what appeared to be a life gone wrong. His faithfulness, obedience, top notch character, praise from God's throne – all these earned Job the top spot on Satan's assault roster. His efforts resulted in his downfall and a world like that makes no sense to us. All ushered in by a God who not only allowed it but *invited* it? Why?

This is the point where our emotions from the fallout cause us to lose focus. We are deeply wounded and thus angry that injustice exists at all. Many of us start raging at God while others grow bitter and cold. We demand reasons for the conditions into which our lives have fallen, knowing in our souls that we did not deserve the magnitude of what has befallen us. As humans, we may not believe we'll receive greatness or even that we deserve it, but all of us at some point believe that exponential injustice should not be our meal's main course. We certainly don't want it as a lifestyle. Life is something we believe should be predicted and controlled, where making good decisions assures us good results. When that isn't how it works, we don't know where to go.

Out of everyone who has ever lived aside from Jesus, Job certainly deserved a better set of circumstances than he was given. We don't know much about the people surrounding Job, but we do know Job was an incredibly good man – as righteous as a human person can come and still be fallible. We also know that his children were not killed as the result of their own or Job's sin. We know that the immense losses dished out by Satan didn't just affect Job. Many people's lives around him were forever altered or ended. His children, servants, wife, household, and their families. His entire community was rocked. The entire *region* knew about Job. If social media had existed back then, Job's devastation would have made headline news across the globe.

Tragedies of this magnitude cause us to understand why people develop disenchantment with God. Injustice changes us and shapes our worldview. It feels impossible to carry on a relationship with someone who allows the horrible. Once we walk a day in those same shoes, we no longer shame people for being angry with God. Instead, disillusioned ourselves, we join them. Having been on the receiving end of the tragedy, we share their stance, "A loving God wouldn't allow this. If that's the way He loves, then I want no part of Him." Or, in Job's wife's words, "Are you still trying to be godly when God has done all this to you? Curse him and die." (Job 2:9, TLB)

A couple of years ago, my husband and I went on a marriage retreat that was given to us as a wedding present. Attendance had been delayed for a couple years due to COVID, so we were looking forward to finally going. It turned out to be one of the worst weekends we've ever had. The shotgun approach to sensitive topics and haphazard tactics only increased the damage to those of us who'd come expecting hope. We drove home feeling like the entire experience was one of emotional whiplash. One of their glossed over sessions was on the delicate topic of forgiveness. I expected that session to be the easiest one because, by nature, I tend to forgive and move on pretty quickly in most circumstances. God however had a different agenda.

Early on in our relationship, a situation had taken place that was deeply painful for me and I'd been carrying it ever since. It became a marker with a date that couldn't be erased. Every year as certain reminders came up, the events replayed themselves, overshadowing our present day. The impact of those events were etched on my soul and shaped the lens through which I saw multiple pieces of our relationship. It had become a burden I was trapped under that grew heavier with every passing conversation about our identity as a couple. They asked us each to write down the event that hurt us and, if we knew the date, include that too. Afterward, we were to fold up the paper, take it to the stage, and drop it into a bowl as a physical representation of leaving that behind at the foot of the cross.

Immediate pain hit me. I knew the exact date. In a mixture of bitterness and anguish, I wrote it down then sat there and sobbed. I couldn't stop. It wasn't just my heart. My *soul* hurt. I didn't know how to let this one go. Forgiving wouldn't mean history erasing itself. That's not how justice works. What was done was done and I knew that was how it would always be. The piece of our story that I carried was a permanent injury and I didn't know how to live with that.

Healing is painful and we don't spend enough time honoring

the space that holds. I wasn't all that interested in letting God tend to my still gaping wounds. He allowed them after all. At the same time, my heart said on repeat, "Alanna, you can't keep carrying this around. It's affecting your heart, mind, body, and soul. All things God wants to be whole. So, if you don't give it to Jesus, it has nowhere to go."

Nothing in me wanted to take that paper up front. I knew what would happen if I did. It meant really leaving it with God. The reality wasn't that I wanted to hold on to it anymore. That was excruciating in itself. It was just that I didn't want it to be real. I didn't want that to be part of my story. I'd signed up to *stop* hurting, not to forgive more. I wasn't remotely interested in God's justice or redemption. I wanted history to not have been what it was, pure and simple, and that plot twist was never going to be available.

I wrestled so hard in that spot before finally making the choice to walk up front. I'm pretty sure I cried the entire way as my husband walked with me, knowing what I'd written down, recognizing that he was as affected by my choice to let it go as I was. As I laid that paper down in the bowl, my heart felt like it might explode. It sounds so ridiculous to even write, but it was honestly one of the hardest things I have ever done.

Letting go of injustice may be the most difficult call we will ever have on our lives. If that is where you find yourself, know that I am holding space for you. *I get it.* Where you are, what you have suffered, how you may feel in this very moment, *it absolutely matters.* Your pain does not go unnoticed. The injustice of how I felt when that event occurred, the incredible pain it caused, no one but me and God will ever know. I could try to tell you, but I am certain even now that my words would fall short. Some injustices are just indescribable.

When I walked away from that bowl, leaving the representation of my choice behind, I felt the burden begin to lift. My heart and soul knew that if I laid that paper down, I wasn't going back to pick it up. I hadn't held back this time. I hadn't spoken the words then denied them in my heart. This time I knew that, although the events would never be undone, my heart would be healed. I didn't have to carry the pain of the injustice the same way anymore. Now, I could hold space for healing, for God to do a new thing where the old thing was broken.

What we often forget about Job is that his healing took time too. His whole life wasn't restored overnight. The injustice was not immediately remedied. Job didn't wake up from tragedy one day to a happy wife, 10 new kids, and a great new world. After his discourse with God, Job still had to walk day after day, week after week, year after year through a long, slow restoration process. Yes, he died "old and full of years" (Job 42:17) but it was a protracted, gradual journey of getting there. I am certain that Job's life after destruction was an ongoing lesson in exercising trust and faith. Job now knew that God's justice didn't guarantee him protection against loss and suffering. In fact, it ensured the opposite.

Job came to understand what none of us want to embrace – that the way to the heart of a God who loves us is *through* suffering, not escape. I cannot even fathom how he explained that to his next generation of kids. The necessity we cannot avoid if we want our pain to have meaning and our lives have aim is that we *need* faith. It sounds unbelievable, but friends, the antidote for injustice is faith. It's not spinning your wheels in social justice. It's not self-improvement techniques. It's not even revenge or killing your enemies with kindness. No, the most valuable resource and weapon you will ever carry is faith. It's what enables us to carry the effects of injustice with us like Job did.

Despite Satan's lengthy time on this planet, he still isn't wise to the ways of God. Satan had the misguided perception that God was the only one protecting Job. Satan thought that once God took His protective hedge away, Job would cave. He was wholly unprepared to do battle with Job's faith. We see that because when Satan attacked Job and took everything except his health away, Job praised God for giving and taking away, so Satan determined his assault wasn't strong enough and returned to God seeking permission to do more. When God granted him the opportunity and Satan took Job's physical health away, he thought that would be the end of Job. It wasn't.

God wasn't ever the one who was going to save Job from Satan. It was always Job's *faith*. We were designed to be *part* of the story. God isn't a superhero and we aren't just casualties in His war with the enemy. No, we are His most precious creation and He loves us dearly. So, if we are going to participate in this part of the story, then we are going to need something to sustain us. That's why we're designed to need faith. It's our only real weapon that defeats the most insidious, relentless enemy. God offers us protection, but it is only to the extent that we choose faith that that protection garners us true saving grace.

I don't want it to be that way. I don't want any of this to rely on me. Maybe you feel the same way. Faith sometimes feels like false hope or as if we're giving up on things. I wrestle with this concept on repeat. The reality though is that faith is exactly how the writer of Hebrews described it: "Now faith is the substance of things *hoped* for, the evidence of things *not seen*" (Heb. 11:1, NKJV, emphasis mine). It is believing in that which you cannot see, being counted amongst the great cloud of witnesses who cheer on those coming behind them, doing hard things and making hard choices, choosing holiness over happiness, no matter the cost. I love how the Amplified version describes it in more detail:

> "Now faith is the assurance (title deed, confirmation) of things
> hoped for (*divinely guaranteed*), and the evidence of things not
> seen [the conviction of their reality – faith comprehends as
> *fact* what cannot be experienced by the physical senses]."
> (AMP, emphasis mine)

When I first read it, that last line really hit me: "*Faith comprehends as* <u>fact</u> *what cannot be experienced by the physical senses.*"

Faith is what tells our injustice that justice will have its day.

It tells us that even a God who allows tragedy and things beyond our comprehension is good and working for an outcome we could never create. Faith believes it as if it has already occurred and operates *as if it is already true*. Faith sees the God who leaves Eden in search of us because *we* are more important to Him than His own safety.

That was the difference in me walking out of the retreat that day. I left the injustice sitting in that bowl, at the foot of the cross, and walked away living as if all had already been made right again. I left carrying faith instead of bitterness, belief instead of fear, hope instead of loss. **My circumstances hadn't changed, where I put my faith had.** I exchanged faith in circumstance for trust in a God who heals. At the time, I had no clue if my future circumstances would contain any form of restoration. I certainly didn't think they could. I chose not to rely on God to redeem the days and somehow make the past not be the past. Instead, I held space for the fact that history cannot undo itself and I allowed pain and injustice to become part of my permanent journey.

Hebrews identifies Jesus as the high priest who empathizes. He understands. He's been where we are. Millions of people have lost their lives because of Him. He Himself took on pains that weren't His to bear. He came here with good intent, healthy concern and care, unselfish in His ways, and loving people that were not very lovable. He sat with some of the worst, most hated people of the day, and broke bread. He had compassion for lepers and touched them, a thing no one else would dare. Yet, somehow it was in doing the *right* thing, the *good* thing, the *holy* thing, things that healed people and made them see just how much He cared, that Jesus found Himself with enemies.

They hated Him, plotted His murder. They tried over and over to trap Him, to keep His truth from getting oxygen. He died for them anyway. His family suffered deeply. His disciples felt lost after He was buried. There really aren't any words I can say that explain the cross, both literal and spiritual, that Jesus had to bear. So, when the author of Hebrews says we have a Savior who understands, a High Priest that cares, a brother who walked in our shoes and carried the weight of the world on His shoulders, he means it. That's why Hebrews also says in that same passage that we can come *confidently* to the throne of grace seeking to have Him meet us there.

Faith is the assurance, the confidence, the *reliance as if in fact* that what we seek has already occurred. It doesn't mean we can assign God a specific outcome. Faith doesn't work that way. It isn't showing up telling the Eternal, "You have to do it this way." Faith is coming to the throne, hands open, knowing you will be met there, that your pain will have a place, and that you can leave your burdens with the One who will go before you, behind you, and beside you all the way.

Faith is the hardest cure for the hardest pain.

When Job's conversation with God concludes at the end of the book, God doesn't give Job any promises. He doesn't say, "I will restore to you the years the locusts have eaten" like He did to the prophet Joel (Joel 2:25). He doesn't bring Job's kids back to life. The hearts of Job and his wife were still broken after immense loss. Their reputations beyond tarnished. What Job lost wasn't easily restored and his healing didn't occur overnight. The Bible doesn't even give us a hint that God ever explained to Job what was going on behind the curtain and why he experienced what he did.

I think the reason for this is because, in the face of the very worst injustice – beyond all we can bear - God is enough. *He alone is our vision bearer.* In a world where we are guaranteed trouble, our only hope is a God who joins us in the mess of a life gone wrong. Where sin and injustice reign and we cannot stop the onslaught, He steps in and says, "This isn't all there is. What you see as devastation I promise holds meaning. I know that you can't see what I see. You're going to have to trust me. I made a way for Eden once and I'm going to do it again."

───────────────

Before I got on my knees and let God have one of the situations that has tormented me for the last few years, I believed I *needed* a certain outcome. If I'm honest, I thought I deserved it and that my idea would be best for everyone. Like Job, my heart was for good things and to this day, I can tell you exactly how they'd play out if everything occurred that way.

The problem is I don't have the foresight God does. My limited understanding only ensures that my version will make me feel better, but it doesn't guarantee the changed circumstances I've entertained. I have no clue whether my plan will have done the work of holiness that is on God's agenda. And that's the rub, isn't it? We don't *want* God's agenda. We want Him to make *our* agenda His own. We want Him to pick up *our* torch, especially if our intentions are good and our motives as pure as fresh-fallen snow.

The cure for me is the same as it is for all of us. It's leaving this situation at the foot of the cross. It's walking away with faith that, in God's hands, as Jesus said just before His death, "It is finished." (John 19:30) The work is done. That situation has been crucified and, just as with the cross, God will reach however He needs backward into history and forward into time, not changing occurrences, but healing hearts and affecting minds.

Never in my life have I experienced the kind of freedom that I did on that absolutely wretched day at that marriage conference. I've come to realize that's what faith does. It gives you the assurance, the absolute conviction of the divine guarantee that *God has got this.* He has you and, even amidst the absolute worst injustice, you can say, "It is well with my soul."[20] He will not let you go. Job had to cling to that with every single thread of courage he could summon. He <u>chose</u> faith.

It is always a choice. We were not created for injustice. That's why it rocks our world. God made us in *His* image and *He* is the epitome of all that is just. We're not going to drum it up. We aren't going to create it. All our social justice endeavors will eventually find their way to ruin. We don't have the power to design Eden in this world. Eden was where *God* ruled, where *His* way *was* the way and His way holds a justice we cannot in all our finite humanity ever sustain. But He will not force it upon us. It is our decision.

Anyone that is fighting for justice like Job was before Satan tried to take him out is going to find themselves an enemy. Satan "prowls around like a roaring lion looking for someone to devour." (1 Peter 5:8b) We don't live protected inside Eden's gates. Out here, this world is at war with itself, and being people who are just is a calling that may cost us everything, including our very lives.

Faith seems like weakness to most of us. We'd rather show up and show out, getting things done ourselves, presenting ourselves strong on our own behalf. What we don't realize is that our strength is greatest when we do the opposite and, like Jesus, who "entrusted himself to him who judges justly," (1 Peter 2:23b, NIV) we live by faith, not by sight. We follow the steps but don't determine the way. If you read the faith hall of fame in Hebrews 11, it says that all those people died living in *faith*. Not in justice, social equality, or presently changed circumstances. They didn't get what was promised before they died, but they saw it coming – through eyes of *faith*, <u>trusting as *fact*</u> that *God* was going to keep His word to them. It all rests on faith's rock.

———————————————————————

There are those of you reading this book that have been through atrocities no human should ever face. You've lost parents, children, spouses, countries, homes, freedoms, parts of your own selves (body and mind) that you will never get back. Some of you will have endured tragedies no human was ever designed to withstand and they have rocked your world. Injustice may be the only thing you truly understand. It has defined every bit of your days and that pain is beyond what you feel you can bear.

If that is where you find yourself, let me just say: There is space for you here. Your pain, the injustice of what you have suffered, it is absolutely not fair. No one should have to carry these things. No one should have to feel that kind of fear or rage. The loss and life altering realities are beyond unfair and not one bit of it is okay. There is room for you here to declare those things because you have a God who agrees. This was never your intended destiny.

Like you, there are devastating realities in my story that will never change. Ones much worse than those I share here. I will walk around with wounds that ache for the rest of my days and sometimes grief still brings me to my knees. The one choice I have made is to carry those with me in faith. One of the situations I've endured for nearly 4 years has ached in a way that has nearly ended relationships and resulted in my need for very strong boundaries. I've cried more tears than I care to share.

Recently, I wrote that situation down on an index card and laid it on the floor in front of me. I got down on my knees before God with that card in front of my face and I heard Him clearly say,

> "This is mine. It was always mine to bear. I have plans you don't know about. There are things you can't comprehend. Your version of events, no matter how well placed, isn't the one I'm creating. My heart and vision for this extends beyond all you can see or imagine. This isn't yours to take. Let me carry this one, child. I'm not promising you a specific result. You need to trust me regardless of what happens. Remember – my ways are not your ways. My justice isn't your justice. It's better."

I don't like that answer, but I am embracing the lightness it carries. I am choosing the path of faith where I don't get to design the ending, but I am free to experience the healing. Justice doesn't mean wrongs are always righted. It doesn't mean the world turns to peace instead of fighting. Injustice is part of the story. It always will be. But so are faith and healing. It all depends on what we choose to carry.

Chapter Eleven:
For the Joy

"Grief and trust and joy. They are just kind of all mixed up together aren't they?"

~Katie Davis Majors[21]

The one person I've known in my life that seemed marked by joy was my Granny. My Grandpa and Granddaddy both had touches of it too, but Granny's was like a living, breathing part of her. Something I often felt like I could reach out and touch. She endured so much in her life that was painful, tragic, or scary. Yet, she had this underlying strength that wasn't a simple grin and bear it, but moreso an "I know this has meaning, so I'm not willing to spend my life complaining and fighting it." There is no one else I'd like to grow up and be like more than her.

I've wrestled most of my life with the concept of the joy of the Lord being my strength. It never really made sense to me. Even in watching my Granny live and hearing her stories, I still didn't have the life experience or context in which to put it. Joy marked her days. It permeated everything she did and was very much a part of who she chose to be. Henri Nouwen once wrote, "Joy does not simply happen to us. We have to choose joy and keep choosing it every day."[22] I think there is some truth to that.

Choosing joy isn't the same as choosing happiness. When you choose happiness, it's like taking delight in your present circumstances or believing that something good occurring is just around the corner. Joy, on the other hand, is a state of being. It's a contentedness in your soul when there is no circumstantial reason for it existing. Joy flies in the face of happiness and makes it take a back seat. It forces you to sit with grief and gives wings to trust. Joy is the anchor that ties it all together.

When life falls apart, people come out of the woodworks with platitudes and explanations for our suffering. Listening to all that can be exhausting. What we really need is solace, strength, and understanding. I think that's where joy comes in. Joy doesn't mean everything gets better. Joy doesn't even mean we know it ever *will* get better this side of the grave. Joy is a mindset that informs our pain, telling it, "This isn't all there is."

When we are in the throes of tragedy, that's often exactly how it feels – that this *is* all there is. Just this morning as I was doing my devotional, I found myself wrestling with feeling unseen, unknown, and that message of not mattering that I've battled my whole life long came knocking. Satan knows that the quickest way to stop my voice is to make me believe I don't really have one. So, he hits me where it hurts most: connection.

Being introverted I don't want to connect with people constantly, but I do want to feel like it's available most of the time. I want to know that my friends and family have my back, that when they say they love me, it doesn't mean they'd die for me but rather that they actually want to live life with me. So, when that doesn't happen, it's painful.

The part of Jesus dying on the cross that I get most is the one where it says, "who for the joy set before him endured the cross" (Hebrews 12:2). Nothing marks my life more than enduring things I don't want and feel like might kill me so I can experience the joy of purpose it'll bring through to the other side. I want to connect with my people, to know and be known. I want my people to know I don't just love them enough to stare down death for them, but also to walk through life with them.

The cross has immense weight and glory, but so does Jesus' life. His sacrifice and dying on the cross for us matters in ways nothing else can, while His life and walking this earth with us for 33 years speaks volumes about His desires. His heart isn't seen just on the cross, it's also lived in His days. That's what we have to understand about joy. Joy mingles with endurance, it lingers with pain, it informs our purpose, and it breathes life into our days. It is not a feeling or, like happiness, a circumstance that comes and goes. **Joy stays.**

One of the things that I love about the end of Job's story is the part where it says,

> "All his brothers and sisters and everyone who had
> known him before came and ate with him in his house.

They comforted and consoled him over all the trouble
the LORD had brought on him."
(Job 42:11)

This tells me that, despite God's restoration of Job's material fortune, he was still aching and his heart still broken.

That's the thing about grief and pain and loss: History never erases itself and what's done is never undone. Redemption isn't a time machine that changes what happened. Job had joy in the knowing, not that things were all perfect and unbroken, but in the understanding that God's character can be trusted. That although He allows and invites trouble to inform our days, He likewise provides comfort and consolation because joy is knowing, sharing, and being present *with us*. We will never know if we can trust Him if we don't choose to try. Joy is a choice. One both God and we will have to make if we ever want to experience its benefits.

There is no doubt in my mind that the Job who lived before tragic disruption and the Job that came afterwards were two very different people. I know because I'm the same. Tragedy has informed my understanding of life, grief, pain, God, and relating in ways nothing else has ever done. I think the same is true of Jesus. Enduring that cross, walking this earth, suffering our shame, and feeling our pain has resulted in us having a High Priest that sits at the right hand of God, interceding for us constantly.

I used to wonder why we'd need an intercessor. Jesus died after all and we now have access to God's throne at all times. We don't need a priest to talk to God. The tabernacle system has been abolished. Jesus fulfilled the law and the Holy Spirit indwells us, so what is the point? Why is Jesus in heaven interceding for us? I think it's because He knows. He knows our world's condition. He sees we're outside of Eden. He's endured battle with Satan and He knows that God values faith in us. He understands that trials and testing *will* come.

Faith isn't valuable if it never has to stand for something.

God pointed out Job and He's going to point out us. Satan threw every weapon allowed at Job and he won't hesitate to do the same to us. The story isn't over. It didn't end with Job. When Satan got kicked out of heaven, he came right here for us. He knew God wasn't giving up, and he's not stopping either. War is war and it doesn't end until someone truly wins. That's why Jesus keeps talking, interceding for us. Where Satan battles for our lives and souls, so does Jesus.

This is why we have to remember our focus. That's why joy is so important. It grants us the ability to endure something as awful as the cross. What we have to understand is Jesus' cross wasn't the same as the crosses the other criminals around him were dying on. Their crosses were the result of their own sin. Jesus' wasn't though because He hadn't done anything wrong. His symbolized injustice at its greatest – the taking on for the first time ever sin He'd never committed, pain He'd never caused, and shame that wasn't His to bear. He didn't just take on one person's lifetime of it either. He took on everyone's.

The magnitude of that is beyond my comprehension. I can't even sit with that and begin to understand. My own poor choices or betrayals, my own regrets, those alone feel like too much for me to bear. Yet, He took on everyone's. The entire world's. Billions of people from history's beginning through to its end with a weight not one of us could endure. That tells me the immense value joy carries.

It was "for the *joy* set before Him" that He did all that. Not joy in His circumstances, that's for certain. No one dies on a cross feeling good about it. It wasn't joy in the present day because that was a day of death. It wasn't even joy in knowing He'd rise in three days and see the disciples again. It was joy in understanding – *there is so much more to the story.*

―――――――――――――――

Job didn't know. He didn't have Jesus' perspective. He wasn't God. He didn't even have scripture to rely on. All the prophets and scrolls and writings Jesus read or quoted in His lifetime were written long after Job. So, what was it that held Job together? What made him endure long and not give up? Trust. It was believing that the character of God was good and that in following God, Job was doing the right thing. It was the utter defiance of his circumstances and choosing to look for the Almighty.

That's what joy does. It endures long and much. Job wasn't the one focusing on joy in the moment. God was. He knew that Job's faith was priceless. That, like Peter tells us,

"In his great mercy he has given us new birth into a living hope through the resurrection of Jesus Christ from the dead, and into an inheritance that can never perish, spoil or fade – kept in heaven for you, who *through faith* are shielded by God's power until the coming of the salvation that is ready to be revealed in the last time. In *this* you greatly rejoice, though now for a little while you may have had to suffer grief in all kinds of trials. These have come *so that your **faith – of greater worth than gold,*** which perishes even though refined by fire - *may be proved genuine* and may result in praise, glory and honor when Jesus Christ is revealed." (1 Peter 1:3-7, emphasis mine).

Faith, joy, grief, and trust are all mixed and mingled together. We can't separate them out and expect lives of nothing but goodness. That's not how life outside the Garden of Eden works. Here faith begets trust and trust begets joy while joy endures grief which requires more faith and trust. Round and round it goes over and over again, mixing and mingling into these jars of clay that make up us.

Friend, here is what I know. Your life isn't going to be easy. If it is, you probably aren't living deep enough. The truth is that life outside of Eden is messy and war torn and it requires vision from One who sees through the smoke and dust right out to purpose. We don't have the ability to create that for ourselves, no matter what culture tells us. That's just not how it works. Joy doesn't sell on earth. Happiness does. Watch any commercial and you'll see one temporary fix after the other as offerings. No one mentions permanent, life-sustaining joy much less mention the suffering you'll have to choose because they're a package deal. That's what we have to understand about joy. It sustains us. It is the foundation that allows us to endure long and much. Joy is like the holes. It's knowing. It's honoring the space they hold and choosing to fill them up with something. Something worthy, something that gives us sustenance.

Joy is the permanent, inherent
worthiness of a thing.

It is not fleeting and doesn't change like a fair weather friend. Joy sits in trenches of grief and holds hands with pain. Joy delights with connection and laughs with hope. It is the foundation on which our days are made worthy of enduring and celebrating, all in one. I think that's what my Granny learned. I think it's why she had the ability to persevere. She leaned in to whatever life threw at her and surrendered it to Jesus. She chose joy where happiness had no place. She looked out with eyes of faith. She entrusted herself, her life, and her future to the One who held her and history in His palms. I don't know that there is anything better.

Joy isn't about things going well or life being wonderful. It's just about knowing. It's allowing pain to have purpose and hardship to be worthy. It's about glorying in things yet to come and identifying with things that went wrong. Joy is an immovable object, a touchstone to which we can return no matter how many times life comes undone. I think that's what my Granny knew. That's why she just kept going and didn't give up. She didn't choose to say, yes, this circumstance is what is going to satisfy me. She didn't expect from today what only tomorrow could hold.

Job's story is the same. It lingered with pain. It held space for tragedy and allowed comfort and consoling. When it was time for healing, in that he gloried, but he didn't forget how trust sustained him. What we need to know, like Job, is that the God who allows tragedy is the same God who provides ways and promises glory. He gives us joy – the inherent worthiness of enduring – so we can make it through things. There is no other way this side of Eden.

That, I believe, is how the joy of the Lord becomes our strength. It is the foundation upon which we stand during trials, tribulations, suffering, and pain. It is where Job found his strength in the midst of a storm he couldn't understand, injustice upon injustice heaped on his head, and what felt like silence from heaven in the face of torment from Satan and his very own friends. Trust mixed with faith in a God unseen but whose eyes never departed from Job for a second. That's joy become strength. That is the joy of the Lord, the One who sees us and never blinks.

It's the very reason we cannot ever chase happiness or look to circumstance. They fail us time and time again. They never last. But joy? Worthiness in suffering? Purpose in pain? Meaning in tragedy? A story beyond yet still encapsulating our own? This is it. That's how joy functions. It's how you look at the cross, knowing what is coming, calculating its cost, and choose to surrender to it anyway. Because joy in what you *can't* control is where you will find your greatest strength. The upside down kingdom many call it. That's the kingdom of heaven come near.

When our circumstances tell us God isn't trustworthy and won't meet our needs, joy is what sustains us and gives us the strength to endure. It is the perspective Job clung to in the absolute worst of his days – that despite everything, my God sees me, and it is in *Him* that I know all this somehow matters. He was right, you know. Job kept saying over and over how it was impossible that his integrity wasn't intact, that God wouldn't allow all of this for nothing, that there had to be a *reason*. It's true. There was one.

The testing of our faith produces priceless character that even Satan can't touch.

There is no weapon he can wield that God can't stop, no assault he can take out on us that won't be repurposed for good. That's why we can *choose* – not to give up, to believe there is meaning, and to *wait* on *God* for an audience.

Obedience isn't simply so we are made holy and can avoid consequence. Job's obedience landed him right in Satan's crosshairs. It cost him everything. God doesn't call us to obedience because He wants us to look good or even experience a life done right. He calls us to it because obedience is where we get to see what faith in action looks like, where we get to partner with the God of the universe in taking the sting out of death and overcoming it.

He doesn't promise us rectified circumstance. He just says, "If you trust Me, if you follow Me, I promise you joy beyond measure, worthiness beyond description, and glory you can't even imagine. With Me, you *will* get there. This side of Eden's gates, you will suffer, but what awaits you is beyond the wildest dreams you could ever conjure. This isn't about you believing in My name and that I exist. Even Satan and his demons do that. This is about you *relying* on Me, setting your sights on Me, allowing *My* joy to inform *your* pain. If you do this, you won't regret it."

It takes faith. It requires sacrifice. It entails everything Job did and it means that, even if your circumstances are redeemed, you'll still need comfort and consolation. Life outside Eden isn't for the weak. It requires strength. There's only one kind that can sustain this place. It's joy. Joy in the Lord of heaven and earth who Himself becomes our strength. It was for this joy that our lives were bought, our price paid, our freedom secured. May we recognize the incredible worth it is to *choose* to suffer and endure and, in its midst, choose to rely on a God who believes in us and provides us with the joy - the reason - to do it, just like Jesus did.

For the **joy** set before us.

Chapter Twelve:
Waiting

"Waiting on God requires the willingness to bear uncertainty, to carry within oneself the unanswered question, lifting the heart to God about it whenever it intrudes upon one's thoughts"

~ *Elisabeth Elliot*[23]

Years passed between the time when my life fully imploded and when I felt like I heard from God again. I saw touches of His hand on occasion, but mostly I felt His silence. My dad died just before dawn on a cold February morning following a major snowstorm. After the funeral, I boarded three planes home and spent the next several weeks immersed in grief, barely making it from one place to another, only going places I had to.

I have little recollection of those days. I put in my earbuds, tugged my hoodie into place, and despite the darkness of winter wore sunglasses almost nonstop, especially indoors. I couldn't bear to have a conversation with anyone and the movie *Venom*, which I'd watched on one of the planes home, became a regular escape from reality. Eddie Brock's was an existence to which I could relate. His world turned upside down, a life where choosing truth meant having one's existence torn apart, and the complete inability to stop what was happening sounded so much like my own.

One of the hardest parts of my situation and of Job's was not knowing when the waiting and turmoil would end. There's something about sitting in the space that waiting holds that makes you feel more present in your circumstances than any other moment. Job's body was wracked with pain and his soul with grief. No matter where he turned, Job couldn't escape. He said, *"Oh, that I might have my request, that God would grant what I hope for, that God would be willing to crush me, to let loose his hand and cut off my life!"* (Job 6:8-9)

I remember about 3 years into the fallout telling my therapist that I felt suspended in the air, like I couldn't land or find my footing. It seemed as if I was going to be trapped in this black hole, floating in outer space forever, and there was no way to get back to solid ground. It took so long for my circumstances to reconcile with my faith. Both needed an audience with God, but my heart wasn't ready.

When we read Job, we don't think much about what his friends needed. We just look at Job and all his suffering. In putting ourselves in Job's shoes, we want an end to his pain. We want resolution, no matter what it takes. I think Job's friends did too, but the thing about suffering is that if you aren't the one in it, it's a lot harder to relate to the grief.

Waiting isn't just for us. It's also for the people we touch, who see us and witness our tragedy. Trouble comes for everyone and sometimes other people are there to see ours because their day is on the horizon. When Job's friends first arrived on the scene, they tore their clothes and heaped dust on their heads. They sat with Job in the literal ashes left of his existence. Their hearts hurt deeply for their friend. Yet, when Job began to speak, to wail and lament, when the words of utter desolation came forth from his soul, none of them had the same depth of experience to grasp what Job was enduring.

Walking through cancer and losing a parent, navigating divorce and the upheaval of family and identity – these aren't things for the faint of heart. These are for people in the trenches, for people who get it. I learned on my own journey through these that you can't surround yourself in moments of this significance with people who don't understand. Like Job's friends, they will sell you platitudes and promise you comforts that don't sustain. When those don't work, they'll start shifting blame and tell you perhaps you just have the wrong perspective.

Can I just say? Those people are not your people. Not for that kind of pain.

I was asked the question recently about what I do when I don't know what to say, when I'm facing a situation or a person and I don't know what words God wants me to use. My response was, "Wait." That's what I do, I wait. I don't want to speak any sooner than necessary. I know from personal experience that if I jump ahead, I'm just going to cause more pain. That's what Job's friends didn't get. They didn't comprehend the power of waiting.

We're all so quick to look for answers, seek solutions, troubleshoot our problems. What if the purpose of the pain is found only in the waiting? I have to wonder – if Job's friends had just sat there in silence or at the very most just validated Job's pain, what would they have seen of God through the wait? What if their purpose was to simply sit in heaven's waiting room, praying for grace, leaning on faith? As humans, I don't think we consider much about why faith is necessary. We're just told we need to have it, as if it is some magical thing we can conjure up. Chained to this planet, our concentration often tends to be on our next steps, on forward progress. There isn't much room or need for faith.

Our hearts long for us to return to Eden, to a land where things make sense, where we are connected and at peace, where life goes according to plan. We develop agendas to make those very dreams come true, at least as much as is within our power to do so. In places like Eden though, faith isn't a necessity. Eden is where we know God and we ourselves are fully known without so much as a hint of misunderstanding in between. We don't have to believe He's real or hope that He's good. We *know*. Eden is the place where all of our heart's desires come true. I think God knew that and it's why "He set eternity in the hearts of men." He knew we'd need that when the Garden was no longer our domain. That longing would both sustain and drive us all at once, causing us to long for Him, for the Garden, for another way of living, doing, and being. Our hearts would lead us to search for that which we alone cannot attain.

When tragedy struck Job's world, I don't think his initial thought was, "God must be up to something good, so I'll just wait and see what it is." Just because Job made the audible choice to honor God by saying, "The Lord gives and the Lord takes away. Blessed be the name of the Lord," (Job 1:21, CSB) that doesn't mean his heart was overjoyed. He spoke those words in faith - before grief turned to boils and loss sat down in the ash heap and time lent his friends the opportunity to add insult to injury. It was before he'd spent so long, whether he wanted to or not, waiting.

Waiting may be one of the most difficult places we all find ourselves at some point. The challenge isn't always tied to tremendous hardship or pain. More often than not, our waiting is for something mundane like the doctor's office, grocery store, or in traffic. No matter where we find ourselves, the difficulty about waiting is the utter stillness it entails. It's as if we are stuck in a holding pattern, going nowhere, and we find ourselves incredibly uncomfortable with the lack of movement.

When Job's life came to a screeching halt, there was nothing left to do but sit and wait, grieve and lament, churn in suffering. Everything was gone. Not one circumstance held the immediate option for redemption. Being unable to change a single thing about his situation, Job was left without a choice. All he could do was wait on God to reveal Himself and, like me, Job found himself doing so yet receiving only silence in return.

What Job's friends didn't realize and what most of us don't either is that waiting offers opportunities we won't find anywhere else. The awful beauty of coming to the end of ourselves is it opens doors for the kind of faith that doesn't sell. No one looks to purchase faith birthed from tragedy. That said, most of us, when we reach the bottom, are either too exhausted or too uncertain to do much else besides wait. Like Job, we may even conclude that death is the only plausible solution to our circumstances.

As horrible as waiting feels, I think that's where God wants all of us at some point to be. I think it's where God wanted Job. I think it's where He wanted Job's friends too. A holding space. A place where only God could show up in ways no one else was able. You'd think a man like Job wouldn't need that, but God obviously knew something we don't.

**It turns out disenchantment is for
everyone, not just the ones in doubt.**

What Job's friends didn't know is that Job's trouble hadn't come as the result of some hidden sin. It wasn't God's discipline. Rather, Job's *faith* is what put him in the direct line of Satan's crosshairs and it was *God* that handed Satan the scope.

I don't think I've ever needed God more nor desired His absence so much as I did during those several years of silence. It was discombobulating because I envisioned my Dad in heaven along with the others who'd gone before me. Yet, here on planet earth, I was *not* okay with God anymore. Not the God I now knew Him to be. This God, He allowed tragedy. He invited trouble. He was relentless in His pursuit of me and I wasn't about it. The God of my childhood was kind and caring. He was someone who loved me and wanted good things for me. The people around me were to blame for hardships and sorrow, not God. God was supposed to be my escape. It wasn't that He owed me, just that He loved me, so surely this wasn't going to be my story.

The harshest reality I've ever had to face is accepting a God who allows severe pain while at the same time claiming to love me more than anyone else. It's almost impossible to believe. I understood that God gave these storylines to Jesus and Job. They're in the Bible. Their pain has a purpose, a saving grace that I didn't expect to have to carry myself. I was wholly unprepared to repeat their history. I'd convinced myself God wouldn't make me. This world is full of injustice and all too often we believe we are its remedy. It is this very notion that allows our hearts to believe that if God were truly good, He wouldn't let us down. He won't let tragedy happen – *not to me, because He loves me and real love doesn't hurt people.*

Until it does. When it comes at the hands of the One who claims to love us most, we walk away, not only disappointed, but in utter disbelief that the God we once knew could even be real. We think maybe God Himself is a figment of our imagination, a crutch on which we erringly relied. Disenchantment rocks your very soul, not just your viewpoint. If you think Job's tragedy and subsequent understanding of God only leveled Job and not his friends too, read the end of the book again. Everyone saw God in His fullness and everyone experienced a Father like they never had. All were ushered to the table.

Disenchantment forces you to reconcile
with the God you once saw and believed
in and the God you now know.

When it comes on the heels of personal devastation, it is the worst kind of disillusionment and leaves you feeling as if you're stuck in a haze, groping your way through. All of a sudden, God becomes the very last person we can trust. Life feels like an incredible injustice. So, what is the point of waiting? Waiting is a crossroad. It is the pause of opportunity. The space we hold for ourselves and God to give Him and our hearts time to show up. We don't wait because we *want* to. We wait because we *need* to. Waiting on God is an art form none of us comes here wanting to know.

Job's friends made the mistaken assumption that Job's pain was entirely about him. It wasn't. It was about them too. It was about Job, them, the community, Job's wife, their families, and even us. There are so many lessons held for everyone in the wait, in the pain of Job's days, in the faith he didn't want to demonstrate but clung to, knowing there was absolutely nothing else left for anyone to take.

For months that turned into years, the one reminder God sent me of His presence was dragonflies. I sat day after day in devastation, a haze of tragedy surrounding my every move, and day after day, dragonflies showed up. Eventually my husband remarked at how unusual it was. I'd moved into his home and, in all the time he'd lived there, he'd never seen them, especially not in multiples. I finally told him what my soul knew to be true but my heart no longer believed. I said, "God knows dragonflies remind me of Him. They're His way of telling me He sees me and is still here."

Sometimes I got mad at Him for sending so many. Everywhere I went, random parking lots, rainy days, sunny ones, at the gas station, winter, summer, spring, constantly He sent them. Some would come right up in front of my window so I couldn't miss them and fly exactly in my line of vision just in front of the car. In time, I developed a love-hate relationship with their presence. They were comforting and infuriating all at once.

Throughout my journey, I've come to learn that the way we move from disenchantment into faith is by letting God be the One who allows tragedy. I didn't want to. Like I said, my heart wasn't ready. What no one ever tells you is that that's okay. You don't have to be instantly ready. You don't have to push through or get over it or move on. Grief takes time. Hardship saps energy. Healing doesn't occur overnight. It's okay to say I need space and time to process it all.

Job's friends didn't know this either. After holding what they considered a reasonable time for grief, they immediately did what most of us do and tried to answer Job's pain, find an explanation, feed him platitudes. They spoke for God without having God's truth. They expected to be able to reason it all away. Some pains aren't reasonable. Some griefs are beyond what we can bear. Some circumstances tear what feels like our very skin away from our bone and we are left raw, exposed, and bleeding, feeling as if no one cares at all. The scariest moment is when we realize God isn't letting up. He sees it all and continues on. No one can help us and there is nowhere to go.

When God intends to use devastation for our good, His focus on us is intense. It is a place unlike any other. As with tragedy, it too is not for the faint. When I found myself there, I was so angry. It seemed as if God was asking me to trust Him when I knew He was the very person I couldn't trust most. His silent yet continual presence both tenderized and angered my heart. He wasn't answering my questions or redeeming my circumstances *and* He wasn't letting me go. Like Job, I wasn't sure I could live with that.

What no one tells you about God using hardship for good is that it feels absolutely horrible. His heart, His care and concern for us may be gentle, yet they feel anything but. Like me, Job didn't want to be God's focus anymore. It felt awful. To be focused on yet at once seemingly ignored, so Job said to God, "Let me alone; my days have no meaning. What is mankind that you make so much of them, that you give them so much attention, that you examine them every morning and test them every moment? Will you never look away from me, or let me alone for even an instant? ... Turn away from me so that I can have a moment's joy." (Job 7:16-19, Job 10:20) Repeatedly Job asked God to shift His focus to anywhere but him.

We all get it, don't we? Being caught in a war between powerful forces that threaten to rip our souls apart, we don't want faith to be our most precious commodity. We'll give it all up for just a moment's peace. A brief pause in the onslaught of awful. Especially when it feels like all we're doing is waiting.

Waiting on things to change.

Waiting for explanation.

Waiting on justice to be done.

Waiting, waiting, waiting.

Waiting felt forced upon me. Maybe it feels that way to you too. It's not something we'd ever choose if we're being honest. When life fails to meet our expectations and God falls short of our dreams, the last thing we are interested in doing is waiting. Finding ourselves in that place, our gut instinct is to move. We want to run as far and as fast as we can - away from the pain, away from the discomfort, away from the death of our reality.

Quite often, we do. Like the Israelites, we wander around, disillusioned, disenchanted, believing the Promised Land we once hoped for now, like God, isn't good enough to be true. So, we set our sights on something more achievable. We make golden calves for ourselves in the desert and worship the idols of our own choice. Some of us die there, not waiting on God, but utterly refusing to do so.

I might have done that myself if I wasn't so exhausted. Life had finally beat me. My Type A personality was done. For the first time ever, I found myself without the ability to push through or carry on. Tragedy took every last bit of fight and gumption right out of me. I crumpled onto that bathroom floor and poured out my soul, not just in grief but in sheer and utter exhaustion. I no longer had what it took and I couldn't force myself to keep going.

We don't see tragedy as doorways to rest. They don't feel that way. We view waiting as time wasted, not a life well spent. I know that was my story. Maybe it's yours too. Maybe you feel like Elijah, completely drained of every resource. The last thing you want to do now is wait on God. The interesting thing is that wasn't the story of Jesus. Even though He was part God, unlike us, Jesus chose in His *humanity* to still wait on the Father's call. He didn't rush ahead. He humbled Himself. He sat in the Father's presence and allowed His soul to be tended to while the world around Him carried on. He ignored the earthly pressure to perform, make decisions, do things that resembled forward progress. He refused to fight battles God didn't call Him to take on. He waited and, in the waiting, He found rest.

Here's what doesn't sound true about Job's story. It doesn't sound like a call to rest. It sounds like turmoil, like a life turned upside down, the complete fallout of every good thing ever known to him. All of that is true. It's also true that waiting offered Job and his friends the opportunity to rest. Rest from striving, rest from figuring it out, rest from trying to understand all the goings on of a spiritual world to which none of them were privy.

Job had spent a lot of time doing great things, helping others, loving his family, praying to His Father. He wasn't out of touch. He was busy. Some things about God, though, can only be found in places of rest. In places of waiting. It is in places of rest that we find the faith we need to bolster us through tragedy. It is in the places of waiting that we find rest. They go hand in hand.

> **Sometimes it is in the places of our worst fallouts that we see just how valuable and precious our faith in God's sight is.**

What I've experienced being on the other side about waiting and faith and rest is: Life doesn't resolve so we never stop needing these things. We will always have a need to wait, to have faith, and to rest. Until we get back to Eden, until the Restoration Day of this place, these will be continual callings on our existence. Therefore, it is here, in the place that we understand Him least and see through a glass dimly, outside the Garden gates, inside a world at war with itself, and here, in the place of our greatest turmoil, that the Eternal calls us to "Be still and *know* that I am God." (Psalm 46:10, NIV, emphasis mine)

Job's friends had no idea that they too needed disenchantment. That they needed to reconcile the God of their understanding with the God who really was. God was granting them the grace of not having to experience the suffering Job did, but they didn't take that offering with much faith. Instead, they whisked it away with lofty opinions and uninformed words where their hearts and mouths weren't willing to wait. That's why God told Job to pray for his friends at the end. Because they had rushed in instead of choosing to wait on Him and, in doing so, had missed God's true identity and His entire heart for them all.

Life isn't just about us, just as Job's story wasn't just about Job. It was for everyone. Nobody *wants* to wait. God set eternity in our souls. We long for it like we long for nothing else. So, of course, we want to get on with getting on. That's what feels like faith. Moving, doing, like what James said - putting our faith into action. The problem, as my pastor reminds us almost weekly, is that if we just start doing stuff *for* God, we aren't working *from* our relationship *with* God. Instead, we're relying on our own strength, our own wisdom, our own understanding and telling ourselves we're doing it God's way.

Waiting is a choice, and it comes with a promise. Isaiah says that "those who wait upon the LORD will renew their strength; they will mount up with wings like eagles; they will run and not grow weary, they will walk and not faint." (Isaiah 40:31, BSB) At no time does God promise us better circumstances. Never does He tell us we won't need faith. He doesn't suggest we push on and forget to rest. Rather, He says, "I promise you that if you *wait*, wait on *Me,* it is the one thing you will not regret."

In the fall of 2021, I took my youngest son to college. It was a beautiful day but my heart ached. No one tells you that missing them being gone isn't the hardest part of letting them go. It's missing your role, your connection and way of relating, the identity you had that came with knowing. Knowing they were home, knowing they were okay, knowing you could go in their room at night and check to see if they were still breathing, even if they were 19 years old. It is missing who you were together as one.

When I became an empty nester, it felt as if everything had changed in the blink of an eye. Like Job, all of a sudden my world was different. Unlike Job, I knew it was coming. I just didn't know what to expect. God did though. It happened during that season where I still wasn't sure He loved me, not how I needed anyway. As we pulled out of the driveway, having made the trip before, I knew the road we'd take, but I turned on my GPS anyway. For some reason, it took us a totally different way. I had to pay close attention because these were new roads. I hoped it wasn't taking us in the wrong direction.

As we turned down back country roads I'd never driven in my life, we came upon fields and fields of dragonflies. When I say there were millions, I'm not exaggerating. Hundreds of thousands of them swarmed at every turn, every corner, every crevice in the road. There were so many that my son who was following behind me in his car remarked at one of our pit stops that he'd never seen anything like it. Neither had I. Mile after mile, God went before, behind, and beside us. Never for a moment did He take His eyes off of us. Laser focus. I told my son as much.

Still, my heart was waiting.

Waiting for change.

Waiting on circumstance.

Waiting and hoping that what I'd find at the end of the journey was something worth all the pain.

It took me a long time to realize that so much of the value was held in the wait, the willingness to rest in that place of not understanding, unable to change much of anything. It was there that God bolstered my faith. Not by changing my circumstances, but by changing *me*. The things He used were the harshest experiences of my life. I wish them on no one, especially in the continual domino way they fell.

I don't recall ever choosing in all that time to intentionally wait on God. My circumstances forced it upon me, but my heart didn't quite heed the call. Instead, God chose to wait on me. I think that's who He is. The One who does first what He calls us to. He leads by example. After having faith in Job, He called Job to faith in Him. First loving us and expressing it to us, He now invites our hearts to love Him also. Dying first on the cross for us, He then asked us to trade in earthly life alone for eternal life with Him.

Eventually, enough time passed that in the waiting I realized what God was offering. It was a yoke. A yoke of opportunity. One that came with a vision I didn't yet see, a lifestyle I wasn't experiencing, and a friend who'd never leave. I'm not sure I'd have ever seen that if He hadn't taken so much away from me. I don't know if Job would either. I'm quite certain his friends wouldn't have.

I didn't understand what it meant before to be yoked in with Jesus. To take on His light and easy call, one that allowed me to set aside all this earthly weight and trade it in for the assurance that I am not alone. I have a brother and Savior who is yoked in beside me, keeping me on the straight and narrow. We both suffer, we both bear pains we didn't deserve or cause.

The burden of walking with Jesus is the burden of being willing to wait. It's walking by faith, not by sight. It's trusting that the One beside You sees what you don't. We're all so sure, aren't we? That what we see, what we know, what we believe to be true is absolute. We don't stop to consider: What if we're wrong?

What if God's love *is* the foundation of our tragedy?

What if waiting is the only way to see clearly? What if silence and solitude fortify our strength for another day? What if waiting on God leads to reconciling our disenchantment, healing our souls, and regaining our hope? What if there is purpose in the wait? What if? Maybe, just maybe, there is so much more to the story than we could possibly know.

THE
INTERLUDE

The Interlude

"While it looks like things are out of control, behind the scenes there is a God who hasn't surrendered His authority."

~A.W. Tozer[24]

I didn't expect this book to have a middle or, as Merriam Webster defines interlude, "an interruptive period, space, or event."[25] Much like Job's life, May 2023 came as a total surprise to me. So, rather than writing this book consecutively as I have chapters 1-12 and the chapters following this one, I find myself 9 months later writing a chapter in the middle. It took me a while to realize that the points tied together from start to finish, but there was a distinct shift halfway through, much like there can be in a play. The scenes before the interlude and the ones subsequent to it.

The disruption this interruptive period created defined the change in my approach from the first half of this book to the second. It's as if I was now in Job's shoes, Satan having come back for round two. My faith was being tested to see if it held true to everything I just wrote. Was I going to live out what I'd been so certain I knew of God? Would I let additional tragedy continue to do its work in transforming my understanding of Him? Most of all, would I hold onto integrity or let it go?

Only time and pain would tell.

It's interesting to go back and read all this as one complete story now. I know the beginning, the end, and the middle. What I thought was over when I started writing turned out to be only the beginning. The conclusions I'd arrived at were still to be tested, tried, and lived out in light of my current perspective. One that has made all the difference. You'll find as you read the rest of this book that there is a space here in the middle where my language goes from past to present. From "I *was* living that then" to "I *am* living it now."

Like Job's story, there was an even deeper season of upheaval that arrived on the heels of my first one. It's as if the space between was like the one between the first and second conversations Satan had with God about Job. I know our stories are different in many, many ways, but I believe the vision God has provided me is intentionally similar. I don't have to be like Job for God to want the same thing for me as He did him. I don't have to be Job for the same truths to apply.

Providence is this space where all the things that go wrong in life are still utilized for God's glory and our benefit.

Providence is *knowing* that trouble is coming and getting ready for it. As Oxford says, it's "timely preparation for future eventualities."[26] Trouble *is* an eventuality and none of us can escape it. We like to tell ourselves that "if we had only" or if someone else had, then all this could have been avoided and things gone on all dandy. That might be true, but that might not be the right narrative.

It's hard, if not impossible, to sell ourselves a version of the story that says the brokenness and loss that occurred were better than if they had never happened. It just makes no earthly sense. But I think that's really the point of all this. Life viewed from an earthly perspective will *never* make sense. Life wasn't made by humans who live a finite existence. Life was created by an eternal being without our limits whose viewpoint and purposes far exceed anything we see. Life, then, *only* makes sense if we recognize that we are living in a kingdom turned upside down.

We are people living in the land between now and not yet, and now just seems so permanent. We may make decisions with tomorrow in mind, but most of us are really deciding based on how we feel today. That's why I think it's so important to hold these stories with so much grace. Grace for ourselves, for the people around us, for the people who are collateral damage that never even intended to be on the page. Grace for the God who isn't the one we thought He was, the one we knew we needed, the one that didn't make a way the way we were certain He would. Grace for a story that feels like it could have been prevented, for ourselves being both participants and not all in the same breath.

The word "grace" defined means "unmerited favor"[27] and that's the perspective I'm choosing to take even though I didn't start in that place. So many of the words on the following pages are my sorting through, finding a way, making sense of the absolutely senseless, and holding space for all the moving pieces that life actually is as you're presently living it. It's knowing all of us play parts that to some seem like victors and to others villains.

It's always our perspective that determines how
we see a thing and what we take away.

So, I ask that as you read the rest of the story, the rest of my leaning ins and running aways, my terror-filled questions, and tear-filled griefs, you too wrestle with things. Life is never something we can make pretty, tie up in a bow, and hand to someone neatly. It doesn't work that way. Life is a thing that comes with a bit of wildness, a need for taming, but also a freedom that allows the chaos a place. A place into which God speaks.

We weren't always supposed to get it right. We weren't always supposed to know the way. We weren't made with the capability of doing everything God's way. Not on our own and not even when we are "saved." Because rescue doesn't guarantee education and education doesn't guarantee grace. Justification may be a one-time deal but sanctification is confined to time and space. It requires a tending to that comes about no other way than living in a world where things don't always go the right way. Know that, as much as you experience that reality, you do not do it alone no matter how you *feel* in those moments.

Many of the pages that follow were written at times when I was actually alone. Physically, emotionally, and in all the other ways a person can be. Isolated was how I spent some of my days and not always as a result of my own decisions. It took me a while before I realized that God too felt this way and part of me experiencing this was so that it was to *Him* that I could relate. He too was trapped in the same reality as me – the one where things aren't going *His* way. His goodness too feels hidden, His heart also missed, His deepest desires and needs deferred or unmet. These facts can so easily disappear amidst all the pain, loss, suffering, and grief. I want us to hold onto them now because they are a lifeline we will absolutely need.

The truth is that God will not spare Himself what we too experience.

He will endure, usually first, the very things we are also handed. So, when I say that you are not alone, that doesn't mean you will not have moments when you absolutely feel it and when you are in all reality the only physical person enduring what you are enduring. Sometimes you are. Jesus was the only one hanging on that cross. He was the only one in completely right relationship with God who felt forsaken by God Himself, His own Father, through absolutely no fault of His own. He was the only person out there in the wilderness with Satan jabbering at Him during an exhausting and trying time that we'd all have tried to save ourselves from and told ourselves we never should've ended up in in the first place.

Jesus gets it. So did Job. You are not alone. Your story, like mine and like so many others of us, is going to have parts you have to traverse alone. Your story also will have many parts where it's the same narrative that you will find other people around the world have endured or are enduring also. During some of my hardest nights, I read the story of Jim Elliot, his family, and their partners in the book *Through Gates of Splendor*. Not because it made me feel any less alone. It didn't. But it gave me perspective. A perspective I needed during some of my very worst hours.

We have to remember that the goal isn't that we *feel* better about what we're going through. That's not always possible. Some things are simply grievous almost to the point of death and maybe even right on into it. Both Jesus and Job said this and they were deemed the most righteous men on the planet. So, if they said it and experienced it, then it's not only okay but also to be expected that we will too. Perspective is important because it is the one version of grace we can hold in the face of things we cannot possibly understand, reconcile, or change. It does not always come to us instantly and it is something about which we must *choose* to have patience.

Our tendency as humans is to believe that, once we get to a different place in the story – one much less trying, exhausting, and painful – then we see what we should have seen all along. The whole "hindsight is 20/20" thing. That's not always the case. The reality is that sometimes what we need more than to know things, to make sense of them, to "see what we didn't see" is to develop character traits. To build faith. To create space. We wouldn't do these things if we didn't have to, if they weren't necessary. We'd go on living in spaces of "peace" and indulging in all the goodness a life of ease offers us.

It's not that a life of "ease" is a bad thing. It's actually how God designed Eden in certain respects and it's how He's creating our eternity. It's just that *earth* is our home today and we need to be prepared for that. We live in the Land In-Between. On earth, subjected to the curse of sin and death, we need *character* to survive well, to endure much, to suffer long, to withstand and fight our enemy, and to love deep. We cannot and will not develop these traits without testing, trying, and necessity.

Suffering is the crucible through which our most Christ-like qualities are birthed.

Suffering is often what forces us to our knees in ways we'd never willingly choose to be. It gives us the gift of a perspective we never knew we needed and one we'd never want for ourselves. To be like God – to have the full knowledge of good and evil - is to know what it means not to just experience shame and "opened eyes"[28] like Adam and Eve did after those first bites of fruit. It's also to have the full knowledge of what it means to be a God who is good in the face of chaos, of disruption, of an enemy, of things getting turned upside down and you having to turn them right side up again. In ways that make no earthly sense. That's our partnership in the gospel. The good news is that this isn't all there is and this isn't how it always will be.

This place is The Interlude. Not just for me. For all of us. It is the land where everything that should be gets turned on its end and we have to find our way through until its righted again. Reconciling ourselves to the fact that this is the journey is a critical piece. It turns out the Interlude is just as important to the story as the rest of our traveling. For me, it's where I thought I'd hit an eye in the storm and things were starting to make sense.

I was understanding a lot of truth and God was bringing me to a place of deep growth, heavy dependency on Him, and a willingness to start surrendering pieces of me that I'd never before considered. I assumed that this was the trajectory in which I would continue to grow and that the worst of the worst was behind me. I didn't know the coming days, weeks, and months would hold betrayal, misunderstanding, a complete lack of seeking truth by certain people around me, and deeper pain than I'd ever before experienced. I had no idea. Neither did Job.

None of us are prepared to be blamed for things that weren't our doing much less things that never even occurred. We are even less prepared for people we trusted and feel safe enough to be honest with about our struggles to respond in ways that do more harm than good, that were the opposite of how we would have responded had we been in their shoes. It's hard to know what to do when you're trying to adhere to the whole "Do to others as you would have them do to you" (Matthew 7:12, BSB) concept only to find that your version of that and someone else's are entirely different things.

Job encountered this also. We all will at some point on our journey. It's part of life – reconciling. Not always with people although that is required sometimes too, but with reality. The reality we are *actually* living, not the one we want it to be.

As much as this is a journey of reconciling our disenchantment with God, it is also one of reconciling our enchantment with the reality we expected – the one it's turned out *not* at all to be.

There are times when sharing the actual details of our stories is powerful and necessary. I've shared the ones I feel are appropriate here and not the rest. Some are saved for another book that is in process. We can all speak to the impact of other people's decisions on us, but we cannot speak from their perspective. So, it is with grace that I think we share our journeys and stories involving other people.

It is also with the willingness to *be* misunderstood, not known, and lacking completion that we travel the road home. All things lead to one place, one Person, knowing what isn't whole here will one day be at the foot of His throne. Sometimes that's all we need to know. I'm trusting what God put on my heart to share here is what He wanted you to hear most. Just like Job, I'm not the point of this story. He is and that's the focus.

PART TWO

PART TWO

Chapter Thirteen:
Eternal Perspective

---

*"If we are the sheep of His pasture, remember
that sheep are headed for the altar."*

~ Jim Elliot[29]

We all say, "It'll never happen to me." Maybe not out loud, maybe not even consciously, but somewhere down in our hearts we believe, "I'll never be the one that has to endure that thing." In between writing the last chapter and this one, my entire world caught fire. Nearly every stable thing I had in my existence was completely upended in a matter of 24 hours. I've never been so in shock nor so terrified. It takes a while once tragedy sets in to get your bearings. At first, all I felt was the searing pain of loss and misunderstanding. I was grasping at straws, headed in every direction that would just *"fix this right now."* Once it reached the point of no fixing and definitely not right now, I still didn't surrender. I started looking for the bigger story line.

I'd been writing this book after all so maybe just maybe, I was living out a piece of Job's tale. Maybe this is what it meant to have Satan come in and literally wreck your entire world, taking one precious thing after another, right down to your health until you literally cannot even function. I started honing in on the attacks, seeing how, like with headline news, you have to ignore the bigger story to see what is really going on behind the scenes. Now, let me pause a second here to say this: That *IS* a bigger storyline almost always. Satan *is* always working to steal, kill, and destroy as Jesus said.

The problem is that if we focus only on that, we're going to miss the even bigger storyline: That Jesus has already overcome the world. One of the blessings of Job's story is that he had no idea Satan was behind anything. He didn't have a book like we do warning us that this could occur. He wasn't privy to one thing taking place behind the curtain. Eternal perspective, in the sense of how we see it by being able to read the entire book now, wasn't made available to him.

As my days went from utter busyness and fullness to a complete crawl where minutes last hours and excruciating is the best and maybe only word I can use to describe existing, I felt a constant pressure to understand and to make other people understand. Someone I thought was a friend at the time said to stop explaining, to stop trying because it wasn't helping. She wasn't wrong, but she wasn't right either. It wasn't that explaining wouldn't have been helpful – it actually would have made quite a difference. However, it wouldn't have gotten me the results I wanted and that was really what I needed to hear.

Right now, I find myself in the place where Job had finally gotten his audience with God. Where the many words of his friends had landed on a battered and bruised heart, where faith was the only sustenance of his days, where his reputation was in the ash heap right along with his body, and where everyone was watching to see a great man fallen – despising his very existence in certain ways. When you find yourself here, although I pray you never do but I am certain that you might, here is my advice: Look for the biggest picture. Not the one that makes purpose from your pain. That is a piece, yes, but the one even bigger than that. The one that makes you like Jesus.

You know what every single person on this planet wants? Compassion and belonging. You know what Jesus did when He got here and started walking around as a grown adult, homeless but with a heart? He *saw* people. He saw them as Scripture says, "harassed and helpless, like sheep without a shepherd," and "he had *compassion* on them" (Matthew 9:36, emphasis mine). The lie we're all sold is: "You need to be able to make it on your own, you don't need community, you need a better *you*." Even Job's own friends told him that. Yet, in reading Job, not once do you hear God say that. Not once does He even mention Job improving himself. He doesn't ridicule or condemn Job for getting his life all wrong and He certainly doesn't side with Job's friends who decided that the biggest storyline was sin.

The biggest storyline is *never* sin. It's always Jesus. Always and forever, it will be the Lord of Heaven and Earth who comes to take away the very thing that ruins and rules our lives and days. He wants it even more than we do and that's what God was trying to tell Job at the end of the story. He was saying, "Job, you don't even *know* what you don't know. There is *so much more to this*." He said the same thing to me. We all need a God like this. The One who shows up in the storm, not simply with hands that wipe tears or arms that mete out justice. We need the God with *perspective* – the One who sees all we cannot, who is already in tomorrow and making a way from today there.

I read a book once called *No Cure for Being Human* by Kate Bowler. Excellent read and the truth of it stands – there isn't a cure. We are all human no matter how hard we try to escape and we are all subject to sudden tragedy, pains that linger, and hope that feels intermittent, stolen, or delayed. The cure isn't to stop being human. The cure is and always will be Jesus.

I don't mean that in a religious way. There is no 12-step program here, no formula for making life better. The only way offered us is death. Death to ourselves, our perspectives, our narratives. Death to the things we are seeking that are temporal. Death to everything that isn't Him. *That* is what God was offering Job. Not a way out, but a new perspective to endure through. Jesus begged the Father for a way out of the cross, and the Father said no – this *is* the way – You Yourself *are* the way, the truth, and the life, and none of these people are coming to me without You, so this is it.

Jesus didn't muscle through. Neither did Job. In fact, they both did the opposite. They both traded in their wills for faith in an eternal perspective neither one of them controlled. It's the beauty of submission – that terrible word no one in the Christian world wants to encounter. We all run away from it these days, but I think we're missing something crucial when we do. We're missing the end of Job's story – the part where he says, "My ears had heard of you, but now my eyes have seen you. Therefore I despise myself and repent in dust and ashes." (Job 42:5-6)

Submission to a perspective greater than all we can see or imagine is what makes this life work. It doesn't give purpose to pain – it gives perspective. It shifts the narrative. It turns us from "What is happening to me? *Why?* How do I make it stop?" to "I trust that whatever is going on, even though I am walking in utter darkness here, is going to matter in ways I could never imagine. I trust because

He who is in me is greater than he who is in the world." It builds relationship.

Satan *is* in this world and his goal isn't to make you suffer, though suffer you most certainly will. His goal is to make you *sin* in your suffering and therefore separate you from relationship with God. Satan couldn't have cared less whether Job felt pain or not. He cared whether Job had *faith*. All he wanted was to steal the one thing that he knew God held more precious than anything in Job's life – his *faith*.

Faith is what sustains us in the dark nights of the soul. I don't mean a faith where you repeat the serenity prayer like a mantra and hope against all hope that things go according to a certain plan. Faith means you live as if the outcome (not the detailed one you've conjured up to make yourself feel safe) is already secured. It means recognizing like Job that this might never be fixed. This right here, this very tragedy, might be the story of the rest of my days. If it is, will I allow God to be the One who walks with me every step, not justifying me, but transforming me?

We all want something to hope for – some storyline we can work towards. We want a future that guarantees us freedom from harm or at least a lot less of it than we'd get otherwise. What if that's not the plot created in heaven? What if God says, "It is in your *weakness* that I will show up?" God doesn't choose strength. If you have any doubts about that statement, go re-read His Words. The entire bible is filled with page after page of people who were weak, homeless, sin-riddled, failing, hurting, lonely, doubters, angry, afraid, proud, and so much more. He didn't look at any of them and go, "Well, she's got her life together, I'm going with that one." He also didn't gaze upon men with strength and say, "Oh, good. There's the strong guy – he's my man." No, "God chose what the world considers nonsense in order to shame the wise; God chose what the world considers weak in order to shame the strong." (1 Corinthians 1:27, CJB)

Why? Because it was never about us. It was always about *His* life *in* us. It was about Him being a Creator who never ever stops creating. The creation story didn't end in Eden. It's still going on. Every time one of us has a new revelation, every time our perspectives are shifted, each moment that we receive a renewed mind about something – *that* is creation at work. *That* is the biggest storyline. God's holiness. His master plan at work. He really meant it when He said that He knows the plans He has for us, that they are good, and that He is working in all things. He is. Even death, even loss, even the most painful utter destruction you can fathom (or not yet fathom until you are in it), He is there.

So, the question becomes – how do we engage with that? How do we live that out? Because I can hear you now saying, "Alanna, that is all well and good but my life's very foundations just busted from the bottom out and I have absolutely nothing on which to hold." I'm right there with you in that boat, friend. So, here's what I've learned: Stop paddling. Stop bailing water out of the boat. Sit down. Sometimes you have to let the boat sink while you sing, "It is well with my soul" even though everything in you *feels* the exact opposite.

That's what faith is – knowing that the boat is going down but choosing to trust God anyway.

I said before that God's allowance of all this in Job's life was also His call to rest. It seems insane to think that suffering would equal rest, but I'm learning in this process that suffering comes with pain and pain forces rest. It is a necessary kind of rest that grants us a perspective we can get no other way. You know how we can focus like the song says of Jesus, "on his beautiful face and the things of earth will grow strangely dim in the light of his glory and grace?"[30] Here's how: "Be *still* and *know* that *I* am *God*." (Psalm 46:10, NIV, emphasis mine). When it is happening to you, it feels like the very last thing you can do. It is the most severe mercy of all to have all the time in the world to do nothing but suffer.

That's how I've spent the last month. Basically in a single room, 24/7, little human contact, little food, little if any ability to cope at all. No social media, no television, nothing to really "keep me company" and some of the times I've had interactions with people have been straight up brutal, battering my soul much like Job's friends did to his own. I kept fighting the process. For weeks I beat my head against the wall of it until I was battered and bloody and no farther ahead than when I started. I was begging God for understanding, begging Him for redemption, grasping at every loose end and thread of hope I could conjure. His answer? "No. I have something better."

I didn't want better. I wanted *out*. I wanted justification and responses and things to *change*. I wanted *improvement* not perspective. I was focused on the here and now because the here and now was more brutal than all the other things I'd endured to this point. You know what I learned? Pain is a severe mercy unlike any other thing you will ever experience. Sometimes it is the only way through and it is the very one you need most. It will equip you with forgiveness you can't otherwise muster. It will strengthen you in ways you could never pump enough iron or believe enough Bible verses to cover. It will reshape your days in ways that give you the grace second by second, quite literally, to endure just one more, and then another, and then another.

There *isn't* another way. This is it. Because this *is* the biggest story. The one of eternity and we are living right smack dab in the middle of it. That is why God never answered Job's questions and just revealed Himself. Because Job didn't need answers. He didn't need justification. He didn't need changed circumstances. He just needed God Himself, and the faith he maintained throughout the process until he saw God was priceless. This is the truest reality we are ever going to know, if we choose to embrace it: Your faith is worth more than anything else you will ever gain in this world. It is your propulsion into eternity, your sustenance in the temporary, and your ticket to a seat beside Jesus. It is only in becoming *like* Him that we get to be *with* Him.

Eternal perspective is the one gamble you can make that will always pay off. It's just going to cost you everything you've got.

Chapter Fourteen:
Desire

---

*"It is our choices, Harry, that show what we
truly are, far more than our abilities."*

– J.K. Rowling[31]

When life imploded in 2023 and I was left just staring day after day at the debris, traumatized and unable most days to even move, I found desire to be an odd place of wrestling. We get confused, don't we, about what we really want? I know I do and I've found that the only way to stay on the path that is true is to decide what I want ahead of time. Before impending doom, before disaster strikes, before all the things level my life. Even in goodness, I have to decide ahead of time where to set my desire or else I will fall prey to the temptation of chasing instant gratification or what looks like "a better opportunity."

Back when life had fallen like dominoes for several years in a row, I'd set my intention on being a person who showed up. Someone who didn't let the bad in another person force me to become someone different than the character I desired. I wanted to reap what I sowed, so I tried hard to be intentional about sowing well. My son has a key chain with the tagline that reads, "Don't Lose Sight." It's so much harder than it sounds.

When you're raising a bunch of teenagers and experiencing all the things that I was at the same time, it's easy to lose sight. When life turns into a total nightmare and all the things you were certain would never happen (but feared they might) actually do, it's easy to lose sight. When life is full of dreams come true and joy permeates your rise to the top, it's easy to lose sight. I thought I'd never lose sight of who I was, who God was, who He says I am, and who God says He is. I thought for sure all of that would remain clear in the midst of goodness *and* chaos because these things are touchstones, foundations we build on, things we hold fast to all the way down the road. Right?

Maybe. Maybe not. Maybe – in the light of doing all the things or experiencing all the gravity or achieving all the greatness – the one thing that gets truly lost is *us*. I think when life feels "off" somehow, we go chasing it down. That looks different for everyone. Some of us change our names, faces, hairstyles, or bodies. Others change our approach, our personality, our temperament, while yet others move across the world, changing our geography, careers, homes, and the environments around us. No matter what – at some point, all of us find ourselves going in search of identity.

In his book *Green Lights*, Matthew McConaughey talks about this. How, in the midst of living, we all tend to get out of touch with ourselves. His response to this is to take what he calls "a walkabout."[32] It's getting *out* of the normal and *into* the discomfort of not having all the "knowns" with which you've surrounded yourself. The purpose? Discovery, reconnection, perspective, integrity. You need to regain sight and sometimes you need isolation in order to reorient yourself.

It feels backwards, doesn't it? Get lost to be found. Sit in the ashes to find beauty. Die to live. All the great paradoxes of reality in an upside down kingdom. It turns out that humility is the birthplace of healthy desire but we see it as the opposite. We feel like if we humble ourselves, we *lose* rather than *gain* what we desire. We believe we are giving something up instead of receiving what's truly valuable. But, what if true fulfillment of desire can only come by being willing to do whatever it takes to not lose sight? To slow down? To *let* your life be burnt to the ground? To say no to every opportunity, no matter how good or even how necessary, that doesn't align with the values of your soul?

I don't think we really recognize just how much Jesus had to face this ongoing battle with desire. We so easily dismiss the concept of His temptations as a human. We see Him as "God," so we disregard the depth of how desire affected Him. As both God and man, He saw people in need and I'm certain that He wanted so much to help every single one of us. Why wouldn't He? He is literally the living, breathing existence of Love. Of course He wanted to help, to do all that He could.

Yet, over and over, instead of taking things into His own hands, His response was, "Not my will but Yours be done." (Luke 22:42) How? How did He choose that every single day? I think it was by the only way possible. He took a lot of "walkabouts" in solitary places, prayed a lot of questioning prayers to the Father of our world, and sought over and over again not to lose sight. I think Jesus knew that if He didn't, His desire could get misplaced and His human identity off course. So, He had to keep those things in line. Identity first, desire second, action third.

That's what most of us also miss in Job's story. Every single time God mentions Job in the book, He refers to him as, "My servant Job." Five times He says it. "My servant Job."[33] I think the reason He says these words *before* he names Job is because God recognizes us by our motives. Consistently, when people are named in Scripture, it is representative of who they are. God sees our hearts. He knows whether we are sure or not of who we are. Job was sure. Job was there – not for Job – but for God. *That* is why he was tested, why he suffered, why he lost so much, why he gained so much more, why his life is a testimony read by billions across the annals of time and history.

God never loses sight. That's why, in His infinite wisdom and eternal perspective, He can allow what to us seems like utter tragedy but to Him is the fulfillment of our identity. What He knows that we can only trust is that our desire is secondary yet wholly foundational to our humility. So, it is in our humility to rely on Him for what we cannot see that our hearts' desires are made complete. What God said to Satan when he came back the second time demonstrates this.

The first time He just said,

> "Have you considered my servant Job? There is no one
> on earth like him; he is blameless and upright, a man
> who fears God and shuns evil."

The second time though, God repeated Himself word for word then added,

> "And he still maintains his integrity, though you incited
> me against him to ruin him without any reason." (Job
> 2:3)

Integrity is defined as "the state of being whole and undivided."[34] The definition itself implies identity – aka, *the state of who we are*. God knew that. He understood that we would wrestle with our desires because, like Paul tells us, we fight them in a continual battle of wills. Desire is never satisfied on earth because it is based in a temporal flesh that is never fulfilled. The flesh is short-lived, not eternal, so it always craves *more*.

Satan knows this and preys on it. That's why his response to God the second time God mentions Job is,

> *"Skin for skin! A man will give all he has for his own*
> *life. But now stretch out your hand and strike his flesh*
> *and bones, and he will surely curse you to your face."*
> (Job 2:4-5)

Satan's hope was that Job would consider his earthly life more valuable than his character and, in his suffering, give up on God. In other words, Satan was counting on the fact that Job would lose sight and that his desire for temporary comfort would outweigh his desire to be a man of integrity, a man undivided. This battle of wills may be one of the most important battles of our lives. Our desires *are* going to twist and turn us in every direction possible, just like the wind. That's why we have to set our identity and chart our horizon *before* anything comes along to change it. It's the only way to maintain sight.

In recent months, things I never anticipated happening have happened. I've lost people I never believed I'd lose and I've found others in the most unexpected places without even looking. What's been most interesting to me is that, once I stopped chasing my version of desire, I started to gain sight of identity not only in myself but in others.

It's bizarre how God clears your path to see what matters most and who you really need beside you. Just today, I received a text from someone I've known for nearly two decades but moreso in a professional capacity than personal. We don't always agree on values, and I don't know for certain where this person stands in relationship to God. What I do know is that she is a person of integrity, a person undivided.

I've watched her endure some excruciating ordeals both professionally and personally, and yet – her horizon is set, her integrity intact, her identity solid. Why? Because she decided it beforehand. She didn't let the desire to fight back and say her piece and prove her innocence or her version of the story be the driving force behind her days. She's had to walk away from some very lucrative opportunities and some very important work. Why? Because of lies and attacks from people with agendas who conjured narratives and preyed on weaknesses, who didn't themselves want to be found out so they tried to make her a scapegoat instead. Because she knew in fighting *them,* she would lose *herself.*

Sometimes you have to let your life speak for itself and you can't do that if you don't know who you are, *whose* you are, and if that isn't the foundation behind why you do all that you do. Eternal perspective is what gives us the identity to endure life well on this planet, to overcome temptation in the temporal, and it fulfills our desires in ways we won't experience otherwise. Everything in us wants to stand on the mountaintop and shout to the world at times, "This is who I really am! This is what is really going on! Here, see, THIS is the truth! Look for yourselves!" Just like Satan offered to Jesus – "just prove yourself."

It is a humbling thing to say no, to choose *not* to prove yourself. Our humanity craves that but God says to surrender it. Losing sight means compromising your integrity. It means dividing yourself up and letting the world cast lots to determine your worth. In God's kingdom, we don't hustle for our worthiness. It's endowed. We don't get caught up in proving our value. It's inherent. We don't trade in our identity. It is in our very DNA, created by an eternal God.

So, what *do* we do when we find ourselves in places like Job where, whether or not we deserved it, pain and loss are what we've got? I think we have to look to his response. Like him, we sit willingly - albeit grievously - in the ash heap. Like Jesus, we retreat to lonely places. We beg for another way from the Father Himself yet still go willingly to the cross if He says we must. We refuse to lose sight. Knowing who we are is essential to our survival. More importantly, we need to know *whose* we are because it is like God in essence said of Job, "my *servant* is the one with the greatest value, highest integrity, and with whom I can entrust the hardest yet most worthy things in the world. It is to *that* one that I can entrust my own identity, my namesake, and *know* - **it will hold true.**"

I think that's why God never did let Job prove himself, never granted him that opportunity to try his case before heaven. Because God knew that what mattered more than anything Job could say about what he'd done and his own heart's motives is *who* Job was. Job's identity. God knew that, in arguing his case before heaven, Job could lose sight and start making it about him instead of about integrity. His humility could dissipate in the effort to vindicate himself, his heart could be divided, and Satan could gain the upper hand. He could've have gotten Job to indict God and thus sin and separate himself from God – the One person upon whom his entire identity rests.

When I said humility is the birthplace of healthy desire, I included "healthy" because pride is the birthplace of *un*healthy desire. We have a choice. We are always in a battle for our souls and the war doesn't end this side of the grave. I am living, breathing proof of that this very day. Your flesh will always fight the Spirit and the Spirit will always work to win your soul. What we think is a battle for our desires, for the things we want most, is actually a war on our integrity, an assault on our identity. Our enemy wants one thing of us more than all else – for us to lose sight, to indict God, and to trade the eternal for the temporal.

As I write these very words, I have no idea where I'll be in another week, another month, another year. I know there are people with whom I'd have trusted my life before that I no longer trust. There are also people I never expected I'd hold so close to my heart whose words have spoken truth in dark places and light over my soul. People with identity, people battling for integrity in their own lives, people choosing humility so they too can have sight. Maybe you can relate because this is where you've also found yourself. Again, I want to say – you are not alone. This journey is one so many of us are on.

When I was a little girl, they handed out character awards at my school at the end of each school year. Although I received many that were good, I secretly always wanted the one labeled, "Servant's Heart." It's taken me until I was in my 40's to really know and understand why. It's because I wanted to be seen for my heart, my motives. I wanted my *identity* to be known. I wanted to be recognized for the integrity that my soul chose. I didn't want, like we as humans so often attribute, for my external actions alone to be what constituted serving someone. I wanted it to be *who I was*.

That's the thing about Job. Being a servant of God *was* his identity – no matter what it cost him. We can't get so caught up in our circumstances that we allow *them* to redefine *us*. Doing so compromises our integrity. We don't want to be people divided. We want to be whole, complete, intact. It is the very feeling of being divided that makes us go in search of something or someone else who will give us an immediate relief from what ails us. The problem is that relief too is temporal. It may distract and relieve us in the short-term, but in the long run, it leaves us hungering for more.

Humility, the willingness to stay in it and seek perspective instead of chasing after desire, is what keeps our integrity intact. It makes us whole. Humility gives our identity sight. And God – well, He is where we find our validation, completion, and capacity to endure well and love much. Christianity isn't some list of rules or regulations to follow. It isn't a Judge in the sky telling us where we're falling short. Those are people. People are what make us want to go running for the hills, chasing after grace, searching high and low for a salve for our battered and bruised souls. We find ourselves desperate for some kind of mercy for simply being human, for being ourselves.

That's what Job was really after when talking with his friends – not vindication, but compassion. Not guidance, but empathy. Not clarity, but hope. Not definition, but sight. All too often what we offer up to this world is a transactional relationship that is based on performance. You do this and I'll do that. If you experience this, then it must be because of that. What if we're wrong? What if maybe you being exactly who you are the way you are *is* the design and what if *that* is the real reason you are attacked? What if when you are made out to be less than you're really exactly just right? What if, like Baby Bear and Goldilocks, we don't need anything bigger or more because what we already have is the right size?

That takes faith. It takes an immense, immeasurable amount of faith that can look as small as a mustard seed yet holds incredible power and is priceless in its value. Life is going to do its very best to disenchant, disillusion, and disappoint you. It will toss you like waves on the sea, to and fro, and sometimes you will want to cry uncle just to get the seasickness to stop. Like Job, you will wonder what is going on and why, and even in recounting all your flaws and faults, you will be unable to conjure a reason that really makes all this tragedy and suffering worthwhile.

What if the reason isn't because you've gotten it all wrong or because the world is fallen? What if the reason is something more? What if suffering is the pathway to joy and the way to show the world who you really are, to maintain integrity, to be undivided, is to let your identity inform your desire? To allow humility to do its work and instead of chasing what seems logical or even what just simply seems more sensible or fulfilling in this moment, you trusted that the answer is in what you can't see and don't know?

What if the way to get disenchanted with God is to take Him down off that pedestal, out of the genie bottle, and sit with Him in the ashes of a world gone wrong? Maybe it's in the ashes that we see a heart of hope. That we understand just exactly what He means when He says that He is for us and not against us and that He loved us before we even knew what love was, when we were still labeling Him as our enemy? What if when we said, "I don't go to church because there are a bunch of hypocrites there," He said, "Yeah, I know. I was thinking of you when I told them so?"

We can't lose sight, friends. Sight of why we're here, what we're doing, who we *really* are, who we belong to, and what eternity holds. This world is going to chew you up and spit you out and enjoy every moment. Then it's going to lie and convince you that God was the one who failed to protect you and made all this happen or maybe they'll tell you it's all your fault. Maybe both. There's a Matchbox 20 song called *Hand Me Down* that speaks to this. I doubt they were speaking for God when they wrote it, but nevertheless the message fits as to how this world treats us and what God's heart is in response.

———————————————

Once Job's friends were done sitting with him in silence because they saw the depth of his sorrow, they lost sight. They started trying to play God. Several people have done the same thing with my life lately. Deciding they know better than God what the truth really is. Maybe you've experienced that too. Other people picking your entire existence apart, drawing entirely incorrect conclusions. Maybe you aren't there now but will be soon. In either scenario, it's a place of having to trust God.

Scripture promises us that we will be hated, misunderstood, and tested. It says that what was done to Jesus and what Job experienced will also be true for us. Family members *will* turn on each other and truth *will* separate the close. Life outside of Eden will not be skittles and rainbows. In fact, quite the opposite. All the more reason why when we find ourselves in places of trial that we don't lose sight.

Louie Giglio wrote, "If you want to do something great for God, you're going to be tested first. You will be *tested* greatly so you can be *trusted* greatly."[35] (emphasis mine). The one thing God entrusts to us that matters more than anything else is Himself. He stamped our very beings with His own. Nothing else in all creation bears the image of God except us.

That is what we are called to – not to *be* God but to be *with* God. It is His name after all – Emmanuel – God *with* us. He desires relationship with us so much that He stamped His very self on us. We are image bearers of the Divine. Nothing we ever do, want, or try will ever fulfill us like our original design. Our deepest desires are met when our hearts are undivided. Our hearts are undivided when our identity is secure. Our identity is sure when we maintain perspective and we do that by trusting, no matter what, the One who designed us. This is what it's all about.

Don't Lose Sight.

Chapter Fifteen:
Whose Story Is This Anyway?

_____

"I'll tell you a secret. Old storytellers never die.
They disappear into their own story."

~ *Vera Nazarian*[36]

Since the beginning of time it seems, mankind has been captivated by story. It's not something we put on resumés, yet all of us know someone who is an exceptional storyteller. My dad was that way and, because of it, there are stories that 40 years after hearing them told time and again I'd still want to hear them ten times more. If I could have another hour with my dad, I'd spend at least half of it just listening to him tell stories from his viewpoint and I'd relish every second.

I think that might be the thing we don't recognize about the story of Job. It wasn't just his. We view it as Job's – as if the story we're told belongs to him, but I don't think it did. Even though he played a starring role, appointed by God Himself, Job wasn't the writer of the script. It was initiated by someone else, someone much greater and more powerful than Job. **It was *God's* story to begin with.** He designed it that way on purpose and everything that happened wasn't riding on Job, it was riding on Him.

What if *that* is the beauty of everything that seems so tragic? What if the author was one with a unique perspective and the story, when told from *His* viewpoint, made sense? What if it was the one story that not only made sense but enraptured us and allowed us to find purpose, meaning, and identity in a mystery we aren't the ones writing? What if *His* version was always the version we were meant to live and that in surrendering to it instead of trying to write our own our deepest joy is found?

This is where eternal perspective and modern day intersect. We don't know where our stories are going or how they will end. What we think are life-altering decisions for only us could be eternity-changing situations for many. That's why it's important to know and be in relationship with the One who holds history in His hands.

At the time, no one knew how Job's story would end, Job included. Only God did and He never told Job the truth behind any of it, at least not that we know of anyway. Only God can see into tomorrow, one place even Satan can't get to any quicker than we can. That's why Satan was betting on Job giving in. He thought that would be the end. The truth is even if Job *had* given in, *had* sinned, *had* done exactly as Satan expected, the story still would have continued, maybe even still been written and included in the history books for all to examine. Why do I say this? Because the story wasn't Job's and it didn't depend on him. How do we know that? Because of Job's friends.

I find it intriguing that God didn't include all the good things in Job's life prior to its devastation nor record the words of his prayer over his friends. He also didn't list much of anything about the remainder of Job's days after He restored them. What He *did* include was the litany of assault and misinformation all of Job's friends spoke, not of Job, but of *Him*. That is what made God extremely upset with them.

I think all of us can relate. All of us want the story to be ours. Like Job's friends, we want to fit it into our own understanding. We like for things to make sense. Sure, we can color outside the lines and do things that are artistic, expressive, or seem other worldly, but even within those things, we want a form of definition. We search for ways to relate, to assign meaning, purpose, or place. We need things to have a story we can narrate, otherwise, we take them to the trash heap.

Jesus said the first commandment is to "Love the Lord your God with all your heart and with all your soul and with all your mind and with all your strength." (Mark 12:30, ESV) The second one is "You shall love your neighbor as yourself." (Mark 12:31, ESV). Both take humility and divine assistance. Where we can't figure out how to do the second one, we return to the first. Where the first seems too challenging, the second reminds us why the first exists. I think this is foundational to our understanding of story because, in light of what Jesus said, it means every circumstance is intended to remind us that - It's not our story to author. It's His.

That's what Job understood by the end that so many of us miss. It wasn't about Job. It affected Job. Deeply. It changed the course of Job's entire history, family, community, and eternity. God knew that.

When everything was occurring, God was the only one with the ability to see into history just how many of us would come to study Job, ponder his life, listen to his words, and seek comfort and solace during our own times of grief, pain, and loss. God never does anything without a purpose and, if it has an earthly one, you can be certain it has an eternal one too.

So, what is it? Why does God do the things He does and why doesn't He always tell us what He's up to? I think it's because, as the word itself says, history is *His* story. Nothing that's done is done merely for what *we* can see. It always carries a greater gravity. Writers don't tell their characters why their parts are their parts in a story. They don't explain the narrative or ask for their opinions. Even if it is a live play, the director doesn't ask the cast to decide how the set should be or what they think of the backdrop or if they are okay with the ending. They say, "Here is the role, play it or not, but the show *is* continuing."

When Job's life was disintegrating, he was given nothing – no explanation, no behind the scenes reading, no foreshadowing of the ending. He was just thrust on stage and had nothing to rely on except his understanding of the Author of his days. *That* is why it's so important for *God* to be the One with whom you have an audience. Not other people. Not even your own understanding. Other people, just like Job's friends, have limits. Like us, they are finite in their understanding. No matter how long a person has taught, preached, prayed, lived, loved, or studied, they will never begin to grasp all that God understands. Just like you and me, the most they can do is trust Him.

———————————

Our modern day experiences are at times going to be just like Job's. We're going to lose things we would give anything to hold onto, endure pain that is excruciating, suffer grief that wracks our souls, and I can promise you from first-hand experience that there is nothing this world has to offer that is going to make it okay. Nothing. The very most you can hope to get here is some kind of medicine or anesthesia to make you unaware temporarily of those realities. Yet, tomorrow is another day, and when you awaken, everything is still the same or maybe even worse than when you started.

I think one of the hardest things for me to encounter in all that's occurred over these grief-riddled seasons has been people who think they know. It's like talking to people who have parenting all figured out. They've never had children yet are *certain* they know exactly how their kids will be. They truly believe how their kids turn out *is* within their control. However, if you ask any parent who's shown up for longer than about a week and they'll tell you – everything I thought I knew, it turns out I don't have a clue about.

There's a woman I know in local ministry like this. She leads things and speaks well. However, if you watch her life, you see how her reality and belief system don't line up. I had to ask myself why because she comes across as rather put together and at least *sounds* knowledgeable about how God works. It finally occurred to me that the dissonance is that she thinks she knows. She thinks the pains she suffered decades ago and her processing of those have absolved her of the necessity of addressing new things going forward. She *says* otherwise but, if you listen close, you hear how she thinks she already has the answers, that things will always be within her control. She believes that, because she's resolved certain traumas and addressed certain principles, she can either keep her life from falling apart or, if it does so without her permission, she won't be deeply affected.

The truth is when life goes exactly the way it shouldn't, it doesn't matter if your friends are like Jesus or like Job, pain is pain and suffering is wretched. Grief will wreck your world and there is little to nothing you can do to make it not so. Reality has a way of changing who you are whether you want it to or not. Adam and Eve would be the first to say so because it turned out this wasn't their story either. It too was God's. The answer isn't to make the storyline your own. It's to let it be His. That is the one and only way through.

At the beginning of this book, I said something that was hard for even me to swallow. If you've ever written, you might be able to relate. Sometimes things just come out and you wonder, "Wait. Is that really true? Do I really believe that? Where did that come from?" Sometimes you have to sit and wrestle with what's now on the page. I've had to do that on repeat with what I shared about how maybe it was always going to be this way. That sin was always the pathway and suffering always the journey and maybe, just maybe, *this* was how we *really* got to know God – the real one, not the one we wanted to know.

When I re-read the story of Adam and Eve, I saw something I hadn't noticed before that now seems so critical. They weren't safe. Not really. The Garden of Eden was beautiful. It was God's creation where He met with them, talking and walking in the cool of the day. They had purpose and plans and there was nothing separating any of them. However, what they didn't have was decision finalized, sin overcome. The choice had yet to be made. The Tree of the Knowledge of Good and Evil stood there day after day and Satan knew it. He waited to see what they would do. Would they eat? Would they be like him and want to choose? Apparently not, at least not on their own anyway.

More often than not us humans are content to be as we are. We don't really want another story besides the one we're already living. We'd rather make our current realities safe and comfortable and stay inside those places where things are familiar or enjoyable. It doesn't mean we can't chase an adrenaline rush or do things that seem out of the ordinary. It just means that we aren't looking to join something bigger than us because our viewpoint is fixed – right here, right now, on the horizons we can envision or see. We are temporal creatures who don't have the perspective of eternity.

The Garden of Eden did not offer one thing that heaven guarantees. Permanent security. In the Garden, the serpent still got in. Snakes still existed and they came slithering in with something we're not going to experience in eternity – temptation. The thing about temptation that we don't often consider is hidden in Paul's letter to the Corinthians. He wrote, "No temptation has seized you except what is common to *man*." (1 Corinthians 10:13, BSB, emphasis mine). *Man's* story is one of temptation.

Temptation isn't from God. It's from Satan. What was the temptation? The same thing it is now. It's to make the story our own. To make life all about you and me. To make *us* the storyline of the entire play. What we often fail to see is that our stories don't matter as much when *we* become center stage. Our stories matter most when we realize we are their *beneficiaries* not their *authors*. Authors have heavy creator duties. They are responsible for the entire thing. Everything that happens is their responsibility.

This is true of parents too. Babies come here without being capable of doing a thing. We make them and then they arrive, entirely dependent and reliant upon our ability to provide for their needs. The same thing is true of a Creator God. He, as Author and Father, is the one designing the reason for our days. The problem is that we get in the way. Much like our children, we insist that we know best and that He's forgotten or, worse yet, doesn't even care about what we need. We issue demands and often add insult to injury when things don't go our way.

God knows why we were created. He's always been the one doing the creating. So, there isn't anything inherently overlooked or missing in the story. We were never intended to be its authors, only its recipients. And, it is in *receiving* life, engaging in the story we were created to live, that we find our own opportunities to generate the stories that we live. Because it is within *that* context that ours begin to make sense. The backdrop has and always will be relationship. It is by seeking out the Author of our stories, or as scripture calls Jesus, "The Author and Perfector of our faith," that we realize our true place.

Job's story was valuable not because of all the good he did to people on repeat and how great he lived before and after devastation, but because in his suffering and temptation *and* in is seasons of goodness and provision, Job surrendered the storyline to God. He leaned on *God's* understanding which is what made him capable of saying to his wife, "You speak as a foolish woman speaks ... Should we accept only good from God and not adversity?" (Job 2:10, CSB).

Our stories are intended to lead us to identity and identity is intended to lead us to our Creator. *He* is the one designing our days. Why does that matter? Safety. Something we cannot, try as we might, create. Peter tells us, "There is no fear in love. But perfect love drives out fear." (1 Peter 4:18) So, where can we find a love that is perfect and guaranteed to keep us safe in the face of danger and adversity? There is only one place, only one person in whom these exist, and that isn't found on this finite planet. It's in eternity. This is where we see what a person with perfect love does in response to temptation, sin, pride, and adversity. He doesn't just design or outline. He enters into the story Himself and becomes part of it.

On earth, even in the Garden of Eden, Satan still had access and he never hesitates to show up. Masquerading as an angel of light, he lures us to envision the one thing we think we are missing. When I re-read Adam and Eve's story, I had to ask myself, how did Satan know what would work? How do you tempt people you don't even know, have never met, and have zero history with? That's a hard one because, back then, Satan had had no time with humans. There was no looking back over history to see what worked with them. So, I think he had to use the one and only sure weapon in his arsenal – what had worked with him.

I think we tend to forget something critical - Pride didn't originate here. It didn't start in the Garden of Eden. It originated in the heavens. Pride began with Lucifer. Before he became the fallen angel we now know as Satan, Lucifer was beautiful. The most beautiful angel God ever created. He had authority just under God's own. For most of us, that would be enough. We'd be grateful to have it. But not him. No, he let it go to his head. It wasn't enough to live in *God's* story. He wanted one of his own. So, he decided I'm *going* to make myself like God, consequences be damned, and I am going to do what *I* want. Then, he did.

That is how Satan tempted Eve. With the very thing that he tempts us with. It should sound familiar, the words we hear. In summary, Satan asked Eve the same question he'd asked himself, the one he asks all of us. "Why are you letting this story be about God? Don't you know what you're missing out on? Don't you know there is so much more to what you could experience than just this? Why are you trusting God when you could write your own narrative?"

We're always tempted to make the story our own because Satan knows that if we can get the focus off the One writing it, we'll lose sight of what's really happening and who's really writing the script.

We'll stop trusting the Author and start trying to narrate a different outcome. We'll allow the plot line to determine the author's trustworthiness and, realizing we aren't okay with how it goes, we'll cast Him to the side and begin writing our own. That's how Satan wins – by making us fight the battle of sin, death, and destruction without any weapons to defeat him and without the one Person who holds them.

There's a scene in one of my favorite movies, *Fred Claus,* that's like a modern day spin on the conversation between the serpent and Eve. Vince Vaughn's character, Fred Claus, is the big brother to Santa. Disenchanted with it all as an adult, he's talking to a kid from a neighboring apartment who still believes in Santa. Fred says,

"Slam, have you really thought about Santa Claus? … The guy's

138

in a big red suit flying around in reindeer because he craves the spotlight. He's a fame junkie. The guy's a clown. He's a megalomaniac. It's all a big shell game. ... Don't be a cheerleader for Santa Claus, okay? Think about it. Watch the angles. Don't drink the Kool-Aid. You're better than that."

Considering his words but not convinced yet, Slam replies to Fred, *"I like Kool-Aid."*

Fred answers, *"Yeah, but don't drink this Kool-Aid."*

Later in the movie after much trial and tribulation, it's obvious Slam decided Fred was right because he repeats the same things to his roommates[37], much like Adam and Eve did to themselves and one another.

Another important aspect about stories is that we get to tell them all we want, but we don't always get to create them. Many of my dad's stories weren't about him. They were told from his vantage point, but he was rarely the only character in them. I think one of the more frustrating parts of life for me has been the storylines that other people have tried creating on their own that are actually *my* lived reality. They've shared a version of my story that's completely wrong.

Have you ever experienced this? Found yourself in a story that held some pieces of truth but overall didn't fit? Or maybe you've been the recipient of narratives other people devised to suit *their* version of the outcome they wanted and it's been at your expense. What do we do with this? Do we right all the wrongs? Fix all the narratives? Shout the truth from the rooftops? I mean, even if it is God's story, we are the ones still living it. We are the people enduring injustice and suffering the results of someone else's sin. Even when it is our doing and our creation of negative events, doesn't that still make it our story to tell? *Especially* when we own our sins and work towards redemption, restoration, and healing?

Apparently not. In the middle of Job's discourse, he lists out the truth for his friends. Not only does he detail everything he was doing that was far more righteous than any of us can claim, especially on a regular basis, but he also says,

> *"I also could speak like you, if you were in my place; I could make fine speeches against you and shake my head at you. But my mouth would encourage you; comfort from my lips would bring you relief."* (Job 16:4-5)

Or, in words more similar to what we would say,

> *"Friends, my heart is nowhere near what any of you are saying. I wouldn't do to you what you are doing to me. Never in a million years would you catch me navigating the story this way. Ever. If you were sitting in my seat, I'd do for you exactly what I wish you were doing for me."*

Maybe you've been in Job's shoes also. Maybe, like me, you know exactly how Job feels and exactly how you would behave were it you in their place. To try narrating the story our own way is so tempting. We want so very much to write the script and Satan knows it. It's a beautiful distraction that can so quickly lead us into sin and separation from the one person keeping us safe.

We live in a world that beckons us to put other people's dirt on display, low key shame them or do so blatantly, and make headline news or at least on social media. The thing is, we *can* do that. There is absolutely nothing stopping us from shouting it across hilltops, publishing it on Instagram, making it known from city to city. We have the freedom to tell other people's stories however we want. Job's friends certainly did. It's the same freedom God gives us to tell His. But here's the thing when you create. As the author, and even the storyteller, you are responsible *not* to tell tales where truth and facts are involved. *Responsible* journalism is called such for a reason.

Most of us have gotten rather exhausted in recent years and months of fake news. It litters our social media feeds and runs like tickertape across our phones. Without even knowing the full story, most of us have emailed it to friends, re-posted it, or investigated things like we have a grip on reality. But, how many of us can really say we want the actual truth? The truth is supposed to be what sets us free yet all too often in this world's currency it's the thing that locks us into place.

The question we have to wrestle with is - Is this *my* story or

His? And, if it's His, then is how I'm telling it making Him known as *He* really is? Or, am I selling a version of Him that doesn't really exist? Those are the real questions I've had to grapple with. Do we want to know the God that allows sin and suffering as the pathway through temptation to salvation ending with redemption that secures our safety for eternity? Or do we want one of our own making that makes us, not Him, the center of the narrative? The latter is deeply tempting despite its cost.

Love doesn't look like this world says. Love bends. It comes near. It binds up broken hearts and heals wounded souls. What it doesn't do is avoid suffering. It doesn't eliminate pain. It won't even just settle for purpose in its midst. Love *saves*. One who loves us *becomes* part of the narrative we choose, He doesn't just write His own. He saves us even when we create a false narrative because that's who *He* is.

Love makes Him part of our story and invites us to be part of His. They are one and the same, and if we want ours to be one we can appreciate, one worthy of telling, we have to tell it from the viewpoint of its true Author. We have to disenchant ourselves with the God we once believed in and get to know the God He really is. Sometimes that means letting go of things you otherwise never would. It means enduring misunderstanding at a price you don't want to pay. It forces you into Job's seat where, at the end, when God says to his friends, "You all spoke wrongly of me, so incorrectly in fact that I am unwilling to hear another word, even of apology, humility, or repentance, from you. Have Job pray for you instead," you're faced with whether or not to do so.

Job had to *choose* them. He had to *decide* whether or not he would stand in the gap for his friends. These were the very people whose words heaped abuse upon injury and rubbed salt in his wounds. The ones who clearly misunderstood God's story yet acted as if they were the only ones who really knew. Job had to *elect* not to make the story about him. He had to submit the storyline to God first for editing.

I'll be honest. If I were Job, if I were still smack dab in the middle of all that suffering, with no promise of when or if it would end, I don't know if my response would be the same as his. I want to say I would, but this season has taught me that there are times when people speak things over you or about you that feel unforgivable. Even if you follow God's commands and choose to forgive them, you may not feel able to immediately go to God on their behalf and ask for anything, especially their goodness.

Job did though. I've had to ask myself why and I think it was because of his perspective. He saw things no one else did. I don't think it was Job's goodness that led him there. I believe it was his humility. God doesn't want us to misrepresent Him. It's one of the things that He despises most. It's why He hates sin. Because sin is what mars the image of *Him* in us. He's not a megalomaniac to say that. He's the one who loves us more than we'll ever know. It is *His* life in *us* that gives us a story to begin with. It is *His* story for us that makes *our* story worth living. And it is only in the willingness to let our stories be caught up in His own that we will ever come to understand and know Him.

The plotline God is writing is bigger than anything we can see. Best of all? It's for our *good*. God doesn't stay in Eden. Not this one anyway. This earthly Eden holds permanent unsafety, constant temptation, and serpents in the trees. To stay here would make Him a terrible Father and even worse God. That wouldn't be loving. That wouldn't be Godly. Love removes threats, overcomes danger, and makes ways in the wilderness and streams in the desert. History – *His* story? It's the one and only plotline that will ever construct an ending that is worthy. God's story is about Him for one reason and one reason only.

Because it is *He* who is our sanctuary.

Chapter Sixteen:
On Being Wounded People

———

"Many people suffer because of the false supposition on which they have based their lives. That supposition is that there should be no fear or loneliness, no confusion or doubt. But these sufferings can only be dealt with creatively when they are understood as wounds integral to our human condition."

~ Henri Nouwen[38]

There is a quote by Maya Angelou in her beautiful, aching book *I Know Why the Caged Bird Sings* that reads, "She comprehended the perversity of life, that in the struggle lies the joy."[39] It's a reality for all of us that life is this intertangled web of that which we cannot control and the things we must. All of these bring us both sorrow and hope, love and loss, joy and grief. Knowing that so much is fleeting, time being one of those things outside of our control, we grasp at straws and strive to make the fulfillment of what we most need stand still.

What I've disliked perhaps most about this season without even realizing it is the space I have to hold for being wounded. Not just by life or other people, but by myself. I've hurt not only other people but me too as I've traversed this world. That's the journey. It's one none of us carries well. No one wants to be wounded. We all want to be whole, healed, and capable. Being these things is what we believe allows us to transcend need or at least to fulfill it.

Yet, that isn't how we're made. Instead, somehow, it is in the wounding that we are found. We feel like damaged goods yet it is our wounds themselves that give us an identity, something on which to build that we wouldn't otherwise possess. It's an odd dichotomy that we constantly search for purpose, meaning, places to belong, and we believe or tell ourselves that, "When I finally get there, *THEN* I will have what is missing." We think that all the answers, resources, or whatever is currently outside our grasp is going to be the final piece of the puzzle.

I suppose it's true to a degree that there is a thing outside our grasp that is the puzzle piece we are all missing. People often say "we all have a God-shaped hole" in us. Perhaps that's accurate but it doesn't really seem biblical or at least not fully so from my perspective. When I read scripture, God is a whole lot bigger than simply being a missing piece of *our* puzzle. It's like we see him as Tom Cruise's character in Jerry Maguire and we're telling Him, "You complete me,"[40] only with a lot less romance and a whole lot more demand.

There are a lot of unspoken expectations surrounding us and God and I think it's here that we find ourselves disenchanted the most because it requires enchanting ourselves with something in order for us to ever feel the loss of it. That's where the missing puzzle piece, the "God-shaped hole" comes in. Like I said in the last chapter, this story we're all living? It's His. What we miss is the outline, the overview, the summary inside the flap telling us what the story is about and who the author is. We believe we've been born into it and, much like our children, we live like God's life began when ours did.

However, the truth is our lives and His existed long before time did in many ways because all of us – everything that lives and moves and has being is wrapped up in one place, one being – and that is *Him*. We cannot escape it. David, in his Psalm about how we are made and the limitations inside which we exist said in essence, "There is nowhere I can go to escape you, God, not even to the grave. Everywhere I am, you are there already. You really are *the* I AM."[41]

Being wounded people means accepting this – that we are *not* in charge, never have been, never will be, *and* that that is *good*. I have wrestled and fought what feels like my very own self into the dirt about the goodness of wounding, the place where being less than is exactly how I was always intended to live. I recently listened to a podcast by Emilie Freeman interviewing Kate Bowler about *No Cure for Being Human* and Kate said that we have to get to the place where we realize that this was never the life we were going to live. So much grief is wrapped up in accepting that perfection, all our dreams come true, this imaginary life we designed for ourselves never was and still isn't reality.[42]

We are all wounded people. Your wounding might look different than someone else's. Maybe yours, like Kate's, comes with stage 4 cancer, surgery after surgery, setback after setback, grief upon grief. Or it comes with dreams delayed, cradles shoved in closets, and couches set in living rooms where the people you hoped to fill them will never sit. Maybe your ache is in the grave where the ones you poured life and joy and everything you could into are now dimensions away from your grasp. It really doesn't matter what the identification piece is, all of us suffer some kind of wounding and there is no making sense of what doesn't make sense.

One of the worst things people can do for you as I mentioned early on in this book is offer up platitudes. "Everything happens for a reason." Likely so, but what if that reason is never extended to you? What if life is full of things that will never, ever make sense? Can we be okay with that? That's the real question. None of us want it. None of us are good with wounding, especially when it doesn't have a reason that tracks. We are trained to believe that life is full of lessons and somehow those lessons transcend the importance of us. As if *we* could be better if we would just fix ourselves. Heal the wounds, depend on the understanding, and this will never happen again. Only it will. It's guaranteed.

Even in what is supposed to be one of the most beautiful unions in all of existence – marriage – Paul says this, "Those who marry **will face *many* troubles** in this life." (1 Corinthians 7:28, NIV, emphasis mine). If you've been married or even in a long term relationship with anyone, doesn't have to be a spouse, you know how true this is: With people comes wounding. Baggage is the native luggage we all carry and Trouble is guaranteed. Even being a hermit, *away* from all the people, has its own set of difficulties. There is no escaping it.

Too often our culture presents us with the opportunity to believe that we can transcend, overcome, or somehow manage our wounding, our baggage, our trouble, our *humanity*. The truth? We can't. And? That's not a bad thing. Being unable to go it alone and being people who need support, those *are* God's plan. He specifically equips us to be incapable of Lone Rangering our lives. He guarantees our frailty and ensures our fragility.

God designs circumstances that make us face realities with which we are unequipped to live.

I think this is why we constantly push, strive, compete, and work towards whatever we deem best. There are world records now for just about everything and people slave over those goals, as if life is found in the achievement itself. I'm not here to tell you that it isn't because it's also true that having goals, striving for things, and being ambitious can be very healthy. God calls us to decisiveness, not complacency. In fact, in Revelation, as He's talking to the churches, He says very clearly that He cannot stand lukewarm. Be hot or cold, pick a place, but whatever you do, don't be complacent. He spits out the ones at room temperature.

Wounding, however, isn't something we're supposed to "overcome" or just learn to live with. It's something we develop the ability to lean into. Just like gifts and strengths, there are ways we need to lean into our wounding and weaknesses. It sounds counter-intuitive but when you think about it, if you are strong in an area and another person is weak, is it better for you to go it alone, accomplishing life only for you and be on the mountaintop alone? Only when you're seeking solitude, which is fine in spurts but not as a permanent existence. If the end goal is to be *with* people – and it is because, remember, this is *God's* story, not just our own - then by combining their weakness, their willingness to lean into that and allowing you to extend out your strength to them, then *both* of you make it. You celebrate on the summit together.

I think that's what God wants us to get. That the journey matters. It isn't the destination. Relationship has no destination. It simply is. My husband and I could be married for 50 years and we won't have ever arrived. There is no arriving. We get up every day and want more of it. More connection, more laughter, more working through things, more understanding, joy, and identity. That never ends. It never will because the journey *is* the destination. It is relationship.

―――――――――――

So, what about Job? Job had already done the mountaintop experience with God. So much so that Satan himself decided Job wasn't even worth bothering with. God and Job were connected, close friends, and Job served Him with a faithfulness that defied existence. Satan had no interest in fighting with God in hand to hand combat. He's more into sneak attacks and damaging what God loves than he is in getting into a brawl with the Almighty, so Job wasn't exactly at the top of his hit list. That's why God was the one who had to bring Job to Satan's attention.

Job had strength, thus the question became - When wounded, what then? On whom would he rely? How would he live? It's really the same question for us all. Are we going to be defined by our wounding or are we going to lean into it? Job was human just like all of us so, while there is much to be learned from his posture of humility, Job nevertheless asked the same questions we all do. *Why me? What is happening? How do I navigate this?*

The answer is still the same. By *being* wounded. By not fighting it. By leaning into all that we cannot possibly understand because the story we think we're telling isn't really the main storyline at all. It's just a detail in a much greater story in which we've been chosen to participate.

There isn't always a reason, at least not one we're made aware of or could even understand. God is God and we are not Him. That is the hardest most wonderful thing we'll ever wrap our brains around. I think what Job did that allowed him to die "old and full of years" – aka with *life* – was he leaned into the wounding. He allowed himself to be a wounded human being and he didn't try, even afterward, to change the narrative.

Scripture tells us that, after all his pain and suffering, people came and consoled Job for all that God brought on him. How many times do we allow people to actually console us and we don't try to fix it? Meaning we don't try to reason our way backwards and find where we screwed up so we can ensure it doesn't happen again. We don't create groups or organizations that prevent life from happening. We just let be what is.

In our modern age, I think we very rarely do that. I think the reason Job was full of life when he died is because he realized what none of us really want to accept – that we aren't living in the Land of Should, we are living on earth, and this place is a place for the wounded. It is where wounding and healing intermix and there is always space for both. There is never going to come a day this side of the grave where you don't experience loss, pain, and grief, just as there will never be a time when your wounding isn't also a gift.

Somehow wounding makes us feel less than. It acquaints us intimately with our limitations and our not enoughness. It introduces us to fragility and frailty we wish did not exist. It motivates us to do something about it and I think God designed us that way. I think we are the ones that take it in the wrong direction. We live like we are supposed to cure our humanity but, as Kate Bowler said, "There is no cure for being human."[43] Getting over it, pushing through, and punching back against it isn't the answer. We can't design our way out of it.

The key is leaning in. If we can't let ourselves be wounded and we insist on fixing ourselves, we won't ever be healed. Not truly. Because *we* aren't designed to do all our own healing. We aren't that well-equipped. We're wired for community, connection, for interdependence. Even our body works together that way. It cannot function without multiple parts of it working in conjunction with the rest. We are no different.

I think the takeaway for us is knowing what God's heart is because that is the cure for disenchantment. Truth and reality take the magic and mystery of what we believed to be so powerful away and put them in their rightful place.

The magic and mystery and power of God aren't found in His ability to give us the specific life we want to live.

They're found in the truth that He knows we will be wounded, designs us to need Him, and *wants* to be our constant companion. That's the beauty of knowing the God who actually made us. He created us this way. In all scenarios, He is ever-present in all the right ways. The ones that give us life the most, just as we need whether we believe it or not. The key is knowing that we have to be incomplete on our own in order to appreciate it. It is our inadequacy, our void, our "God-shaped hole" that allows His fullness to shine because Him filling us *is* the glory of God.

We were reading the other day when Romans 3:23 came up. It says, "For all have sinned and fallen short of the glory of God." My whole life long that verse has been presented in one way – that we are all failures, that if we all had just gotten it right in the first place, done enough, been enough, and acted better, then we'd have made the mark. Life would have been good. It's a lie we sell ourselves and it's all performance based.

What if that was never how it was intended to read? What if that's not what it really means? Sin *is* missing the mark, yes. Sin also is separation from God. When we look at it in that context, we realize that falling short of the glory of God doesn't mean we just are not good enough and didn't hit the mark. It means we are separated from Him.

The truth is we weren't designed to be capable of demonstrating God's glory on our own. We can't. *We aren't Him.* **The** glory of God is *His* life *in* us. *We* are His crowning beauty, His greatest expression, His most beautiful creation, and *sin* is the separation piece that keeps us from living and experiencing that. Falling short of His glory is missing out on His existence within. It's that hole in us that we continue to try filling.

Wounding is necessary because it reveals God's true heart for us. It shows us that what He longs for most is relationship – *with us*. He isn't looking for our achievements and He isn't that worried like we are about everything going just so. Not at least in regard to circumstance. He knows He's bigger than that. He can work in and through everything to bring about good, so our circumstances just aren't that big of mountain to Him. He can handle them. It's us that's the issue. *Our* hearts, *our* minds, *our* willingness. That's the real battlefield.

That's why the weapons He equips us with to navigate the trouble this world guarantees us aren't tangible. They aren't intended to make our circumstances better and achieve for us the glory and strength we think we need to have in the here and now. Does He care about social justice? Absolutely. It's just that social justice isn't the end in itself. The end is us – it is *our* hearts – it is our willingness to let Him be the power in our clay jars, our bodies, our very existence, life, and breath, that extends everything He is to a world in need, a world created to reflect Him.

Life, as God designed it, was always intended to be immortal, eternal, and supernatural. It is divine. It extends across dimensions and into spaces we cannot comprehend. That is God Himself – infinite. So, we have to expect that our lives are going to resemble it because we were made *not* in human image but in His. Humanity is simply our form and it was intended to be filled with *Him*. That's what true glory means.

Glory as we've redefined it cannot exist in this place the way we dream because ours is a watered down version of all we were meant to be and experience. We can't fix ourselves into being the glory we all seek. We have to submit. If I'm being honest with you, this is what I hate. I hate having to accept my own humanity. I want to, if not control it, at least design it. I want to know that my input guarantees certain output. That's just not reality though and none of us really know how to accept that. It isn't our story, but oh how we want it to be.

I don't write fiction, but I read a lot of it. I love character development and watching how authors give one character a completely different personality from another. I love seeing the interplay and how circumstances affect even fictional people differently. Here's the thing though. Never in any of those stories is the story one that belongs to the people in it. They aren't even real. Even in nonfiction stories where someone may even been sharing their own autobiography, there is a running undercurrent of – this doesn't matter just to me, it always has been and always will be bigger than just me.

Wounding allows relationship in.

It invites us to look at God through realistic eyes and ask the question, "Who was I intended to be?" We don't have to keep chasing it. We can set all our demands down and let our strivings cease once we realize that this world is only going to volley up struggle. It's not something we can escape. It's a promise we will all live. Satan wants to use it to convince us that we are the issue, that we have the problem we need to fix.

The truth? He is. Satan is the epitome and fulfillment of sin itself. Pride originated with *him*. We are where his battle with heaven plays out. That's why humility is so critical. Because when you lay down your own script, when you discard your narrative, when your insistence upon the life you wanted to live is something you're willing to let go of and grieve, you can enter safely into a place of wounding, knowing it is the very glory you are seeking that you will find in the end.

Glory only matters if there's someone there to see it. That's why glory really, at its core, is relationship. Always we come back to this. Wounds are meant to hurt, yes, to stop us in our tracks and force us to take stock of where we're at. They are *not* meant to define us. They are designed so we can lean in. Lean into our not enoughness, into leaving the Land of Should for the Land that Isn't, and reach out for someone who has not come here to make our lives better or our circumstances fulfilling but rather to make our hearts a place He *lives*. *We* become *His* very dwelling. There is nothing more intimate and beautiful than that. We are His home, His temple, the beautiful place in which He exists.

That is true glory. God *in* us.

That's why Jesus left. Because the Holy Spirit living in our very beings is life itself. Wounding reveals just how much we need Him. May we be people willing to let our wounds inform our perspective so that they no longer simply hurt us, they also *heal*. We are designed to embody the very places of sanctuary that we seek. So, the question is – do we really want to see God, to be disenchanted with who we saw Him as so we can engage with Him as He really is? Are we really willing to be *His*?

Chapter Seventeen:
Managing Expectations

"Life is about learning to live with loss."
~ *Gary Thomas[44]*

I attended a Lysa Terkeurst retreat recently where she shared the story of the very day her life imploded again. As the truth surfaced in a repeat of an all too familiar and painful past, the pages of a book she'd written a year earlier were spread across her bed. God had specifically designed her, as she says, "to work through what I walked through" and it was her very own words, used in ways she never in their original writing expected, that ministered to her in that moment.

We so rarely expect life to be what it really is. God always sees though. He always knows in advance. He exists outside of time and holds Time itself in His hands. It too is His creation. There is nothing that escapes Him. It's why He sends His word out and can assure us that it never returns to Him void. He has that power. We are the ones who cannot see, who do not have a window into tomorrow nor a time machine back to yesterday.

During that same retreat, I had the immense privilege of staying on a farm that I had no idea existed. I was just scrolling through the travel website looking for a hotel when an image popped up. At first, I checked it and then moved on. Days later, I found myself coming back to it. I couldn't believe no one had booked it yet. It was at a lower cost and definitely nicer than any hotel listed. I took it as a sign and registered, ensuring I'd have plenty of time to get there the day before and settle in.

Realizing I wouldn't arrive at normal check in time since I was driving in from several states away, I emailed the owners. Not long after, I received a phone call in response asking for more details. Why was I coming, what was the story, tell her about the retreat. So, I did. Her call came on the one good day I had in the midst of an immense ongoing crisis that had consumed my life for several weeks. In a season where the people I needed most to surround me well weren't available and didn't reach out, her words leveled and encouraged me. She said,

> *"God gave us this farm and He's sending you here now for a reason. This place you're coming to is holy ground."*

I can't even write that without tearing up. Providence always goes before us in ways we never expect. When I got there, a sign hung out front with verses from Romans 12 claiming, "He Will." As I told them, I will tell you – God goes before us and He knows exactly the safe havens we will need. He prepares ways in the wilderness and streams in the desert and sometimes they come in the form of farms as we scroll through random travel websites looking for a place to land.

When I planned this trip and booked my spot at the retreat, I had no idea where my life would be at the time I went. I thought I did at the outset because back then everything seemed fairly predictable. Things were stressful and difficult to be sure, but life always is somehow, isn't it? That's what I told myself, so I reasoned that when I went, it would be for the things I thought I knew then.

I couldn't have been more wrong. God sent me there. He knew exactly the words I'd need to hear, the prayers I'd need to pray, and He even knew just how far into this book I'd have written. He'd put it on Lysa's heart to share with us her story of writing and re-reading her own book *Forgiving What You Can't Forget* on the very day she'd have to relive and at once newly encounter that topic again in deeply painful ways. He knew that her story would prompt me to journey back in this book while laying in bed in that farm over a thousand miles away from the physical realities plaguing my days and provide me with a respite to read not only what He wanted me to say to you, but what He was saying to me.

I cannot even begin to tell you how painful this journey has been. If your travels carry any similarity, know that I hold for you so much space. Life can be downright brutal and the truth is that it doesn't matter whether we've landed there at someone else's hands like Job or if we've brought it all upon ourselves. Life is just a challenge and the reality it seems we so often rush past is how much of it comes with an unanticipated amount of loss.

The trouble with managing our expectations is that we don't come here really knowing what we're in for. We figure it out as we go along and, even then, we still try to work our way towards something we can handle or at least navigate more than not. We don't like being ships tossed about the sea, writhing to and fro with the waves. We, like the disciples, look at Jesus and think how insane it is that He is asleep on a cushion and we ask Him as they did, *"Don't you care about us at all?"*

Expectations are a bittersweet pill that we can't help but swallow. We love to have them when they are fulfilled and we ache when they are not. It takes an immense amount of strength to walk out of the fire scathed but not dead and reach back in for others who are still struggling to escape. Expectations are the same. Having them yet managing them is a harrowing tightrope to navigate.

———

Job's story doesn't explicitly tell us about his expectations. Like with most stories, we have to look deeper at the details. It seems that Job was similar to all of us in that he expected life to go well. He expected that to be a servant of God meant you would make sacrifices and respect the King of Heaven. You would bring water to thirsty souls. He didn't expect to be God himself and he clearly stood in great reverence of the Almighty.

That said, Job, like the rest of us, seemed to believe that life shouldn't hold so much inexplicableness, so much unnecessary pain, such deep grief. He wrestled with night terrors, people's abuse heaped on his already suffering body, and his friends' perspectives that were nothing like his own. Job seemed to know what community was supposed to look like, what it meant to be God's servant, and how integrity was to be lived out. At least he did until he didn't. As I said before, there comes a point when Job says in essence, "I don't care anymore, I just wish I'd never seen the light of day. It wouldn't even be enough now to be dead. I wish I was never even born."

Recently, I was listening to a podcast and they were discussing death. They explained how, back before modern days, there were no such things as funeral homes, hospitals, morgues, or undertakers. We didn't have places or people to take the dead. We buried them ourselves and death was a natural part of our existence. Now, that is no longer the case. In current times, we've separated ourselves so far from death that death no longer seems inevitable. Instead, it now seems unexpected.

One of the reasons existing feels so traumatizing in modern day is that it doesn't meet our expectations. We've set ourselves up for failure by refusing to acknowledge the realities that existed long before we had a place on stage. We've conjured up a version of the story we want to live and demanded, or at the very least expected, God to bless it. Yet, that's not how this works. That's not who God is. We have to remember the story we're living is *His*.

When I got to the farm, I was literally walking into someone else's narrative. The entire place represented them. It was very Carolina-esque, decorated with taste and intention. It made you feel both welcome and wanted. As I walked the grounds, I began to see there was much more than met the eye. This wasn't just the owners' story. It was far beyond them. Like the sign said, "He Will," He had and He still did.

It was clear that God had designed every inch of this place and put it on their hearts to display. Right down to the goats, the flowers, the hammock swing in the back. Every detail, even the sign on the fireplace, spoke of Him without ever saying His name. Just like the book of Esther, without even mentioning God once, His fingerprints were apparent on every page. I think that's one reason we need to manage our expectations – because if we don't, we'll miss out on His.

I quoted in the introduction to this book a passage from Hosea, the prophet whose wife wouldn't stay put but whom God called to loving her deeply anyway. God said some interesting things there. He said He'd lead us into the wilderness and that there – in the wilderness – is where He'd give us back vineyards and make the valley of our trouble a door of hope. In the wilderness is where we would respond as the Israelites did in the days of their salvation from slavery. Because it is in the wilderness that God speaks to us tenderly and there that we are finally willing to listen.

Disenchantment is part of the journey whether we want it to be or not. God doesn't offer us a Promised Land without a wilderness.

He doesn't give us summits and mountaintops without requiring we climb to them. Valleys are discussed on repeat in scripture. They're described as "trouble" and "the shadow of death." Valleys are where we get hemmed in and life starts to feel sketchy. Loss looms on the horizon and the hairs on the back of our necks start standing up as we feel Satan's hot breath. This is not at all the journey we expected.

That's why we're called to things like discipline and reconciling – because there is just so much that we don't understand, so much we *can't*. We have to trust the process because we can't see its end. We have to rely on the Author because our part in the story is the only thing visible today. Doing the next right thing is the only thing and it's the one thing we tend to prefer least.

Brené Brown wrote about expectations in her recent book *Atlas of the Heart*. She describes them this way, "*Disappointment is unmet expectations. The more significant the expectations, the more significant the disappointment.*" She goes on to define "expectations that are unexamined and unexpressed" as "*stealth* expectations"[45] which seems exactly right. It feels like this is where so many of us live. As if reality sneaks up on us unexpectedly.

We walk into life with an imagined storyline, a tale we think we can reasonably expect. The problem as Brené describes it is, "*the movie in our mind is wonderful, but no one else knows their parts, their lines, or what it means to us. ... Our expectations are often set on outcomes totally beyond our control.*"[46] Therein lies the rub.

We always want what we cannot have – the power of being God.

I used to think that wasn't true of me. I used to think I didn't want to be God because I don't want to carry that responsibility. That's true to a degree. I *don't* want the responsibility. Having been a parent for nearly three decades, I know exactly what comes with being responsible for things that affect other people and I'd rather not be in charge of any of that. No matter what you do or how hard you try or how great your heart is, things have a way of falling apart for at least one person under your care.

What *is* true of me though is that I do want to be God over myself. I don't care to run the world or line out anyone else although I'm certain it sometimes comes across that way. The truth is that all my attempts to control the narrative are about *me, my* safety, *my* needs, *my* expectations. Me trying to control things that affect you isn't really about you. It's about me fulfilling things how I think is best. I want to ensure that things go as planned or at least in a way that works out. I'm not so good with letting God be Himself, at least not as He really is.

In the story of life that I've conjured up, God doesn't allow pain. At least not any that's truly significant. In my version of reality, He doesn't let loss join the party. In fact, He does everything in His power to keep grief and sorrow away. That is my expectation. I'm even willing to do what it takes. I'll perform, practice, show up, sacrifice myself to the point that may even be unhealthy at times – if it means my expectations are fulfilled.

What I don't realize is that all of that is complete futility. I don't hold tomorrow in my hands and, even if I did, I don't have the perspective it takes to ensure what I decide will work out for the best. I might *think* I do, but the truth is that I'm not God so I can't. I might get lucky on a few things, but that's it. The reality is that, while God may lend me His strength and offer a helping hand, His throne is not up for grabs.

Scott Strode of The Phoenix shared some insight on this topic during his interview on Mike Rowe's podcast. He said, "*I think there is some risk in folks that step into recovery in this sort of more extreme way of thinking - they sort of now have their act together and everyone else is sort of broken and they have reached the pinnacle. Because when you feel like you're at the pinnacle, the ability to fall is always there, you know? Whereas I kind of think of it more as - I developed an awareness in recovery that I think we're actually all in recovery from something and we're all sort of healing from the human condition in some way.*"[47]

Expectations have the ability to set us up for failure in unanticipated ways. They lure us into believing the lie that we *can* arrive and that, once we're there, we stay. God knows better than that. Job did too. That's why he prayed – on repeat – "God, forgive even the *unintentional* sins that my children *may* have committed." There was no assuming God just understood. Job expected that God's position was so high, so holy, so perfect that even our best human efforts wouldn't withstand divine scrutiny. What I think he *didn't* expect is that serving God and loving Him would come with so much loss and grief.

Isn't that where we all resonate? Being mired in pain, aching with loss, and reeling from unmet expectations whose very opposites are now our stories? All of us know to some degree or another how this feels. Wretched. Awful. Anxiety inducing on a level that pharmaceuticals just can't reach. The thing is that, when we realize that we *are* in fact all healing from the human condition, that *we* are the condition itself, we experience the freedom of releasing the expectations that it would ever be anything else. As the meme says, we let go of the expectation that it would have ever been any different. *This* was always going to be the story.

Managing our expectations well requires that we embrace what isn't and what never will be. **Life will never be about learning to live *without* loss. It will always be marrying ourselves to it.** Our storylines will only ever make sense when they're set inside the backdrop of the bigger History that God is writing. In order to embrace that, we have to exchange our expectations for His. In His plotline, loss is necessary and grief is imminent. Pain is inevitable and suffering is a requirement. None of us want it to be this way. God Himself doesn't.

That's clear by what Jesus says in the Garden of Gethsemane, *"Father, if you are willing, take this cup from me."* (Luke 22:42) He doesn't want it to happen. He wants to be with us and if it is at all possible to do that without pain, without the cross, without suffering, He will choose that path. Yet, it is in what He does next that we see His heart. He says, "Yet, not my will but Yours be done." (Luke 22:42)

Not only does He humble Himself before His Father, but He chooses *us*. He doesn't give up when the going gets tough and He doesn't get tough Himself. In fact, throughout the ordeal, He remains silent, never justifying Himself, never answering for His innocence, never speaking up on His own behalf. He silences *His* hopes and expectations of the storyline and replaces them with what *ours* need most.

This is what I've witnessed time and time again: where our deep lack exists is where His deep fulfillment begins. There is zero chance I would have leaned into God at this level, would have understood submission, surrender, and peace, or would have glimpsed what really walking by faith and not sight means if I hadn't endured the things I've written here and things I haven't shared. Zero chance. It's just not in me. I'm not Jesus.

I don't want there to be missing pieces. I don't want the grief. I can carry it, sure, and I can navigate sadness. God has gifted me in deep measure the ability to do sad without drowning or getting caught in the quicksand. That said, doing hard things isn't the journey I expected. I thought with time and experience, living would get easier. Things would be more fun. I'd have more freedom. *Life* would be better.

None of this is biblical. None of these things come from God. He put us on notice that life in this world guarantees us trouble. What He came to give us is the thing we traded in when we ate from the wrong tree - life and life abundantly. Just the fact that it is His gift alone implies that it's something we don't inherently already have. It's not something to which we are entitled and it's not something we can earn or otherwise get outside of Him. He alone holds the keys. The timing is His, the story and plotline are His, and the life extended to us too is His.

I've said it over and over and over again. *He* is our deepest need. *He* is our greatest fulfillment. *He* is the expectation of everything. If you find that nearly impossible to grasp, accept, or hold onto amidst living in reality, trust me when I say I get it. Even as I've written these words and gone back to re-read and edit them, I've found myself caught up in God saying to me yet again,

*"Alanna, where circumstances don't look like they should, you're missing the point. This world offers you a life focused on what doesn't matter. What I'm offering is different. All of this – people whose hearts aren't aligned with yours, people whose actions have hurt, betrayed, or dismissed you – all of this I am repurposing. Every single bit of it is intended to lead you to the same place as everything good, everything gone the right way does: **Me**. It's all intended to lead you to Me."*

This truth is one of the most beautiful, hard truths we'll ever encounter. *He* is what we most need, *He* is the one who loves us the most deeply, and it is from *Him* that we are separated. He will do and allow anything and everything it takes to ensure we have a place reserved in the kingdom. Everything except choose for us. He will make a way where there is none. He will pour out blessings we don't deserve. He will woo us, protect us, and give us good gifts even when we spit in His face and demand what we think is better. But never will He force Himself upon us or make us trade in our expectations. Those are up to us to manage.

The beauty of a God whose heart is *for* us and not against us is that He is good no matter what. It is His character. He cannot help but bestow grace and mercy and love upon us, whether or not we've earned it. He knows that we have an enemy who seeks our destruction daily and He gets that loss is an inevitable part of the story. His goodness is what makes Him not leave us alone to navigate it but makes Him enter into it.

God leads us into the wilderness and speaks tenderly to us there because it is in the desert that we are most likely to be aware of our need, lack, and insufficiency. Rather than making light of that, instead of expecting us to pull ourselves up by our bootstraps, He *appeals* to us. He uses that place, that time, and those conditions to soften our edges and restore our souls.

Hosea tells us it is in the very place of our trouble that God gives us vineyards and a door of hope. The hope is not in escaping the valley. Vineyards aren't portable. They are rooted, planted, and remain alive only when connected to the soil. The soil is located in the Valley of Trouble.

It is in our very place of deep pain and suffered loss that we can trade in our expectations of a life gone right by this world's standards for a life abundant by God's. Fruit can grow in the midst of struggle.

Remember how I said sometimes we have to lay our hope down? Our hope isn't sustainable any more than our expectations are. So often we place our hope in what's earthly, temporal, finite, and based on what we can see, not what we don't. That's why we're called to walk by *faith*, not by *sight*. Where Satan lures us into temptation, things so far beyond our control, storylines that affect things we can't even comprehend, God *allures* us into the wilderness so that He can restore to us what we've always needed most. *Him.*

Being willing to reconcile our disenchantment means being willing to accept what's already going to happen. It's trading in our earthly viewpoint for an eternal perspective. It's allowing our expectations to drive us to our knees not our pulpits or soapboxes. It's being willing to accept ashes because we trust that the One writing the story wastes no pain and always makes something good come from tragedy. It's choosing to participate in a story we cannot write but on whose stage we are invited to act.

Setting our version of God aside, we pull up a chair at the table He's set for us and let Him tell us the truth about Himself. We get intimately acquainted – not with a life gone wrong, but with a perspective that sees beyond it. We surrender like Job to a narrative not of our making that is nevertheless for our betterment. We die to live. We get lost to be found and we remember – God made deserts just as He made mountaintops. One is no better than the other. In fact, both hold things of Him we couldn't know unless we traversed each of them and maybe that was the point all along.

Knowing Him is the greatest treasure there has ever been. Relationship is critical. It's as Solomon said, "He has set eternity in the hearts of men yet we cannot comprehend all that He has done from the beginning of time to the end." The reason for that is - He wasn't ever intended just to be *our* dwelling place.

We were designed to be *His*.

Chapter Eighteen:
Sanctuary on a Desert Road

———

"The first question which the priest and Levite asked was: 'If I stop to help this man, what will happen to me? But ... the good Samaritan reversed the question: 'If I do not stop to help this man, what will happen to him?'"

~ Martin Luther King, Jr.[48]

One of the best things I've ever done in life is move. I've moved states, homes, and cities. It's been so good to not only have different surroundings and learn to navigate those, but also to be forced into finding a place I can occupy everywhere I go. We're all drawn to this need to create a space where we belong, even if it's on the go. We want to feel at home, whether in our bodies, on the road, or just in the world period.

Safety in recent years and months has taken on a whole new meaning for me. It used to just mean my physical being was not in danger. However, the older you get, the more you realize how important it is to be emotionally safe. We all need places that feel like havens. Spaces where we can lay our burdens down and know that it's ok. I care more than ever now about knowing there is somewhere safe I can take everything life has thrown at me and me at it and set it all down. A place that is inviting, where my vulnerabilities are celebrated rather than shamed, a place to escape to instead of from.

Sanctuary is defined as "protection or a safe place, especially for someone or something being chased or hunted."[49] I had a friend once whose home felt like that, one who had been to hell and back, and every time those of us who needed a safe place to go entered its doors, we felt an almost immediate peace not just in our bodies, but in our souls. There's a reason we call refuges for animals "sanctuaries." It is the place where they too can go to be cared for, avoid attack, and ensure their safety. Every time I went to my friend's home, this is exactly how I felt. It's where I let my guard down, felt safe enough to cry or laugh, to be real, and to say things only the walls of that home will ever know.

Churches also have sanctuaries. That big space usually in the middle where everyone gathers to worship. Tragedy has reshaped how I view that place. After my dad died and again in recent months, the church sanctuary has at times been a place that feels the opposite of its definition. The building itself has felt painful to be in, a place of harm, hurt, and betrayal. I'm still learning how to navigate that physical reality because the truth is that same place was also one where God met me.

I listened recently to a podcast on walking out of a room by Emilie Freeman. She explains how rooms can hold gifts that we take with us while the room itself was meant to be experienced only for a season.[50] The thing is that we walk into and out of rooms on a continual basis, yet we rarely stop to consider our expectation that each one will be permanent. It's only when a room is uncomfortable that we look forward to leaving it.

There's a song by Building 429 that says, "All I know is I'm not home yet. This is not where I belong. Take this world and give me Jesus. This is not where I belong."[51] I love that because it's true whether life is good or life is tragic. It holds fast in happy times and in sad. There is never a room on this earth that will fit us for long. They're all temporary. It's what we do when we come face to face with that fact that matters most.

As a child, I never understood the significance of the temple in the Bible or history books. It had little to no meaning to me. Sanctuary even less. A sanctuary was just the center of the church where everyone gathered but, in Hebrew, the word for sanctuary is a derivative of the word meaning "to be set apart as sacred."[52] When the Israelites were wandering through the wilderness, God asked them to make a portable sanctuary where He could come be with them. In essence, He requested they make a "set apart or sacred, holy space."

It was intended to be a refuge, a place of rest, beauty, and worship. He didn't ask them to set it up somewhere then leave to wander the wilderness. He wanted to be *with* them. So, He told Moses to encourage the people whose hearts had moved them to willingly give to do so and said, "*Let them make me a sanctuary, that I may dwell in their midst.*" (Exodus 25:8, ESV) Dwell in Hebrew means to "lodge together or lie down with one another."[53] This portable tabernacle was the safe place for people to come experience intimacy with God, rest from the outside world, and a refuge in which beauty and worship were celebrated.

I'm fairly certain after over four decades of living that we as humans don't understand the value of God's holiness. It's something we've mostly conjured up a negative connotation about, seeing it as unattainable or maybe only for the most devout. When we left Eden, we left the only place where we could be with God face to face and unashamed. If we understood God's holiness for what it really is, I am convinced we would spend all of our days seeking it. Why? Because *God's holiness is the only safe place outside of hell this side of the grave.*

God does not acquaint himself with the intimate knowledge of evil – meaning He does not dwell with it, make a home with it, or allow it any ground to influence His ways. Thus, we are in complete safety when we are at home with Him. This is why He insisted that the tabernacle go with them while they were wandering the wilderness. He knew they would need a refuge, a place of rest that allowed their souls to be at peace. The ark of the covenant where the most holy items of the Lord were placed was so sacred that if people mishandled it, they died. It was serious business. So, why do we expect any less today?

It seems we rarely take time as humans to consider how the sins against our own bodies – whether committed by us or someone else – affect our souls. They are inextricably intertwined. Likewise, what feeds our souls will feed our bodies also. Numerous scientific studies have been conducted on the power of prayer. Over and over and over scientific research has proven that prayer has resulted in lower blood pressure, unexplained healing, reduced anxiety and depression, longer life spans, happier moods, and in general – calmer people. There is something about being connected to the heart of God that soothes what ails us and brings us peace.

The presence of God is also where we experience the absence of the power of evil. God's holiness doesn't allow it to remain. Satan is only allowed nearby when God has a purpose for his presence. Otherwise, he flees upon God's command. His demons look at Jesus and shudder. Scripture tells us time and again that evil and holiness cannot co-mingle. This is why our consciences shout at us, our bodies go into upheaval, and our lives feel like they are in an untenable state when we try to do both at once.

Friend, your soul is not neutral ground. We are either for God or against Him. We belong to heaven or to hell. Earth is a temporary living space. The only place where we can escape the tragedy this world brings is in the tabernacle where God lives. Our bodies, souls, and spirits have become that place. When Satan came into God's presence and they discussed Job, he wasn't allowed to wreak havoc in the heavenlies. That's not how God operates. He'd already given Lucifer his day and he'd opted out. If he wasn't going to be like God, he wasn't staying. So, to roaming the earth he went.

When Satan shows up to talk to God about us humans, he's not capable of disrupting the place. God's holiness won't allow it. Just as people died for mishandling the ark of the covenant, if Satan were to fail to abide by God's protective measures, he'd be gone in a heartbeat. Satan is smarter than that. He's not interested in challenging God's authority where it's already established. That's why he picks us instead. We are vulnerable, weak creatures who need boundaries and protection. Our hearts are ground much more easily gained.

Time and again, we can read Job and find little to no comfort in it in certain ways. God doesn't assuage the pain. He doesn't stop the onslaught or make it all go away, at least not in any kind of immediate time frame. Instead, when He does speak, He makes His holiness very evident. He knows what Job had tasted but didn't yet intimately know: God's holiness is the only Eden we are going to find outside the Garden gates on this side of the grave.

As an adult, I've come to realize that safe places are priceless. We need a place to go where our spiritual safety is no longer in question. Where the devil doesn't reign and temptation can't reach us. We need a serpent-free zone. The problem is there is only one place we can find that and it isn't on this planet. Yet, this planet is where we're stationed so we find ourselves like the Israelites having escaped captivity in Egypt but now on the run in the desert, uncertain of our futures and even our right nows.

When my Granny died, she left behind several Bibles. I've had the immense privilege of inheriting one of them in which she took a lot of notes. It's in the King James Version so, for several years, I mainly read the notes not the scriptures. In recent months, I've started reading the scriptures too and found them fascinating. Words we rarely use are commonplace in the King James and it's forced me to be more intentional about understanding their meanings. They're richer, deeper, and more descriptive in certain places. What I've also noticed is that sometimes newer translations leave certain words out that were originally included.

For example, this morning I was reading Psalm 100 again and verse 3 jumped out at me. It says, "Know ye that the LORD he is God: it is he that hath made us, and not we ourselves; we are his people, and the sheep of his pasture." (Psalm 100:3, KJV) In modern versions, the part about "not we ourselves" is missing. Also, the punctuation is significant here because, in describing how we know that the Lord is God, it includes a colon which signifies that the definition – our ability to see exactly how that is true – is next. The *way* we know that the Lord is God is by realizing that *He* made us and we didn't, that we are *His* people and sheep in *His* pasture.

All along, the story that's been occurring is *His*. That's why we are **safe** here in His holiness. That's why sin that separates us from Him isn't about the sin. He cares a whole lot less about the sin itself and a whole lot more about its effects. The separation is what gets to Him. He wants us near Him. He knows that is where we are safest.

I don't know if you've ever been to the desert but it feels like a place of utter contrast. There is incredible beauty, sunsets like no place else in existence, against a backdrop of what feels like lawlessness. The rules of nature don't apply like our rules in civilization. Out in the desert, it's survival and not necessarily of the fittest, just of the ones willing to work with instead of against the elements.

I think maybe that's what God is trying to tell us. I think He's trying to say, "People, there is no way to survive this with your own understanding. Nothing is as it seems. It's all upside down and backwards. You were designed for something different. So, when you try to go at surviving life in this wilderness, it's going to beat even your very best. You're going to need a guide and your entire life is going to depend on Him. I am that guide, so if you're willing to trust me and rely on me, I promise that together we will make it through this."

How often do we see God through that lens? The one of safety, protection, guidance, and direction. We seem to speak from pulpits and book pages as if God has this plan, a very specific one at that, that

166

we are supposed to figure out. As if life is this series of decisions that will make the world make sense if we just follow Him. I think the truth is closer to this – the longer you follow Jesus, the less you understand about life on this planet and the more you just love Him.

We humans will never arrive. It's impossible. We will never be holy enough, wise enough, good enough, smart enough, or capable enough to become what life on this planet really requires of us. Like the verse says, we didn't create it, He did. Therefore, we arrive here equipped to be – not Him, but dwellers of pastureland. We are created with intention – as sheep. The Bible says this on repeat. Sheep in need of a shepherd. Sheep who require safe grounds, guided direction, and protective care.

That's what is so significant about Jesus coming here. He made Himself like us by taking on the form of a man. He didn't lose His divine identity, but He did give up the right to use the power it came with however He pleased. That's what we often miss about Jesus. We say over and over again, "Yeah, but He was God." Of course He was. His divinity, His identity never changed. His exercising of that authority did. He chose not to do it in the way He would have from the throne of heaven and instead made Himself a man so He could show us how to live.

We don't have Jesus' identity apart from Him. We don't have His power without His intervention. We don't have the capabilities of battling life in the desert elements without someone teaching us. Sure, we can make it through some skirmishes, some washouts, some flash floods and scorching heat waves. We might even find ourselves the occasional oasis. But we will never make it and certainly not well.

Sheep aren't designed for desert sands. They're made for pasture dwelling. Not one of them is created to lead or rule over any of the others. Sheep travel in packs, herds, and they are quite prone to wander off into random dangers unaware, especially when left to themselves. Wolves, lions, predators – they are sharp. They never lose sight of their prey. In fact, they're so attuned to what's going on that they don't attack the middle of the herd. They always go for the outliers and the truth, whether we believe it or not, is we are all outliers in some way.

All of us have weaknesses. All of us have blind spots and places where we are likely to drown. Anywhere the enemy can get us to look the other way and miss the ravine or cliff face right in front of us, he will. He wants us lured by the temptation of quenching our immediate thirst and then he laughs when following him sends us spiraling over the falls in Niagra. It's a brutal picture but that is the plight we are in.

That's why sanctuary and God's Spirit residing within us is so significant. It's why Jesus said how important it was that He leave and that the Holy Spirit come in His place. Because it means we *can* traverse this world and all it contains and still be safe.

I've been reading Ezekiel lately and, if you haven't read it, it's a prophetic book with a number of visions God shares with Ezekiel that help him convey the dire straits in which God's people find themselves. For the most part, no one listens. Everyone, like sheep, has gone his or her own way. I was reading chapter 8 and God's revealing to Ezekiel all these wicked deeds and sins committed in the dark by God's priests themselves when He says something so telling. He said, "Son of man, do you see what they are doing – the utterly detestable things the house of Israel is doing here, *things that will drive me far from my sanctuary?*" (Ezekiel 8:6, NIV, emphasis mine). Just like Eden, we are driving Him out of His own home. Not because we are so powerful but because we are so loved.

God's *heart* is to be with His people. Always. There is *nothing* in all creation He desires more. The beautiful thing is that He doesn't expect us to clean ourselves up in order to love us well. He does it. He reaches out. He makes a way before we ever even turn our faces His way. He does so because He knows that we aren't capable. This is *His* story. We didn't write the script and we don't have the power to influence the outcome. So, He does it for us.

His sanctuary is wherever *we* are.
Ours is Him.

When we aren't in sync, He is driven from the place He designed for Himself to live. With us. There is absolutely no reason for any man, woman, child, or even God to endure all the pain, suffering, and awfulness that a place like earth holds if there was no gain in the end. It would be utterly futile and pointless. Since God is one of order, not futility, who holds time itself in His hands, whose word never returns to Him void when it sends it, then there must be a reason. The reason is you and me, friends. It's everything our hearts long for but can't create in our current reality. At least not without His assistance.

I think Job believed this prior to all the devastation. Job's heart posture and later his description of his days lends itself to a man who, for all intents and purposes, really lived out his belief system. He wanted to serve God and he didn't do it for personal glory or gain. He did it because he saw its effects and he loved God with a reverence few people on this earth have ever attained. That said, I think Job learned a lot more about God being a sanctuary *after* God spoke to him in the whirlwind. God came at Job with a lot of questions, even telling him to brace himself because God was about to question him like a man. That right there should give us pause. All of us are aware that we are not gods of any kind, but few of us settle for the powerlessness of being human.

You've probably heard the phrase about being lions instead of sheep. That is exactly what God calls us to live as – sheep who carry the power of lions within us. We aren't to be mere followers of wherever life beckons. That's how you get caught in the thicket as easy prey for your enemy. Living like a sheep with the power and wisdom of a lion requires that we have something within us that supercedes our external limits. It requires divinity.

God stamped us this way – with *His* image. Think about it. He made us as sheep, to dwell in safe pasture, yet knowing that we were going to leave that place. He knew we'd be traversing the desert, deadly valleys, mountain ranges, and waters that will drown us in a heartbeat. He knew every predator we'd face and every temptation that would come along to lure us away. Yet, He did all of this anyway. It's not the story we'd write. That's basically what Job said too. He let God know despite God's resounding silence that he wasn't okay with all this. He was enduring it, yes, but he didn't understand it. He would rather die than continue. He would prefer to never have been born than to have seen even one of these treacherous days. At least that's how he saw it until it was with God that he had an audience.

———

Most of us extend some compassion when we see someone in deep grief. Most of us reach out, even if in silence, and sit like Job's friends did with him for days. That may have been God's heart for Job, but it wasn't His response to Job's commentary. Instead, God came at him with an intensity that reminds me in certain ways of what He says over and over in Ezekiel. Repeatedly God told the people of Israel that He was going to make sure they *knew* He was God, not them. I believe scripture says God relayed that message 65 times through Ezekiel. He was *not* going to let their iniquity go unaddressed or their hidden sins performed in darkness remain as is. He loved them too much to do so.

God never accuses Job of sin. In fact, the opposite, yet His clarity on who He is and who Job isn't is extreme. After all this pain, it makes you wonder why. Wouldn't God be more tender, more considerate, more gentle, even more loving because that is the God we believe we have come to know and expect from scripture, isn't it? I have to say – I don't think so. God *is* all those things – gentle, kind, loving, good, considerate, tender - yet, as we discussed in the beginning, God is not safe. Not the real one anyway.

Safe gods only serve us well so long as they stay with us in the pasture. The ones who aren't so safe can handle walking with us through dangerous valleys, treacherous ravines, and raging waters. They make ways where there aren't ways, and they work *with* the desert elements, not against them. They see what's coming that we don't. They do things behind the scenes that we'll never understand and all we can do is trust them. I think that's what God wanted Job to know.

> *"I AM your sanctuary. I am the only safe place that exists on this extremely dangerous scorched earth. You can see that all of this is temporary. None of it here is safe. Everything is up for grabs. Even your own being. However, there is One who holds the stars in place, who gives might to the weak and peace amidst the storm. I promise no better circumstances than the ones in which you are already living, but I guarantee you that I know what I'm doing. I'm writing a story beyond all that you could ever hope. You have to trust me. Let your not knowing of all this life holds fall away in the face of your knowledge that I am the only sanctuary you'll ever need.*
>
> ***With me, no matter what,*** **you are safe.***"*

Sin separates us from God and not in the performance-based way we think. It separates us from relationship, from intimacy, from understanding who we were designed to be. We aren't ever going to achieve enough for God. That's not what sheep do. That's not even what lions do. That's not even what we need. Creation isn't here to *achieve* anything on God's behalf. It's here to *dwell* with Him.

This earth? It is His footstool. Our hearts? They are His dwelling place. And Him? He is our sanctuary, our home, the one and only location *set apart* where we can be safe from the effects of sin on this world. It doesn't mean they won't touch us – they most certainly will this side of the grave. It just means that we don't have to be overcome by them because He is with us and where He resides, where His holiness is present, evil has limited reach. That is Providence at play. We just need eyes of faith to see.

The beauty of being a temple in which God dwells is that we can remain right here in the midst of all the pain, all the struggle, all the grief and instead of running *away* from it, we can run *into* the fray. A quote I once read said,

> "If God has you in the palm of His hand and your real
> life is secure in Him, then you can venture forth – into
> the places and relationships, the challenges, the very
> heart of the storm – and you will be safe there."[54]

He is the power that equips us to become the beauty amidst ashes, to extend peace inside chaos, to give grace within unmet hopes, needs, and expectations. We aren't designed to do any of these things on our own. We are sheep, remember, and it is in His pasture we are intended to dwell. He knows we won't stay though, so instead of sharpening our hoofs and trying to get us to be better, stronger, wiser – aka, not ourselves – He does the one thing we need most. He goes with us.

God is one with whom we can reconcile ourselves because, as Job came to see, this was never outside of His hands. The story was always going to give us a fighting chance. Not to be better than we are. Not for improved circumstance. Not even for the outcome we want and seek after so desperately. No, it was going to grant us the opportunity to choose Him. To know Him intimately. To have *Him* be the very power within us that makes us everything we were always designed to be.

There is, however, another side to that coin. Just as two trees stood in the Garden, two trees offering two options, the same is extended to us. We also have a choice. We don't have to be temples.

We can defy God's image within us. We can distort and damage and work our very best to become people who let God know just how wrong He is and just how much we refuse to represent Him. It is our one and only right as humans. That said, it is also our only lifeline. The question is – when everything is hanging in the balance and you realize your plight, will He be your sanctuary in the desert or will you keep trying to create it yourself?

The choice belongs to us.

Chapter Nineteen:
The Redemption Piece

"God will not protect you from anything that will
make you more like Jesus."

~ Elisabeth Elliot[55]

There is no coming back from certain things. Death especially carries with it a finality that reminds us in its wake, "Things will never be the same." Who I was in 2017 and who I became in 2019 feel in certain ways like entirely different people. Tragedy will do that to you. It isn't that I'm carrying unresolved trauma with me. I've processed so much. It's just that you can't unsee things once they're seen. You can't turn back the clock and not experience what is now and forever a part of you.

What I never expected was to have to reconcile myself to the redemption piece. There is a terrible ache that lingers with the way things have come to be. I think it's the thing we all run from most. The knowing, the holes, the space lingering between hope and fulfillment. Life, despite its brevity, all too often just seems too long. It's way too lengthy to wait on hope realized.

I didn't understand that the purpose of redemption was to bridge the gap. It's what connects the seen and the unseen. It is bringing the kingdom of heaven near. Supernatural power showing up in earthen vessels and holiness dwelling alongside ordinary people. I think we miss the invitation being offered us when it comes to partnering with God in displaying His holiness. There is a glory that exists outside time and space. It wasn't confined to Eden and it's not confined to heaven now.

It's the harsh beauty of taking things we hold dear and offering them up to God to be transformed into something better. Sin mars our understanding of what's offered. We have no idea the glory and beauty bestowed on us at conception, so we spend lifetimes trying to change God's ideas into our own. We want *Him* to change to meet *us* where *we* are at instead of recognizing He already did and that redemption is the way home for us both.

As I wrote this chapter, I found myself struggling with circumstances that felt all too familiar, history repeating itself, but this time I'm paying attention to the choice with which it comes. Grief, tragedy, and longing call us to give ourselves over. It is a temptation all of us are seized with in one way or another. Whether it's one small compromise after another or a literal giving in of what matters most, in some fashion not trying to make life good or stay true to our deepest selves anymore coaxes all of us.

If we want to live a life that doesn't end in repetitive consequences, we have to choose the path of great resistance and stop our insanity. To the world, our choice will seem the exact opposite. In fact, we'll be told we are insane, probably many times over. Job certainly was. His wife, his friends, his neighbors, and the people who heard of the tragedies he suffered thought he'd lost it. They told him in essence there was no reason to keep believing and having faith in God the way he was.

I love Job's response. It reminds me of Davy Crockett when he said, "You can all go to hell and I will go to Texas."[56] Job knew what he wanted and no amount of earthly tragedy, suffering, or loss was going to change his viewpoint. My problem is that I want redemption without the cost, the outcome without the process, the prize without the work, and the glory without the suffering. I don't think that's wrong. That is Eden after all. It's where we originally started and it's what is set inside my soul.

Once upon a time, work was a good thing. Effort didn't result in laborious exhaustion. It was partnering with God. It was beauty become. It was holding creation in your hand and not getting stung. The problem is that is not the land in which we now live. Outside the Garden, things are undone and toil doesn't guarantee specific results. It's what we all keep chasing though. "If I just do this, then surely I'll get that."

Job could have given up. It would have been so easy to listen to his wife, community, and friends. If he had, there's a chance Satan may have relented. Knowing he'd won and that Job wasn't really the man of faith God touted him to be, Satan could've said the battle is won and gone off to gloat. But Job didn't do that. Not even knowing what was going on, Job still refused to tie himself to a specific outcome. He didn't insist on his version of redemption. He just chose God.

I don't know about you, but that's where I so often fall off. It's pretty common that I prefer to avoid staring down my insecurities, fears, temptations, or even potential outcomes. I just want to know that I'm going to be okay, even if it means giving up long term gain for short term comfort. It seems like it would be easy to recognize that and change, but it's not. Emotions are powerful tools and, when we don't regulate them well or challenge them against the backdrop of a truth greater than ourselves, they easily become weapons we turn on ourselves.

Sin's lure is such an illusion. If we only realized that all sin leads us eventually to Satan's doorstep where he is lying in wait to strip us of our truest identity, then we'd run hard and fast in the opposite direction. Instead, he teaches us to mar it ourselves. He tempts us to take our God-given desires in ungodly directions then convinces us it was who we were always meant to be. We have no idea the glory that has been bestowed upon us by being created in the image of God with divine purpose, power, and authority. Our identity is so precious that Satan has given up his entire time in existence to do nothing else but assault it.

That's why reconciling ourselves to God not doing life our way or being who we want is so important. Because it is in Him remaining true to His own character that the very best of us comes to life. It is *Him IN us*. No wonder Satan wants to snuff out every hint of our identity. Imagine seeing your worst enemy's image everywhere you look. No wonder he wants to crush us – we represent God and there is no one Satan hates more than Him.

Redemption forces us to come to the end of ourselves and give up on all the notions of being enough.

We aren't enough. None of us. We never will be. God made us to *need* Him. Not because He wanted glory but because He loves to give Himself fully to those He loves. He invented generosity. Ever heard the phrase, "You can't outgive God?" Well, it's true. He didn't just give us life and His Son. He gave us part of Himself.

It is hard to live without a piece of you. I learned this when my dad died, when my husband moved out, when my kids left home. These events are life changing not simply because the roles I played are now over, but because *who I was as a result of the relationships I was in is now missing.* That's what eternity is – it's either living in relationship *with* God or living forever separated.

All too often we've been presented with this image of a God up in the sky who keeps blaming us for getting it all wrong. Somehow, the script has been flipped and *we* have to be good enough for *God* instead of recognizing *He* is the one good enough for *us.* Our hearts long for the very things His does because that's how He created us. The reason we feel sick when our hopes are deferred is the same reason He feels sick when we wander off, get ourselves trapped in slavery, and cry out for freedom. We have a God who *sees* us. He knows our pain, He aches with our grief. Our sorrows are carried in His heart, our tears stored in His bottles, and our names etched into the palms of His hands. We *matter* to Him.

I think this is why there is no place that Satan attacks us harder than the redemption piece. Because, like Jesus, he knows. He knows what it means when we believe in the One who made us, when we trust that our identity isn't the one this earth would remake us into but is something so much more glorious, beautiful, and powerful that we can barely contain it.

> As C.S. Lewis once wrote, *"It would seem that Our Lord finds our desires not too strong, but too weak. We are half-hearted creatures, fooling about with drink and sex and ambition when infinite joy is offered us, like an ignorant child who wants to go on making mud pies in a slum because he cannot imagine what is meant by the offer of a holiday at the sea. We are far too easily pleased."*[57]

The difficulty of being human is how finite everything seems to be. We have one thing in common with Satan: we too are short-sighted. Our mission in living is usually focused on the temporal. We'd rather have earthy ambition than eternal gain. We'd prefer to avoid earthly pain even if it means eternal separation from our true identity.

Where I've found myself wrestling so often with redemption is in discovering that it's so similar to boundaries.

Embracing redemption is like embracing boundaries
we may need but desperately do not want.

If I'm being honest, I think redemption is the thing I dislike most because it means trusting a God I can't control. It means letting the outcome be chosen by Him, not me, and dealing with a reality I'm not sure I want. Redemption is choosing Eden over my current reality and, if we are all honest with ourselves, we want the *benefits* of Eden without the dependency. We want the freedom of here with the perfection of there and that's just not an option. In essence, we want to have our cake and eat it too. Who doesn't?

Reconciling ourselves to that is a process. It's rarely once and done because desire is one of those things we continually return to, butting our heads against it over and over again. It forces us to choose between what we think we want in the moment or what God designed us for in the Garden. Redemption means embracing needing God to make it through a world at war with itself. That's the purpose of the redemption piece. Not that the ache goes away, but that we know – *this was never how it was intended to be.* God doesn't want us to believe that this is the life for which we were made.

When Jesus was here and He looked around, He had compassion on us because He *understood.* "This isn't what I ever wanted for them. This is *not* the life I created. This? This is awful." Scripture wasn't lying when it said that we have a High Priest who relates. The truth we cannot escape is that we are stamped with and created in the image of the Almighty. That piece will go with us right through the grave and on into eternity. It is not limited to our body. It is part of our souls. What we mistake as an intellectual exercise of simply "believing in God or not" is actually us embracing or denying our true identity.

This chapter has been so hard to write. I don't think I've wrestled with any of them to this point as hard as I have this one. I think it's because it means the most out of everything. It is the one where everything really is on the line. Redemption isn't required. It is entirely optional. We *don't* have to choose God. We *can* walk away from our truest identity. We can elect to be and live however we want. Being disenchanted with God isn't a requirement for survival.

So, the question is this: What does redemption look like? I believe it looks like rubber meeting the road. Not in a man up, cowboy on, or shoulder the load kind of way. Rather, it's where we lay down our resources, climb up on the altar like Isaac as Abraham's sacrifice, and say, "Lord, I don't have a clue what You are doing or how You are going to provide. All I can do is trust You that my sacrifice will be worth whatever is on the other side." And then, we let go.

It is the most brutal, painful thing in the world to do – letting go. Cultural Christians are going to tell you how wonderful it all is and how Jesus fills your life with physical prosperity and a whole lot of other nonsense that isn't biblical. I can say from personal experience that "letting go and letting God" has been one of the most painful, difficult experiences of my entire life.

There's a song we've sung at church a hundred times whose chorus says, "I run to the Father. I fall into grace. I'm done with the hiding. No reason to wait. My heart needs a surgeon. My soul needs a friend. So, I'll run to the Father again and again and again."[58] This is what we need to know about redemption: It isn't a once and done thing. We do it over and over, time and again. It's a continual returning to, an ongoing leveling up of trust and faith. Once you've gotten your feet wet and realized how far out you can swim, the sandbar disappears and you're forced to dive farther in. Just like Job. Faith? It cost him absolutely everything.

**Redemption requires us to get out of the driver's seat
but remain in the vehicle.**

It forces us to rely on a vision we can't see. It lets someone we can't touch, control, or manipulate make all the decisions while we're traveling. During the trip, we are still offered the opportunity to take over anytime we want and sometimes we do but it rarely goes well because our job is to cooperate, not coordinate. It's an incredibly hard position in which we find ourselves.

How do we know the vision of the one driving is trustworthy? How do we know they have our best interest at heart? What if they fall down on the job? What if we get hurt on their watch? Then we'll be mad at them and ourselves. We think it's easier to do something ourselves because at least then we believe we did all we could and we discover it wouldn't have turned out different anyways. It's easier to let ourselves down than it is to turn the reins over to someone else, be let down, and feel like we betrayed ourselves. We end up with a case of the "If Onlys" and, if there is one thing we all want to avoid, it's regretting our decisions.

Regret can put you into a prison of your own making faster than just about anything else. It too can become a weapon in Satan's hands. Redemption requires that we usher regret out the door and drive off, leaving it standing on the side of the road. We refuse to entertain its company and carry on knowing that we are right where we are meant to be no matter how the highway looks. My problem is

I've allowed regret to become so much of a permanent passenger that I now find it hard not to ask its opinion about my decisions before I ask God Himself.

The truth is that God's vision for my life requires the kind of faith and courage and lack of actual sight on which I don't want to lean. It's a stepping out of my comfort zone instead of creating one that makes my skin happy. It requires risk without guaranteed reward. It means like Paul I may look like a fool for Christ. It is certain I will be challenged, misunderstood, criticized, and probably ostracized for it. It means my family may be injured as a result of my decisions and I will have to suffer for things I'm doing *right* according to Jesus.

———————————————————

I didn't expect to be at the place that I was when writing this chapter. When things start "getting better," you can't help but start assuming that trend will continue. We aren't really prepared for another setback. Life is supposed to move forward – at least that's how it works in the Land of Should where things go the way we know they ought to go. We all return in some form or fashion to that place. We can't help ourselves. If we don't start at some point holding again to hope, then we are going to quit.

Earlier this year, my husband and I sat with our community group and said hard things about the hard places where we found ourselves. Tears were shed and words of life spoken over us. In those moments I felt held, seen, and known. I also felt fragile, frustrated, and uncertain. Redemption is this bittersweet relationship where I want to plant hope and run away from it at the same time. Even in the coming back to oneself, we expect it to be easier than it is. We expect for things to stop getting broken. Yet, holding space for what *isn't* is something we never get to stop doing this side of the grave.

Redemption is the place where truth and reality anchor themselves to the hope of what is still on the horizon. It's the land between now and not yet. It's where we are at our most vulnerable and Jesus has the greatest opportunity to change our direction. It's also the one where we are most likely to run, quit, or give up. The truth of being finite creatures trapped in infinite souls is we are always longing for more. Our hearts desperately desire the benefits of forever in the here and now. It's why instant gratification is so hard to stop. We weren't made to live unfulfilled.

When I was a little girl, I was at times incredibly impatient. Teaching others something tedious to this day can make me almost instantly lose my mind. It took having kids of my own, living some life, and realizing some people never mature or grow up for me to recognize the value of waiting, of having patience for the not yet.

What we don't often understand about maturity in Christ is that we can't handle instantaneous fullness. We aren't equipped to go out and be Jesus overnight because maturity in any form takes time. Being filled with the Holy Spirit is wonderful but it doesn't automatically mature us. We still have to learn how to use the tools we are given. We build skills and develop muscles by repetitive use, not through one-time experience.

One of the aspects of the fruit of the Holy Spirit listed is patience. You'd think with the urgency that eternal salvation is, death always on the horizon as a guarantee for everyone, patience wouldn't be so necessary. But I think patience might be the most critical piece. Were God not patient, He'd have no tolerance for being kind. Because as scripture says, it is His *kindness* that leads us to repentance and waiting on someone to reach that point can take years and years and years. A lifetime even.

The thing about redemption that makes it so beautiful is the way it stretches like a canvas between here and eternity. Where we want restoration now, the Garden of Eden in the present, redemption steps in and bridges the gap. It offers us both life with Jesus in our modern day and the fullness of His story inside eternity. Somehow that is where Job ended up. In the middle, with the redemption piece. I think Job's life being restored wasn't as easy as it seems. I think his conversation with God marked the remainder of his days.

I think Job realized things most of us don't quickly face. That loss and pain and grief *are* more often than not the way. Nothing is guaranteed. Only God is truly trustworthy and everything depends on Him being exactly the Person we need. Our faith is priceless, but only in the light of His redeeming grace. The things of this earth fade in importance once we encounter the God of the universe. I think *that* is where Job landed.

All the things God gave him after his life was torn apart were wonderful in so many ways. He relished relationships in ways I imagine he never had before. I think the fullness of his years following devastation were rich because he realized the truth of his own words in ways he hadn't upon his original utterance, "The LORD gives *and* takes away. Blessed be the name of the LORD."

It seems like utter foolishness to us to praise God for taking things away. We spend our entire lives trying to hold onto and save. People start putting money into retirement when they're 20 years old and wait an entire 40 or 50 years to use it. We build empires and businesses, launch enterprises, and plan for things our own eyes won't even live to see. So, when we're called upon to praise God for what He takes away, it just seems downright absurd.

Yet, that's where I've recently found myself. Just today, I had a conversation with a dear friend I haven't spoken to in months. She's in this incredibly humbling position of being asked to stand up for truth and justice in ways I know she is uniquely gifted to do but will cost her so very much. Nevertheless, it is clear as day this is what God has called her to do. In an odd (read: divine) turn of events, someone she doesn't know but I do has been appointed to a position that affects her own. She's found out in the strangest way the exact same thing as me – that when trouble comes knocking, you find out who your friends are and, more importantly, exactly who they are not.

I think this is the crux of so much. We have to *know* who it is that we can trust and, at the end of the day, there is only one Name, only one Person, only one Author whose character we can consistently rely on. It's God. Not the one we conjured up. Not the one who makes Eden our permanent home while letting serpents roam free to tempt or attack us. The One who enters in and, while ushering us out of the Garden for our own good, goes with us Himself, closing the gates behind Him too. It's there in that place that we find ourselves asking Him what is going on and why He is doing this. We don't want redemption to bridge the gap. We just want back into Eden. Only that's not an option and we don't understand.

As Holly Furtick so aptly put it, "I'm learning that *not* knowing *is* the faith part. Maybe I'm not supposed to know."[59] She says it's as if God's asking us, "I know you want answers, but can you accept the invitation to mystery?"[60] That's really the question. Mystery is part of the redemption piece. It's beyond all we can know or understand. It was for Job and it is in our modern day. What we have to do is trust is that, even though His way makes no earthly sense, it is the only heavenly way to exist. Life was always meant to read like this.

As a child I created my own newspaper and titled it the *Heavenscope* because I wanted something good to contrast against how I perceived a horoscope being. Even though I was only about 8 years old, I think my little self just might have been onto something. We were always intended to see life through that lens. The one of eternity. It's in the very prayer Jesus directed us to pray. "Our Father which art in heaven, Hallowed be thy name. Thy kingdom *come,* Thy will be done *in earth, as it is in heaven.*" (Matthew 6:9-10, KJV) We're right here in the middle of the now and the not yet. Exactly where the disciples found themselves when Jesus left and they stood there staring up into heaven. This, what we are living in our modern day, *is* the redemption piece and we are the ones intended to carry it.

A quote I came across on a calendar in my algebra teacher's class once read, "Christians are the keyhole through which the world sees Christ." If that is true, then we have to ask ourselves – what does He look like? Because if I'm His representative, then it's *His* life I'm living, not my own. Maybe that *is* what it means to be a *living* sacrifice. Although it's the one thing we all never want – redemption – because we want life to never have gone wrong in the first place, maybe, just maybe, this is what it means to see what life going right really means. Maybe "right" was getting to know the God He really is afterall, not just the one we wanted Him to be. Maybe leaving Eden *wasn't* the worst thing that could've happened to us. Maybe the worst would've been us staying there.

Maybe the greatest beauty *is* the redemption piece.

Chapter Twenty:
Grief

———

"It is doubtful whether God can bless a man greatly until He has hurt him deeply."

~ A.W. Tozer[61]

I'm not much of a storyteller, but this year has been one for the storybooks. Not the Cinderella kind either. There's been a lot of loss. Exponential in fact. Most of it I don't really have words for and much of it I'm not sure I ever will. I've been shocked by God, shocked by myself, shocked by people I love, people I don't, and people hanging out in the woodworks. Sometimes when life runs aground, you come up entirely caught off guard at who is and isn't in your corner. I've had to shed some things in this season that I didn't anticipate and that quite frankly have deeply stung. People I wanted to call friends for a lifetime. People I did call friends and still consider as such to some degree but with whom relationship has changed. Other people with whom it cannot continue. People I care for, people I always will, people with whom there is now an undeniable healthy distance for us both.

When I think of Job, I wonder how that ended. His friendships. It appears no other people were around during their discourse. The entire story for chapter after chapter only involved him and these four men, one of whom God entirely dismisses and doesn't reference at the end of the book. We are given no glimpses, no insights into how their relationships moved forward or whether they did at all. We know his family came back around. We know that other people with whom he was once close or somehow associated came and consoled him after all that befell Job. But how his friendships landed after it went down remains a mystery for us to discover on the other side of eternal.

Until this season, I'd been through grief but never thought I'd need a support group through it all. Turns out some seasons are so deep that the people closest to you just aren't enough. Some of the best conversations and most lingering support I've had in the last year have been with people I'd consider random. Friends I see every few years or maybe here and there at public events. People I haven't spoken to in so long I couldn't tell you the last time our paths crossed. Strangers in other states that landed at a retreat I never imagined I'd attend. New faces in homes where I never again wanted to walk.

Although I've done an immense amount of grieving this year and I've taken a considerable amount of time off to wade through it all, I've also found that grief has a ripple effect, an impact much like the shockwaves of an earthquake that can go on for days. You never really know when one will erupt. I've gotten used to the disconcerting nature of them and no longer feel like the world is ending when the ground starts shaking beneath my feet. But nothing stops you from the instinctual need to reach out and grab onto something stable you can hold.

I really don't know how to write this chapter without tears. They're both cleansing and sad, healing and disappointed, relieving and sorrowful. It's the story of life as a whole. As an Enneagram 4, I've learned we always have this longing for what makes us complete – this yearning to find the missing pieces. It is a beautiful tragedy and a tragic kind of beautiful that can be very meaningful. Yet, it's also one that if we spend too much time dwelling in, we'll lose ourselves inside of, kind of like a black hole. It's taken me years to realize that at the bottom of the hole is what we all long for. It's what this book started with. Eden. Eternity. Perfection inside the temporal world. Emmanuel. God with us – but unveiled, unshackled to our finiteness, real, tangible, known, accessible, *safe*.

Drew Newkirk says it like this, "*We are born kind of with a homesickness for Eden.*"[62] He's not wrong. We are. All of us. How it manifests may look different amongst personality styles, but all of us feel that tension – that not enoughness that makes us go looking for more. Grief has a way of stirring that up in an approach that tethers you to things you never anticipated would come.

If there is one thing grief is not, it is safe.

There is absolutely nothing safe about grief at all. In fact, quite the opposite. Grief has this way of threatening everything safe you've come to know.

I never expected apathy would be one of its side effects. Yet, it makes sense in retrospect. The loss of certain roles – most especially that which turned me into an empty nester – have really thrown me for a loop. It's a forced exile from caring about things and people in ways you were *required* to care for every moment of every day for decades. One day you're a full-time parent whose entire life is going one way with a definitive purpose and goal. The next day, quite literally, it's over and despite your best efforts to prevent it, apathy can make its way through the back door and set up shop in the sunroom while you're cleaning out the basement in hopes of moving on.

What no one tells you or at least no one tells you enough is this season is going to be one you can't prepare for. It will shift the foundations of your identity in ways that no amount of preparation will stop. I think that's what grief is for. No one talks about it much, but there is a reason the book of Lamentations is included in the Bible. I think it's because we are created to be people who grieve. We have to have a place and way to express all that brings us sorrow. It is the only thing a soul born for eternity can do in a mortal world.

What people also don't say enough is that a person doesn't have to die in order for you to grieve the loss of them. That's what I've spent 20 years telling people going through divorces. You aren't just separating out your assets and starting a new life. It's never that beautiful. You're also grieving the loss of identity. You're burying something because new life first involves death.

A death of the known. A death of the expected. A death of relationship. A death of marriage and who you are in certain ways all in one. Although it may come with relief, newness, things that allow you to breathe for the first time in many years, it also comes with pieces of a story that cause you to lament, to lay down on the floor and allow your soul to weep into the floorboards.

In so many ways, it's the same thing when your children leave home. Grief is a story that says at once, "It was never supposed to be this way" *and* "This is how it was always going to be." I think that's what it means to reconcile disenchantment with God. *Reconciling isn't just about making peace with the God we thought He was and who He actually has turned out to be.* It's also about reconciling with disenchantment itself.

It's recognizing enchantment was always going to sell us short, dump us on the corner, and leave us out in the cold. The word enchantment alone kind of lends itself to this. Enchantment is other worldly and magical in a way that reality reminds us isn't sustainable.

I think that's why we have to introduce it to a real God. A God who breathes life into dust. Who makes ashes beautiful. Who shows up in the desert and makes our wandering fruitful. Who is Eternal. It is life swallowing death and death swallowing life all in one.

I will tell you I don't know how Job did it and I'm not sure I'm supposed to know. One thing is certain – I am grateful that his story is not my own. Although I've endured enough tragedy to know that God's grace is timely – it shows up when we need it, not early nor late, but right on time – I also know that it's not a type of grace I want to have to need. The amount I've had to tap into this year alone is more than enough to last me for another lifetime. Brutal doesn't come close to describing it and I don't think there are any words I could conjure up that would adequately encapsulate 2023.

This makes me wonder how Job told the story. When his kids were born long after their siblings had died, when his wife and he sat around the dinner table with 10 different faces staring back at them, what did they say? Did they speak with tears over the graves outside their door? How could they not? Clearly Job loved his people – deeply so. You do not grieve or lament the loss of people for whom you have no concern or empathy. Job's grief was so great that he wasn't merely tortured by physical suffering but by deep emotional anguish also.

If you've ever endured a single hour of a day like that, you know how he felt. It's like a dead man walking with your body eating you from the inside out. There is plenty of research out there that shows the effect grief, loss, and trauma have on our bodies and brains. However, there is no measure for the effect it has on our souls.

I don't know about Job, but I know that's where I found myself in 2023. With an ache that is so deep my soul is almost a felt thing. It is one where I know at once that God has me in the palm of His hand and I am safe and secure there without the shadow of a doubt *and* one where I equally know with complete certainty also that there *are* things which will kill me. Quite literally. Broken hearts are a cause of death and anyone that tells you they are not has not loved another deep enough yet.

The place that has stuck with me throughout all of 2023 is – I wouldn't wish this on my worst enemy. We all say that but I don't know if we really mean it. When your worst enemy tries to take your entire life apart, disassembling it piece by piece, when they watch you fall to pieces and glory in the triumph of what they can get for themselves while you're on the ground, when they make your sorrow about themselves and your tragedy about their feelings, most of us would rather get revenge than care how devastation will result in their fallout.

Enter grief.

Grief has this way of tenderizing the soul so that you no longer hate your enemies enough to wish on them tragedy.

Instead, you understand the depths of what the pits of hell can entertain and you wish them well. Even if your paths no longer cross and you no longer spend dinners across the table, you stop short of wishing upon them evil. You know. You understand. You have caught a glimpse, a taste of death, and there is nothing that makes you recoil faster than seeing into hell.

I wonder if Job had the same experience. The one where you see God with eyes of reverence and awe that make you realize there is nothing on this planet worthy in comparison to a God who is so much more than even the very worst experience this world can lob. The one where the absolute depths of grief, sorrow, and death force you to come face to face with your own true motives and realize that there *is* a suffering you truly would wish on absolutely no one. The one where both of these are true at once. The one where disenchantment and God meet in the middle of the circle and that circle is your world.

Right now, I find it a struggle to leave this place. The one where I'm both watching and experiencing all of this play out. I don't *feel* like I'm on solid ground. I think that's how grief is lived out. I know what is true and I feel uncertain of it all at once. I find myself brimming over with gratitude and at the same time in the throes of a sadness like I've never known. It allows me to hold space for the ones who don't know what I know and to pray they never have to. It grants me the freedom to tell those who think they know that their version of the future isn't what God is calling me to. It enables me to say – this is a moving story. It isn't over. It's still ongoing. God is still writing my tomorrow.

The thing we all wrestle with is this need for life to be settled. For it to be still, something we can hold onto, something we can ensure will remain stable. Although I think that too was birthed in

Eden, the same is true now as it was then. What made Eden stable wasn't Eden itself. It wasn't a geographic location where Adam and Eve dwelt. It wasn't even a set of certain circumstances that made them safe. The only safety that existed both before and after the curse was the same one that exists for us now. It was God Himself. The indwelt. The Alpha and Omega – Beginning and End. The omniscient, omnipresent, Almighty who is Himself the only safety and certainty we can ever have.

I don't want that to be true and at the same time I have never been more comforted and certain of a thing than this. I wonder if that's how Job felt. He definitely wanted his suffering to end. He wanted his audience with God. At this point, I think we can all agree that once he got it, it did not go at all how he imagined. When it ended, Job saw what I think it takes for all of us to reconcile with reality: A God who is dangerous enough to love us at all costs. A God who leaves Eden because we had to also. A God who doesn't make suffering a punishment but a revelation tool. A God who grieves, sorrows, and laments the same as we do. A God in whose image we were made.

A.W. Tozer may have described it best when he wrote, *"To have found God and still to pursue Him is the soul's paradox of love."*[63] He is the God of invitation, not exclusion. The God of grace because there is grief abundant. The God of mercy because sorrow is the other side of the coin's face. The God of suffering because His image in us is what it takes for us to be complete. He is a God who longs for us to be near in ways we can only taste. I think that's why Lamentations has a place. Because it reminds us that our God isn't angry, unforgiving, a tyrant, a perfectionist, or one of impossible expectations. He is one who takes on flesh, just like us, so that He too can bleed.

I never like this part of the story. The one where Jesus bleeds. I cannot make myself, no matter how many times I tell myself I will, watch *The Passion of the Christ* and the scenes where Jesus bleeds. It doesn't make me upset with myself as some people feel. I am not burdened with guilt. Rather, I feel His suffering in a way I cannot explain. It's one that brings me to my knees and I think it's because I know what it means to choose suffering. To allow misunderstanding. To nearly faint with grief. It makes my heart long for Eden – for home – for the way things *should* be in a way all else fails.

I think we know. Our hearts *know* it shouldn't be this way. At once, they also know they *have* to be this way. That's where I am. The knowing in between. The unchangeable reality of a space in which I don't want to dwell and yet must all the same. Maybe that's where you find yourself today. This is why I wrote this book. Because of the desert place. The dusty road. The sand dunes and valleys and shadows. The knowns that aren't okay. The unknowns that restructure all your days. The uncertainties and the things we cannot change.

We have this tendency as humans to want to make everything okay. How we go about doing that looks different depending on how we're made, but all of us in some form or fashion want things to be okay. There isn't a humanitarian organization, philanthropic effort, or social justice mission out there that, at its purest core, doesn't have the goal of making life in this world better for the people whose lives they want to change. Likewise, so often the efforts we call aggressive really have the same stance.

Repeatedly David asks in Psalms for God to bring destruction, to allow calamity an opportunity to make an impact. It's the same story couched in a different phrase. Most of us have the same mission God has: Redemption. Make the places, relationships, and people better. Heal things. Change things. Give goodness a chance. The thing that we all have to wrestle and reconcile with is that sometimes it takes things we aren't okay with for things to be okay. Like broken relationships. Divorce. Death. Devastation. Storms. Grief. Loss. Change. Earthquakes. Disruptions. Difference. War.

I'm a big believer in things happening for a reason and an equally big believer in that being a wholly uncomfortable statement because, more often than not, we don't know the reasons. Some we never will. This isn't our story and we aren't writing it. We don't get to know all the reasons because *we don't have to*. That's a burden we don't have the responsibility of carrying. Where we might see it as freedom, just like a child who sees the adults "getting" to make all the decisions and "getting" to stay up late, the truth is these things are a responsibility that can come with a lot of weight.

We were invited to the table to participate. There is a glory in that that we often don't realize we carry. God created us as people of favor. All of us. Not a chosen few. Everyone that has ever crossed this earth and ever will. We have a place. A place where we are both comforted and chosen to instill character. One where we are both served and servants. One where our glory is made evident by things that cause us to suffer. It's why knowing why doesn't matter the way we think it does. Having all the answers doesn't make the pain any easier.

I think that's what Job discovered. I think it's also what made his heart tender enough that when God told his friends Job had to do the sacrificing and praying on their behalf because He wasn't about to listen to another one of their words, Job did it without a second thought. He understood that knowing God was knowing all he needed to know. His suffering paled in comparison to a God who held everything together, even pain and loss and terror.

Separation may be one of, if not *the*, most excruciating experience a human being can endure. We anticipate it with fear. We endure it with sorrow. We try to change it with longing. We do everything we know to escape being separated. We even self-sabotage by separating ourselves in an effort to not be separated. Even our isolation can be a self-protective measure to keep us from intentional rejection, misunderstanding, or the loneliness that comes from reaching out but having no one reach back the way we needed. That's happened to me more times than I can count in 2023. It's been a year filled to the brim with misunderstandings and failures to care. Years like that have a wear on them unlike any other.

My tendency when life gets tough is to get going. I do something more often than not about where I find myself, even if I have to pause first to get my bearings. I rarely just sit and stare. 2023 changed all that. I ended up in positions where my body wouldn't even allow me to do anything but stay in one place, sometimes for hours upon hours. Not because I was physically sick with an illness but because grief completely wrecked my world in a way all other griefs to date couldn't compare.

The place I am now is no longer sinking sand. It's a sad understanding of truths I don't want to bear. It's an acceptance of grief that so much of life is temporary. It's a recognition that tomorrow will hold new things God is preparing but I'll live in those spaces with new scars I now bear. Much like the graves of Job's children in his backyard, there will always be reminders of what was and now isn't. They'll hold both joy and sorrow. Glory and sadness. Pain and hope.

I've wondered why the Bible bothered to mention that Job's daughters who came after his first set died were the most beautiful in all the land. It seems like a superficial, frivolous detail. One that a God so holy and righteous and busy wouldn't bother to manufacture much less care about. Yet, of all the things that could have been shared about Job's second set of kids, God chooses to impress upon the writer of Job to share how his daughters were beautiful. You know why I think He mentions it? I think it's because when God redeems something, it is made *truly* beautiful. It comes to be what it was always intended to be. Pure, full, and complete in its glory. God *is* beautiful and His redemption is not just eternal. It is beautiful also.

Redemption may always signify pain. I can't fathom that Job didn't see the likeness of his other daughters in the faces of his younger ones. I imagine he did every day. Yet, their beauty reminded him that God makes everything beautiful in *His* time. Even tragedy. His ways, His perspective, His thoughts, His storyline. All of it is wrapped up in something so far beyond what we could ever dream that even devastation becomes a beautiful story we don't just endure but one we get to tell. Just like Job. His story has been told for thousands of years, continuing on long after he left this globe.

We too are all Modern Day Jobs. Our stories worthy. Our pains purposeful. Our griefs deep and scarring. Ours hold the same potential. The potential to be made beautiful. To rise from the ashes, to age, to be filled with life. Our sorrows, sufferings, struggles, and griefs are also reflections of redemption with each valley we traverse, each desert road we walk, and each mountain we climb. Like Job, may we learn to see not our own reflections in the water of the lives we live, but the image of our God – the One He always was and always will be. A God bigger than all our enchantment could envision and all our disenchantment could dismantle. The God with whom reality forces us to reconcile.

The God *with* us. Emmanuel.

Chapter Twenty One:
Agency

"Any sacrifice in the hand of God,
God can bring good from."

~ Lysa Terkeurst[64]

I went to the retreat in June with my life seemingly in shambles. I had no idea how to navigate anything forward. Not one single step made sense to me so all I could do was whatever was in front of me, whether or not it was "the next right thing." That's the thing that people don't tell you about grief. There isn't the brainpower left for you to even decipher "next" much less "right." All you can do is something – or, in my case some days, nothing. I went thinking that I was going to find some healing, some place to take everything that was happening. As if some sense of it could be made in the woods of North Carolina that didn't exist on the Texas roads. What I found instead was agency.

Prior to that retreat, I had no real understanding of the additional meaning of the word agency. Even now I find it a hard word to use. Yet, it is so applicable. At the end of the retreat, just before we all left, we gathered in a circle around Haven Place and Lysa asked us to state in one sentence what we came in feeling like and what we were leaving with now instead. She'd come in feeling heavy and was leaving with a sense of hope. I was one person down from her and at that moment so aware of how uncomfortable I felt to be standing in what seemed like a place where everyone else saw what I had been carrying around for so long. This sense of not togetherness, of not knowing, of feeling behind the curve and like I just didn't measure up. Yet the words that came out of my mouth were, "I came in feeling paralyzed and I'm leaving with a sense of agency."

During the one-on-one sessions where our individual groups got to gather with Lysa and ask her questions personally, the one I'd asked was how. How do you go from being paralyzed to moving forward? Because I feel trapped, stuck, and usually in a prison of my own making, only this time my story is more like yours and I didn't create this narrative even if there are pieces I contributed to or caused, and I need to know how to move on. She paused for a while before answering me. Although I don't remember her exact words, I do remember that the general gist was keeping looking for God, keep showing up, keep asking, keep praying, keep pursuing because this isn't the end of the road and eventually you *will* get to the place that you feel like you too have some agency.

One of the things I've learned on repeat in seasons of loss and grief is that we have to be seen if we want to heal.

I've also learned there are only a select few people who are really going to take the time to see you. Like Job, in seasons of deep grief, we have to let ourselves off the hook of being good with everyone. We have to take some agency over our own experience and say, "I know that everything that is happening to me may not be within my control, but who I share my deepest pain with and how I carry it in the world is."

God tells us that He gives us "treasures of darkness," (Isaiah 45:3) that there is a richness that exists within the confines of all that grieves our souls. These things handed us are losses, sorrows, griefs, and pains to bear that unite us with Jesus in ways not everyone around us will grasp. Jesus didn't share all of His with everyone because He knew not everyone cared, not everyone would understand, and not everyone had the capacity to bear it. So, it is with some level of *not* caring, *not* making it necessary that others care, *not* allowing other people's version of your story to mar your understanding of it yourself that you have to carry your own grief. It is with a level of abandon and inhibition that you have to take agency of what has been entrusted to you by God to bear.

We talk a lot about all the pain Job carried, all the suffering he endured, and how his friends just didn't get what they didn't get. All true. Yet, we spend very little time considering Job's response to his friends as they spoke. For all the loss he was bearing, Job never lost sight of the truth. He may not have known the reasons behind it all, but he did know what the reasons *weren't*. He knew what real comfort was and he knew what his friends were offering didn't measure up.

I think that's the thing we start to grasp a bit more the closer we get to God. The more we endure our own pain and seek God's comfort, the more we begin to realize what kind of comfort is truly palpable and healing. Rarely is it the kind we think we need most. What soothes our bodies and what soothes are souls are two entirely different things. Sometimes we need both, but the kind that brings peace to our souls isn't creature comfort. It's knowing. It's accepting the holes. It's the brutal truth that life hurts and there is no way around that. In equal measure, it's the fixture of God in a place where, no matter what, He doesn't abandon us.

At the end of the story, I think one of the things that Job felt most comforted by is that God knew all along. He had not abandoned Job nor was He just unleashing His wrath on Job for something unknown. Job had a strong enough sense of His Father to know that God would never just arbitrarily do something like deeply wound and injure him without cause. Job also knew that he was in an upright place with God. He walked with God close enough to know that, if there was some sin in his life, some place where he needed to make a change, God would convict him of it and work with Job on changing his heart. He wouldn't, in a fit of merciless rage, say He'd finally had enough and throw Job to the wolves. No, Job's God was better than that and Job knew it.

Job also knew his own heart and soul. It'd been years and years of trial and error, failure and success, seeking God's favor and grace, and working with God to navigate his own growth. Job *knew* the heart of the One he'd entrusted his life to. That's why he could say with all confidence that his friends didn't know jack about what they were talking about. He was right. His friends *didn't* know. They were just as in the dark as Job as to what was going on in the spiritual realms. All of them were caught in a cosmic battle between Satan and God and not one of them had the first inkling as to what was going on.

I don't know where you are today and what you walked into this book carrying. I just know that everyone is given our own burdens to navigate. So, it is with the recognition that we already have our hands full with things God has entrusted to us that I remind us both to let ourselves off the hook of pleasing everyone. I've had people tell me that I needed to handle the situations that have arisen in 2023 with grace, with me being the first to reach out, to try to right wrongs, to do all the same things that Job's friends told Job to do.

Like Job's friends, mine were at times wrong. Unlike Job, I tried to take their advice. Mired in grief, abandoned in pain, and lost in a sea I couldn't control, I thought maybe they knew something I didn't know. After all, they were God-following people, so surely I could trust their judgment in a situation where I was struggling so much, right?

Wrong. If there is anything I've learned about spiritual warfare in this all, it is when the battle belongs to the Lord, any efforts we make to redeem what He's allowed to be destroyed are only going to end in futility. We are not redeemers. We are the redeemed ones. The ones bought with a price. The ones for whom sacrifice has been poured out and so the story only makes sense when we play our role.

The problem is that so often we don't want that role. We don't want to be the betrothed, the ones pledged to Christ, the ones who don't know what's going on. We want to see the bridal suite, the home He's building for us. We want to know what He's up to instead of waiting until the day He comes to take us home.

Faith is this place that isn't intended for us alone. It's one where our friends, family, and community also belong. **What Job endured wasn't for Job alone. It was for the people watching also.** They needed to see and trust that what made no earthly sense was a heavenly essential. In the upside down kingdom, the battles we fight aren't the battles we think we should. We are so often focused on the here and now, the temporal, that we lose complete sight of what we're really here for.

The thing about pain and grief and loss is that we have to surrender those things to God in order for the sacrifice they are, even when imposed upon us, to hold any value. They are going to happen no matter what. You do not traverse this earth for any significant amount of time without being guaranteed trouble.

If the first two humans on the planet couldn't do it and their own kids started out with one murdering the other, then it is clear that the problem doesn't lie within society as a whole. It lies within the reality that this world is cursed and it is a curse we cannot undo or escape this side of the grave. It is a curse that has to be overcome by someone and something so much stronger than we are.

We live as Lysa said – between two gardens. We live between the now and the not yet. We are stuck in the remnants of the Land of Should, where things are not at all as they *should* be but nevertheless constantly remind us that they *could*. If there is one thing that remains true, it is that loss is guaranteed to us all. Just as the start of Job tells us that "Man is born to trouble as surely as sparks fly upward" and Jesus says, "In this world, you *will* have trouble," we must all come to the place of not only accepting but *expecting* trouble, loss, grief, and sorrow to be part of our experience. They are promised. What is not is their outcome.

This is where we can either become like Jesus in His sufferings or ours can continue without point, purpose, or redemption. There is a phrase in scripture that contains the words "sacrifice of praise" and sometimes I think that's exactly how praise feels, doesn't it? Like a sacrifice. Like something we're giving up, not something we're joyful about or grateful for.

Sometimes praise is surrendering to a reality we would do anything to change.

Especially when things are exactly as they *shouldn't* be, when we have grief unbearable, when "sorrows like sea billows roll."[65] So, the question is how do we, like the writer of that song, come to the place that we *can* say, "It is well with my soul?"

I think we have to take Job's approach. His response to his grief, loss, and suffering was one of agency. He couldn't control God. In fact, he had no idea what God was up to and desperately wanted an audience with the Almighty to vindicate himself. However, what Job *could* do is choose his response to his suffering. He first *chose* sacrifices of praise. He is quoted as saying, "The Lord gives and the Lord takes away. Blessed be the name of the Lord." This wasn't a happy response to tragedy by a man who had just lost everything. This was a sacrificial posture of the heart to things inevitable.

Agency isn't taking control of the situation. It's taking control of ourselves. It's taking loss and putting it in the rightful place it belongs. On the altar.

If our lives truly don't belong to us, then neither does our loss.

It too belongs to God. What He gives and what He takes away are not just things within His control. He doesn't play chess with our lives. He invites us to be part of His family and, in His family, nothing is off limits. His love is no holds barred, thus the same is true of His loss. If He will give everything for us, the same is required of us in response.

The beauty of it – though it feels like anything but in its midst – is summed up so well in what Jim Elliot wrote, "*He is no fool who gives up what he cannot keep to gain what he cannot lose.*"[66] Our lives are not ours to keep in the first place. We may design our days but we are not their authors. Their timing wasn't begun by us and cannot be controlled by us. We do not have control over the breath of Life. Thus, it is not a loss to give back to God what already belongs to Him anyway. It just *feels* like it.

What we are really surrendering is our expectations, our *need* for things to go a certain way, to have certain experiences, to know that our security is indeed secure. From personal experience, I can tell you that the hardest things to let go of haven't been visible things. Those seem inevitable. What has been hardest have been my versions of fulfillment. Fulfillment of my dreams, hopes, and wants – the things that I feel like make up so much of who I am and what I was put on the planet for. Yet, God expects that I will let go of those things too. He doesn't force me to though. He just invites me to the altar and allows me, like Abraham, to make the *choice* as to what I'm willing to sacrifice.

The reality is that we only want to sacrifice things when we know what we're doing. When we are certain of their outcome. We sacrifice our time, our money, our belongings for other things we want. The problem with sacrificing ourselves to God is that we know we can't control the result. We don't know what we will get in return and sometimes it feels like getting Jesus or salvation in response just isn't enough. We want something more tangible. God with skin on. Present day results.

That's the place I've found myself wrestling so much lately. The one where I know that Jesus is better than anything this earth has to offer – I've tasted and seen as scripture says, and I know that there isn't a person on this planet who can meet my needs or fulfill my hopes like the Lord. Where everyone else has failed me over and over, He is a sustaining force. I didn't always feel this way nor want this story of hope. This kind of hope requires loss. It acquaints itself with grief and it allows Jesus to be the Son of Suffering, not just the King of Kings and Lord of Lords.

It's that piece I don't want to witness again. Yet, it is in the witnessing that I think we learn what makes all the difference. Job's friends thought they were witnessing a man who was out of line with God, a man who needed as someone told me in the midst of all this: "pruning." The truth is we are *all* in need of pruning in some form or fashion until our dying day. There is never a person who doesn't have room for improvement somehow. Yet, there are parts of scripture where God tells us Job was righteous enough to save himself, just not anyone else. So, whether or not Job needed pruning wasn't the point.

The point was so much bigger.

I think it's critical to remember that in seasons of growth. Pruning doesn't save us. In fact, it's not even required. Ask any gardener and they'll tell you that pruning definitely helps and is absolutely preferred, but it is not *essential* for a plant's survival. Pruning is used to make already existing fruit or flowers even more bountiful. It is intended to take abundance and make it flourish more. Pruning exists to take the measure from full to overflowing. Pruning stimulates growth. We often think of it as something that hurts and is required because we aren't growing right. The reality though, as any good gardener knows, is that pruning is designed to take the pieces that *naturally* grow and cut them off so that the energy spent on their growth gets channeled more deeply into other already existing growth.

We're all going to grow many branches and produce fruit of some sort. However, pruning allows us to channel and shape that growth into something very specific. That's what Job's friends didn't know. They thought Job was being punished, faulted for something he got wrong. But he wasn't. Job was being pruned into deeper growth and *not* because Job had done anything wrong but rather the opposite. Job's growth was so strong that God knew he could withstand pruning that wasn't even required but would nevertheless reveal more of his heart, integrity, and God's character. How do we know this is true? It's how the story began. *God* brought Job to Satan's attention. *God* enlisted the fallout. *God* offered up the sacrifice.

When God sacrifices, it is always and only for good.

It may involve loss and suffering. That is how pruning works, but the focus in pruning isn't on the immediate cuts and instant pain. It is on the fruit and abundance to come.

———

Last year ended on a good note despite all the suffering. Usually, at year end, I try to take some time to reflect, to consider the last year, and think towards the new one. I don't make new year's resolutions, but I do choose a word of the year and usually try to find a verse that seems to correspond. 2023 was so disruptive that I changed my word of the year mid-stream and it absolutely fit - then and now in retrospect. So, going into this year, I really expected to be excited and happy about a new year, new word, new verse.

Yet, a month in advance, the word that started coming to me over and over was, "Invitation." It turns out there are exactly zero verses in all of scripture that contain the word invitation. There are things that discuss it generally or variants like "invite" but not one verse uses the exact word, "invitation." I painted it on a page to see how it would land, if I would stick with it or change it into something else. I didn't particularly like the word in light of how 2023 had played out. Everything in me has been in certain ways on lockdown, careful consideration mode, and extremely cautious in stepping back out into things.

I wonder sometimes what those days were like for Job. The "returning to normal." The thing about grief and loss and suffering is that, to a degree, people care while it's occurring. Even Job's friends, however misguided their perceptions were, still cared enough to be there, to come, to sit in silence for a week, to *be* with him. Yet, when it was all over, as often happens after the funeral has passed, the casserole dishes have been washed and returned, and all the flowers have died, people start returning to normal. The one left in deep grief doesn't usually move on so quickly and that's when the silence settles in and reality is a brutal companion that you don't have the energy to escape.

All of a sudden, "moving on" carries no joy, no hope, no desire for forward momentum. It's often at these points that you find yourself in your pajamas, day in and day out, laying in bed with an exhaustion that seems almost from another dimension it's so all-encompassing. There was an energy about the initial occurrence that keeps people going. The forced activity makes it seem like life to a certain degree is still possible, but the after effects shroud your days in a grief that swallows light and life whole.

This is the part where I wonder how Job coped. Scripture gives us no words of solace, no comforts, no insight into how Job moved on. All we know is that people came and consoled him, gave him physical necessities, and God restored the prosperity Job lost. In addition, as often comes with pruning, his life was more abundant, more fruitful, and more prosperous after it all occurred. But none of this happened overnight.

Every day, Job still got up and went through the motions. His body had to heal, his mind and emotions had to reconcile, his wife and he had to grieve the loss of their children, his reputation had to regrow – and look different than it had before because now, it wasn't just him saying something or extending some goodness out of his abundance. Now, Job was speaking from a place of deep understanding of darkness and even greater comprehension of the power of God. He was speaking from *loss*. He'd been invited not only to taste and see that the Lord was good, but also to join Christ in His sufferings. To not only lead his family, but to be a full member of the family of God.

Our lives are not our own and that's not a thing to say or take lightly. It's a pain that leaves behind holes in our hands just like Jesus' as we too learn to let go. To choose sacrifices of praise. To accept the wounds and hold fast to truth. Truths we don't want, truths we feel we cannot bear, truths as Job said of God, "too wonderful for me to know."

There is nothing about suffering that feels wonderful, but what Job spoke wasn't of his suffering in the end. What Job got at the end of it all was perspective. It was agency over his own experience. One that, in the light of knowing a God big enough to wipe away the nations with one breath, could recognize He was up to something so much greater than just Job's experience.

He was conquering death. He was demonstrating life. He was making the invisible visible. He was providing treasures of darkness so that the magnitude of glory could outweigh them all. We were born to this. All of it. Darkness and light, suffering and joy, glory and raggedness. It is the upside down kingdom where earthly things only make sense in eternal sight. This is why our disenchantment *must* be reconciled. Because when we enchant ourselves with a version of God that only fits *this* life, we will never be enchanted with a God Eternal. And *that* is the God we need most.

Chapter Twenty Two:
Bearing Witness

"What if God is teaching us that there are times when your suffering is so deep, so visceral, so present, so enduring that you don't have sentences or verbs or pronouns or adjectives? Like you don't have syntax for what you're going through but God still responds anyway."

~ Jackie Hill Perry[67]

An interesting thing happened about a month into life imploding in May 2023. One of our friends had died in a tragic car accident a month earlier and the Sunday before Memorial Day was her memorial service for all of us who knew her as a local musician. She was one of those souls that knew exactly who she was and lived it without apology. Her music would make a believer of even the hardest souls that there is life beyond all we can see. Since my husband and I were still separated, I went to the service alone. I decided to be brave and showed up in a space that had felt in so many ways like *his* friends and *his* space and *his* reality up until that day.

I may upset some people with what I say next, but I've learned that that too is part of this whole journey. I don't believe God divides and separates Himself into "secular" and "Christian" cubicles. He is God. He is and was and will be before, during, and after all that we as humans create. It is in Him that we *all* – every single one of us – live and move and have our being no matter what we believe. That is the beauty of God when you think about it.

So, I showed up and I am so glad I did because God did that thing He does. The one where He meets your needs through and with people that you'd never expect Him to if you're raised with a specific system of beliefs. The beliefs that say "Only Christians can get you. Only church-goers know what you need. Only people reading scripture can witness to you." If you've spent much time in evangelical circles, you know the one I'm talking about. It's very religious, very unlike Jesus, yet has an insanely large following. It adheres to the whole "us vs. them" mentality like God didn't make everyone the same way: Human.

I wasn't even out of the parking lot before I started seeing God's fingerprints all over this day. One of our long time musician friends whose music I fell in love with the very first time he played in our downtown courtyard was getting out of his car right in front of me just as I was exiting mine. He had no idea about the events of the last month of our lives and didn't even know to ask me. Sometimes the innocent interactions and questions are the most freeing. I don't think it was accidental either that the very building where we were celebrating our friend Ace was literally next door to the building where my life started to unravel a month earlier.

I could have hidden. I could have said it was all too much. I could have kept the truth to myself or put lipstick on a pig and tried to make it all sound better than it really was. But I didn't. I'd decided to be brave so I was just honest. He asked where my husband was and I told him the truth. That we were separated, that things were rough, that I was holding out hope but it was hard. We were already friends before but hadn't connected on this level. We talked about a few important life things here and there but nothing this significant. This one mattered. It was going to define whether this group of people were "our" friends, "his" friends, or mine. It turns out they were all of the above.

What you need to know about my husband and me is that, at times, we have had an unintentional presence that even we don't know how to define. It's become like a living breathing part of us. We've had complete strangers come up to us more times than I can count and say things like, "Y'all are literally the best. I've been watching y'all all night and I don't know what y'all have but it's awesome." We'll both tell you on the back end of this storyline now that we haven't always stewarded that well. We didn't know that love is a gift you steward too. We thought it was something that just happened to you. Something you fell into. Something that just arrived one day on your doorstep and, yeah you may have had to do a few things to keep it intact, but steward it? Well, that just never occurred to us.

It turns out love is a gift that's both handed to you and one you build. It's not complete when you're given it. Rather, like Adam and Eve, it's something you develop as you go. I think we understood the basic concept of that, but we didn't understand the real world application process. We'd been given something a whole lot bigger than us and it seems the world around us saw it better than we did. We felt it and thought that this was something we just needed to hold onto, not something we had to keep developing, building, or give. We made love more about what we individually received not what we were called to together creating. So, it was an absolute shock to the system when the way we'd been approaching it stopped us in our tracks. We thought it'd always just be and then one day it wasn't. Neither one of us knew how to handle that.

God was so gracious to our journey. These friends of ours, some of whom I'd venture to say probably don't have a relationship with Jesus, nevertheless saw and reflected back to us what we were confused about and couldn't seem to figure out. Rather than the non-welcome, the shut-down, the avoidance, the trying to explain it away, the trying to fix a problem that wasn't theirs to begin with that we'd received elsewhere, this group of people that you'd never expect took a different approach. Love. They just showed up, loved me, loved my husband, cared for and about us both without trying to do, explain, or solve a thing.

They listened, hugged it out, cared, and spoke realness over it all. They didn't act like humans aren't or shouldn't be messy. They didn't say we needed to get it all together. They didn't say we'd even gotten it all wrong in the first place. They said things like, "Yeah, been there, done that. I get it. No matter what happens here, you are individually and together still accepted here and loved. We aren't choosing sides because we aren't choosing division at all. We just love y'all."

I can't tell you how freeing that was. How much of a weight was lifted to have someone hear your story and *not* try to condemn, figure out, or get involved in ways that weren't theirs to take. Unlike so many others around us, this group of people gave us the gift of just being. Of bearing witness without trying to change a thing. I think that's exactly what Job's friends needed. They needed to reflect God's heart for Job, not try to reason out his circumstances or make sense of his sorrow.

Grief isn't a reasonable thing. It is devastating and there is no logic that fits. I think that's why, instead of coming in with our own perspective, we have to seek God's. We have to ask, "God, what role do YOU want me to play in this situation with this person?" So often, probably more often than not, He's going to ask us to simply bear witness. To just *sit* with someone in their suffering and *not* take it upon ourselves to speak, reason why, or change things.

When you read the entire story in the book of Job, it seems that Job's friends were sent there to bear witness to a God who holds together all things, even griefs unbearable, suffering unexplainable, and pain beyond reason. Knowing that God – the one who allows that kind of tragedy – was just as important for them as it was for Job. Their role was to be one of stabilization and humility amidst the chaos, not people who understood what was happening (they didn't) but people who still trusted the One who did. Their job was to be present without losing sight or compromising their integrity. They weren't called to speak on God's behalf, but rather to do as Paul directs us to when dealing with the enemy, "to stand your ground, and after you have done everything, to stand." (Ephesians 6:13)

Your reason for being here might be totally different than you think. All of us should check before we assume. That mattered in Job's friends' roles because, at the end of the story, we find out that what they chose to do instead incited God. God-fearing men upset the Throne in their well-intentioned attempts at helping Job. That should make all of us pause and consider our own responses. We should all ask ourselves why their response is what angered God. My best guess is because this was not *their* battle to take on. It was His. *God* was doing battle in the heavenlies and they were called to bear witness. Instead, they involved themselves in things they knew nothing of and misrepresented the Lord and it made Him very angry. He was so angry that it is the only time I can think of in all of scripture when God specifically *tells* someone that He will *not* accept their prayers.

Until then, Job's friends were not only *certain* they were right but reinforced that certainty with their ongoing arguments. They'd developed a bit of the mob mentality that comes with feeling vindicated in your own perspective when other people agree with you. They kept spewing words that, for all intents and purposes without any glimpse into the heavenlies, would make a modicum of sense to humanity. After all, we believe in cause and effect and so does God. He invented it. It's just that *His* cause and effect in the storyline of Job was not at all understandable nor visible from the human perspective. It required faith, trust, and a view of eternity.

I think it's important for us to remember that these men

weren't terrible people who just didn't know. They were men of integrity, faith, and wisdom. They'd lived a while, had strong relationships with God, understood His ways to many degrees, and were in close enough relationship with Job that they were considered his friends. The only friends and people in Job's life period who showed up when his world imploded. Keep in mind that, before destruction, Job was the most righteous man on earth. God endorsed him as such – one whose heart posture and external actions lined up. He was a dedicated servant of the Lord. So, the people with whom Job spent time probably weren't fools or men dragging his life off course. Job's friends were very likely men worth their salt.

In the modern church, I think we'd see these same people as elders in the faith, maybe even leaders, who know and walk regularly with God. People devoted to the ways and service of the Lord. People we can trust to seek the heart and mind of God. People we'd expect to have discernment, wisdom, and advice we could trust. People we believe would be present, caring, compassionate, and praying for us. However, all these things were only true of Job's friends during their arrival on the scene. After seven days, which is a pretty short time period in light of how long life is, they began leaning on their own understanding. Given long enough inside suffering, just like us, they turned to human means rather than asking God for the endurance He was setting them up to need.

Scripture tells us *suffering* is what produces perseverance in us. It also says that perseverance, not repentance, results in character - the kind built in the crucible of enduring the most difficult things - and *that* is what produces hope. A hope that "does not disappoint." (Romans 5:5) That seems so strange considering it is birthed out of suffering. Here we are again, inside paradox and it just makes no sense. How could it?

It's hope in the temporal that we seek but hope in the eternal that we need.

We are all dependent creatures in need of the God He is, not the one we've defined Him to be. I find myself returning to this point again and again and again. We don't need the God we enchant ourselves with. We need the one He really is. The one who allows us to suffer and Himself does the same thing.

Job's friends called Job to something he didn't need: Repentance for unknown sin. Something that wouldn't cure his condition or save him from reality. They told Job he or his children *must* have sinned. Otherwise this all made no sense. They couldn't have been more wrong. Not only so, we know that Job already did that. He'd *already* prayed on repeat for himself and his children to be forgiven for any unknown sin. There was nothing left from which to repent, nothing yet to be forgiven.

I think it's important for us to remember that we all do unhealthy things at times with very healthy motives, often without even realizing it. I imagine that if Job's friends were men worth their salt, men of integrity, fortitude, and compassion as it certainly appears, then their motives in speaking every word they did were good. They probably wanted their friend's suffering to end and also wanted answers for themselves, a reasoning that made sense of why God was allowing the worst of things to happen to the best of people. They just didn't know what they didn't know and part of what they didn't know is that God intentionally was allowing Job's suffering because of his *faith* and *not* his sin.

Today, I went to see my friend who is dying. She has a degenerative disease that is guaranteed to result in eventual death. There is no cure, no hope that her life will be extended or even that the life she has now will get any better than it is right this very moment. Her sister died last year of the same thing. Her daughter buried her aunt knowing that she'd soon be in the same place doing the same thing, only this time it would be her in her cousin's shoes. My friend said today that it had to be like looking into a crystal ball. I was at the service and told her it was. I said even our friend who isn't very emotionally expressive was somewhat emotional at the service.

We've all been friends for 40 years, since we were barely old enough to read and write and really talk. Even though all of us have the same disease – not the degenerative one our friend has – but the one of being terminal, none of us ever anticipated this day coming. Not like this. Yet, here it is. The one God isn't sparing any of us from experiencing. Not only is He *not* taking away tomorrow's eventuality, but He is leaving us all in today's reality. We all have the cursed blessing and blessed curse of watching her body waste away. It is wretched. It is precious. I cannot help but carry both.

There is something about the loss of a thing that helps you own its value. There is something precious about the gift of time and knowing that it is coming to an end. It helps ground you in today. I know that, as the time passes and the day this all ends gets closer, we will have more and more opportunities to visit, to make memories, to say all the important things. The things we've already said a thousand times over in a thousand ways because that's what true friends do.

Today, though, isn't that eventual tomorrow. Today is where we're called to do what Job's friends were called to – bear witness to our friend's suffering and to God's allowance of it. To be present in the pain – both for our friend and ourselves also.

For a while, we all ran away. It was so painful and so debilitating to watch our friend deteriorate. None of us initially knew what to do. How can you? We tried to make the allowances we could, but there came a time when we didn't know what else to do so we did nothing. We didn't speak like Job's friends did but we also didn't do anything else either. We didn't stay there with her in it and bear witness to her pain. We were carrying our own and instead chose to escape.

I want to hold some grace for all of us for a moment in that because the truth is that none of us really know what to do. Not the one suffering. Not the people witnessing. Not anyone at all. I think this is what love is though – it's showing up despite what it costs you. Yes, there is a place for healthy boundaries and all those things, but this isn't a book about that. This is about when we *know* we are called to be present, bear witness, and it is going to cost us something to show up.

Love is never non-sacrificial. Sacrifice is its inherent definition. That's why God Himself is Love. Because *He* is sacrificial. It isn't something you have to get Him to do. It is part of His actual character that doesn't have to be produced. When scripture says that suffering is what leads to character, it says that because humans don't come here fully formed. We have to develop. We have to learn through experience what is healthy and unhealthy, right and wrong, good and bad. God doesn't. He already knows.

He allows us to suffer because He is developing
***Himself*, His life, in *us*.**

We were made in His image afterall and the knowledge of good *and* evil means the knowledge of suffering too. That is what we asked for when we ate the fruit and that is what we are being handed: the knowledge of being like God who knows good and evil. We need Him in order to be the people we were destined to become. People who suffer well because we love much. People who shut their mouths and open their arms.

If we were able to take ourselves to the scene with Job, I wonder if we could conjure up what he needed most. His body was wasting away. His soul ached with a pain deeper than anyone he knew at that point could even begin to comprehend. His physical suffering was only barely relieved by scraping his boils and causing his skin even more tearing. His reputation was obliterated and people mocked his condition. His wife was in the deepest grief of her entire life and could not save Job from his own. There wasn't the option of putting Job into a medically induced coma or taking him to a hospital – physical, mental, or otherwise. He just had to deal with all of it as it was handed to him.

As his friends in that situation, I don't think I would have a clue what my friend Job needed most. I barely know what my friend of 40 years in her own situation needs where she *does* have care and *does* receive attention unlike Job. I know that nothing I say or do is going to change how she feels or her circumstances at all, but I also know that she still needs me to show up. Bearing witness and being present make more difference in her life than anything else I can possibly do.

I imagine it would've for Job too. That's what Job's friends didn't seem to realize was valuable. Not their words. Not their explanations. Not all their solutions or trying to figure things out. None of that helped. In fact, it made it all significantly worse. So bad at one point that Job called them all "miserable comforters" and he wasn't wrong. They not only provided zero comfort, but they added to his misery, blamed him and his dead children for things that were in no way their fault, completely failed to provide any kind of demonstrated care to his wife or to Job that is recorded at all, and even tried to convince Job of things that were wholly untrue of God.

One of the things about Job's friends that no one ever mentions is that Satan didn't necessarily know they were coming until they were on their way. He was so busy attacking and tormenting Job that he may not have known he'd get the bonus of having Job's friends show up and have the opportunity to tempt them to play God too. Job's friends didn't know that their bearing witness or failing to do so was going to either aid God's agenda or Satan's. They had no idea they too were locked in this cosmic battle.

Neither do we.

Do you realize that when your friends' marriage is falling apart, Satan and God are warring for it? Do you recognize that if it lands on your doorstep, you're being commissioned into battle? Not the one here on earth like you might think, but the one happening in the heavenlies.

It seems that is so rarely our first thought – the one of spiritual warfare. Yet, that's how God starts the book of Job. God. Not Satan. *God* commissions war and incites battle. Why? Because He **loves** us. This is the point we keep missing and must return to time and time again. If God is really good and truly loving, He is *going* to defeat evil and destroy every last remnant of it.

We chose this battle, this captivity, this life outside the gates of the Garden that we weren't prepared for. If we think for one instant that God isn't going to involve us in this war we have chosen, we are wrong. Of course He is because we are *partners* in battle. We are citizens of heaven – the coming Eden, and Satan is going to do everything in his power to stop and slow the arrival of it. Paul reminds us that is our true reality, the truest one we have, thus we've been given divine armor for a divine battle.

When the spiritual warfare I was involved in last year came into clear view for me, I wrote everything I saw down. I dated and time-stamped it which is something I rarely do. However, it seemed purposeful in the moment and it was only later that I would come to know just how much that was true. The invisible battle going on wasn't going to be defeated by me merely concentrating on God being good as I was told to do. That was a given. His goodness is what had equipped me with armor – the shield of faith, belt of truth, shoes of readiness, breastplate of righteousness. These things aren't necessary when we're relaxing in the hammocks of God's goodness. Yet, these things were *essential* to my making it through.

Paul tells us what we actually need in these moments is "the whole armor of God, that you may be able to stand against the schemes of the devil." (Eph. 6:11, ESV) Our job is more invisible than visible and that's why Satan tries so very hard to shift our focus. If he can get us concentrating on the temporal and feeling stuck in our own circumstances, trying to fix something that has no lasting value, we'll be completely ineffective in the heavenlies. We need strength, vision, awareness, and a willingness to participate in the invisible war that is playing out through our visible world.

The hardest part of this entire story for me has been and continues to be the times when I'm standing alone. The ones where, like David, I am facing Goliath by myself. I've come to realize that sometimes you are *going* to stand alone and I want to encourage you just like Paul that, when that is where you find yourself, take up your shield, and just stay standing. Don't move. Stand still. Remain firm. Resolutely plant yourself no matter what comes and trust that your resolution is what equips your shield of faith not only to protect you but to actively extinguish *all* the fiery arrows of the enemy. I can promise you that everything in you is going to want to run for the hills, to hide out in the desert, and to give up the faith. Job felt it. Jesus felt it. You will feel it too.

When that day comes, *do not quit*.

One of my very favorite verses in all of scripture is found in Revelation. God is talking to the churches and He's telling them what He appreciates about them and identifying the areas where they still need to grow. I've always related to the passage in chapter 2 and what He says to the church of Ephesus, the same people to whom Paul wrote about their heavenly citizenship, roles, and spiritual warfare that comes as a result. He said,

> *"Whoever has ears, let them hear what the Spirit says to the churches. To the one who is victorious, I will give the right to eat from the tree of life, which is in the paradise of God."* (Rev. 2:7)

There is no victory if there is no battle. God has called us to something so much bigger than our own storyline. Our mark isn't on this earth alone. It is a legacy eternal. When God initiates war, expect to be part of the process. We cannot eat of the fruit of the tree of the knowledge of good and evil and expect not to live with the consequences. In His holiness, God grants us our request – to have the knowledge of both. In His goodness, God equips us with the armor we need to stand in the day of battle because now we know our enemy and his schemes.

There will be times when each of us stand alone, when we know things others don't and have an awareness that is ours alone. There will be times when that will all be true. Even in Job's story, I think there was a degree to which each of his friends and Job himself felt that. However, what none of them had the perspective to know is that God was the one who initiated the battle and their job was to stand, not to redefine the strategy of divine warfare.

I don't know how many times or all the reasons why I continually feel the need to be cautious as I say these things, but I think it has a lot to do with the fact that we all are Job but we are all Job's friends also. Like my friends and me with our friend who is dying, we all find ourselves in their boat. Looking for answers, searching for reasons, and trying to make sense of the unknown. We all feel the responsibility. We love people and want good for them. We do our level best to help their circumstances stop being so awful. Yet, God doesn't give any of us a window into exactly what He's doing most of the time, so we're all running on our best laid intentions, life experiences, and wisdom available to us to do the things to which we believe He has called us.

As much as we are Modern Day Jobs, we are also the other people in the storyline. The mockers gloating over a good man fallen, the ones stealing the reputation of the innocent, the people who think we know and speak on behalf of God to our loved ones, telling them, "Give up, repent, change course, get out while you can." We just don't know what we don't know. Even with good hearts, well laid intentions, and a deep love for God and His ways, we still mishandle people and circumstances all in an effort to avoid our own ways of not wanting God to be the actual God He is. The God who allows tragedy and makes way for suffering.

It's an easy intellectual exercise until you're the one in the shoes of experiencing it. Then everything changes. That's what Job figured out and, now that I'm on the other side of things, it's the thing that makes me wonder how much of this was about Job's integrity being tested and how much of it was for all the people bearing witness to Job's reality. It's been said that God wastes nothing, even our pain, and I believe that. So, if He really does waste nothing, then He didn't waste Job's friends', community's, or family's witnessing.

Sometimes our bearing witness doesn't mean we speak. Sometimes it means we take Solomon's advice: *"Do not be quick with your mouth, and do not be hasty in your heart to utter anything before God. God is in heaven and you are on earth, so let your words be few."* (Ecclesiastes 5:2) We watch and *later* we speak – after everything has ended and we know the full conclusion of a matter. That's what Jesus told the disciples to do when He left for heaven. To go be His *witnesses* in all of the world now that they knew what they knew.

While the disciples were waiting on the Holy Spirit to arrive at Pentecost, they were discussing who to select to replace Judas Iscariot as one of the 12. They didn't leave an empty spot. They filled it. Their one requirement? That the person be one who had been *bearing witness* to Jesus' life from the beginning of His ministry right up to the present day.[68] That person needed to be as certain and dedicated to Jesus as they were, even though he hadn't been in the inner circle as a disciple like they had. Why? Because they were all doing the same thing - bearing witness to the fact that Jesus, the Messiah, had come and saved humanity from the power of sin and death.

I wonder if we know how precious that kind of faith is. None of Job's friends heard from God in the whirlwind as far as we know. God didn't reveal His plans, His story, or anything of Himself to Job's friends other than His righteous indignation at their misrepresentation of Him. That was it. All of His revelation was to Job, to the one He'd allowed to suffer, just like His communication of Himself to the people was through Jesus back when He walked this planet. There is a reason our *faith* is what gets tested. It's because *faith* is the thing that sustains us. It is the crucible of our integrity and Satan knows it. That's why God has designed it as our shield in times of attack by the enemy.

I had to have faith, just like Job did, that what I saw that it seemed like no one else around me was seeing was still true. That what God revealed to me was reality. I had to trust that what some of the most well-meaning, God-honoring people around me thought was reality wasn't in fact reality at all. That they were missing the boat and, even though they didn't believe me, I had to still cling to what I knew was true. I still do. Some are never going to come around. I wonder if that was true of Elihu. He was the last one to speak during Job's situation and he was pretty riled up when he spoke. God doesn't mention Elihu and in fact makes a very distinct dismissal of him entirely when He speaks to Job and Job's friends at the end of the book. Elihu is very clearly missing.

We aren't told whether he left, stayed, or was simply dismissed for reasons unknown. We could surmise, but that's what Job's friends already did that led them here so I'd caution us all not to make the same mistake. I think the takeaway instead is this: God isn't going to tell everyone else what He tells you. Instead, He is going to give you opportunities to test whether what you think He's said is true. *Your* faith will be tried and refined and any impurities in *it* removed. He did that with Job.

Job was convinced that he wasn't suffering as a result of his own or his children's sin. He was right. He was convinced his friends were wrong about many of the things they said. Right again. However, if there *was* any reason that Job was trusting God because God had him all shored up, secured, and safe from all trial, trouble, and danger, that was entirely removed. Satan had complete access to every thing in Job's life just short of killing him. His faith, no matter how strong it had been before, was now refined, stronger, purer, more solid.

People of integrity in times of trouble they can't control find their deepest testing to be the substance of their faith. Because it is there that we either allow God to be the God He really is or we try to take His place. None of us *wants* a dangerous God because none of us wants to need a God like that. The problem is we still always eat of the fruit. We still always want to know what it means to know what God knows, so we fall prey to the temptation of doing things ourselves. No one escapes eating the fruit of our choices or the choices of people around us. We are designed to seek nourishment somewhere. The question is whether we are willing to seek nourishment from a God dangerous enough to make goodness come from tragedy.

I think our hearts were always intended to be enchanted. I think disenchantment is the part where Adam and Eve's eyes were opened as Genesis 3 tells us. Scripture never says we fell or that we are "fallen." It never even says we are broken. It simply says that our eyes were opened. I think they were opened not to the truth that *God* cannot be trusted but rather to the fact that *we* can't. We sought knowledge we cannot handle and enchanted ourselves with wisdom that wasn't actually being offered. The only thing we can be enchanted with and hold fast to being trustworthy and true is a God dangerous enough to allow and conquer evil for all eternity, and do it *with* us in the process. I think our eyes revealed our dependency and that is what changes everything.

Sparing us trouble isn't going to make us enchanted with God. Rather, it often makes us prideful and entitled. Involving us is what shows us what true enchantment with the right source can bring. That's the thing we were missing. We didn't even know what we had until it was lost. We needed to be thrust outside the Garden gates into the Land of Should in order to appreciate what Eden held. In order to value eternity, we had to experience degeneration.

The knowledge of good and evil is tempting when you believe it is something you get to use for your own benefit. That's the lie that Satan sold Eve. But a lie is inherently a lie because it isn't true. We were never going to get to use the knowledge of good and evil to enhance our lives, to enchant ourselves, to get things we thought we didn't already have, to fulfill our own needs. That was the deceit. We were created to be in *relationship* with God, not to *be* God. THAT is what we've really enchanted ourselves with believing. That we *can* be like Him, have His knowledge, and do His job.

> **If we're really going to reconcile our disenchantment
> with God, then we must surrender our enchantment
> with ourselves.**

That is the real issue. It turns out we are not all we thought we were cracked up to be. Just ask the friends of Job.

Chapter Twenty Three: Vessels

———

*"Is He going to help Himself to your life, or are you taken up
with your conception of what you are going to do? God is
responsible for our lives, and the one great keynote is reckless
reliance upon Him."*

~ Oswald Chambers[69]

Much of my life has been a perpetual struggle between what felt like the pendulums of "too much" and "not enough" and it's only been in the last few years that I've really come to the place of accepting that we all have to teach ourselves and other people how to love us. Perhaps that's par for the course for most people hitting their 40's, but I've found it is especially so for those with my or similar personalities. There's a quote whose original author I cannot identify that says, "Be careful what you allow because you are teaching people how to treat you."

I think that was a fundamental element in the stories of Job and Jesus. Neither one of them compromised their identity and neither one of them allowed the things they *knew* were not true of them to become parts of it. They both worked from that place of security and allowed the certainty of it to rest in the hands of the Father while they were the vessels that lived those things out. It's what all of us are called to do, but most of us want to be more than vessels. We want to be important in our own right or at least someone that matters much.

**Another element of the upside-down kingdom is
recognizing that our greatest "being" isn't found in us
filling ourselves up but rather in emptying ourselves so
that God can fill us with what we were always destined
to hold: Him.**

While I was talking with my friend who is dying the other day, we discussed raising kids, God, and all these things that go in ways we never anticipated. There's been a rather fanatical person in her daughter's life that subscribes to a version of "God" so based on human emotion, radical extremism, and intensity that it's impossible, at least for me and her both, to believe that the God He really is is any of those things. It's turned her daughter off so much to even the idea that God could be that that she'd rather believe there is no God than to believe in the one to whom she's been exposed.

I think that's the better option. Maybe that statement will upset some people and maybe I am wrong, but I think we have to at least consider that we might be leaving God a whole lot more ground to work with when we say there isn't one than we do by following a false one down the road paved to hell. I was watching a video this morning by one of our favorite singer songwriters, Drake White, and he mentioned this. He said how he thinks one of the greatest tricks the devil has ever pulled is convincing us he isn't real.[70] I'd go another step and say, it's not just convincing us he isn't real but convincing us that who we think God is is actually the devil disguising himself.

One of the problems with living in a temporary world and acting like this is all there is or like the spiritual realms care more about what's going on here than they do there (as if here and now is the most important thing in all of existence) is we begin to forget or fail to acknowledge that the real battle isn't here. It's there. It's invisible. It's the war we cannot see because, unlike Eve, we don't have live serpents speaking to us personally. All we witness are its effects much like wind across the sand.

Satan is named in scripture as the Father of Lies, a master deceiver, and even Eve noted that when God asked her point blank why she ate of the fruit. Her response was absolute truth. "The serpent deceived me." (Genesis 3:13) I've heard it said that her reply was blame shifting. That's certainly possible. Nevertheless, she still acknowledged the reality of what had occurred. The irrevocable truth that had opened her eyes to more than she was prepared to know. Until then, deceit wasn't even on the table as a thing *to* know and now she'd experienced its intense effects.

We all fall prey to this. We deceive ourselves and we're deceived by others. I think that's one of the reasons Job prayed the way he did for forgiveness for things which he and his kids might not even be *aware* of. Because the human heart, without the Holy Spirit's indwelling presence, is underneath the power of the curse. It is blind, deceived, and bent to wickedness. It needs regeneration lest it become wholly hardened like stone.

This is something none of us want to think about, admit, or believe is true, especially not of ourselves. Yet, it is. People are not born "good" as the actual definition of good is. We may think we are born "good enough" by human standards but even in that scope, there is always an incompletion there, something missing, a weak spot that most of us spend our entire lives trying to compensate for in ourselves and others.

My friend and I talked about being vessels and understanding that we were created to hold things. Memories, feelings, health, disease, thoughts, life, death, the very breath of God Himself. We were designed to do this, created to be messengers, to carry, embody, and contain things. Even if we try our hardest not to, we cannot overcome our designed destiny. When Jesus was talking to the disciples, He shared the story of a person possessed by a demon and compared it to a house. (Matthew 12:43-45) While the house had a demon living inside, it was messy and torn apart. Once the demon was banished, the house was cleared out, things put right, and rooms swept.

You'd think that'd be enough right there, but it's not. We miss the critical piece if we walk away before the story ends. It isn't enough for your house to be in order. It was meant to be lived in. The story continues that, as the house stood empty without anyone good coming to live in it, keep it in order, bring life and light and joy to it, it was an open breeding ground. The demon saw that so he gathered up a group of his friends and they descended upon the home, coming back in forces nearly impossible to evict. They desecrated and took over every square inch of the place, making it exponentially worse than it was when only the first demon lived there.

When someone says they don't believe in God, I wonder if they really mean they don't believe in the God they've been shown or told exists. The one people say He should be instead of the One He is. There are so many times when I have to agree because I don't believe in that God either. Many false ones exist and there is a reason the Old Testament is full to the brim with exhortations for the people to avoid, tear down, and rid their entire lives, countries, and world of these.

It is not merely that God is a jealous God as some like to focus on, as if His jealousy is the same as human jealousy seeking to be the only thing that matters. He doesn't need that from us. He created us and everything else that exists. Things we haven't even seen yet. Things we don't even know to imagine. He knows all that we can't possibly comprehend. There is nothing we can give Him or do for Him that He hasn't already done for Himself. That's not the foundation of jealousy for Him.

His jealousy is different. It's one that comes from a place of love, a place of providence, a place that says, "How dare you take the ones I have created to hold light, life, and breath and destroy the beauty of them!" He is not jealous for Himself the way we imagine He is.

God is jealous for OUR benefit.

We are the ones deceived. We are the ones enslaved. We are the ones begging for escape. We are the ones trapped by our own decisions. None of this is true of Him. Still, He chooses to enter into our captivity and become captive Himself, not to sin, but to its effects upon creation so that He can rescue us from the consequences of things we have no ability to free ourselves from apart from Him. It is an intentional servitude.

God knows that when our house is filled with His Spirit, there is no chance of defeating it. He knows that His life is so full and His Spirit so great that any demons, any powers of spiritual darkness, will *not* be able to take up residence within it. He never loses sight of His own identity. That's why He never loses sight of us. Because *we* were created to be vessels that hold and reflect Him. So, it is in clearing our houses out and opening the door to Him filling them that we are rendered safest.

Only a dangerous God can make a way like this. Only a dangerous God understands the gravity of deception. Only a dangerous God would implement a curse as a response to sin that He Himself intends to lift – with the same requirements of us as He gave Adam and Eve of free will, choice, and decision. That empty house *will* be indwelt. That empty house *will* be a vessel. A vessel that offers shelter and abode for whatever comes there to live. We get to choose who enters in. We get to select the residents.

This is why it is important to know what we value, to know who we are in light of the God who designed us, to know that *we will wrestle*. Those demons do come back, but this time they bang on the doors and throw things down the chimney. They break windows and try to burn it down from the outside in. They only win when we give them ground. They lose when we stand in our identity and say, "No matter what comes against me, I am a conqueror because of who lives in me."

We teach people how to treat us by what we allow. We teach them how to treat us by how we treat ourselves. How we tend to our house is how others will tend to it as well. That's why Satan tries so hard to get us to doubt our own value. He doesn't want us to know that when God comes, like C.S. Lewis so beautifully depicts,[71] and dwells in our home, He makes it bigger, better, more beautiful, with so much to offer that we never could have imagined. That's why our identity matters so much that it is made in His image. Because He Himself intends to live in it. Not just as a king, but as The King who *loves* us more than anything.

We are a *treasure,* a gift, a delight beyond all that we could ever imagine. That's why all the things the world throws at us that seem like things that will fulfill us (and do hold some level of pleasure and enjoyment) are never things that complete our identity. They satiate a level of desire as God intended them to, but they don't make us complete. It's a sappy scene and you either love it or hate it, but the truth is that we all need to recognize that it's actually true in the right setting what Jerry Maguire says, "*You* complete *me.*" God *does* complete us. He's the one that created us, began good works in us, designed good works for us to do *with* Him, and even now is preparing a place for us to live with Him. An immense, magnificent, glorious one that far exceeds our imaginations. Beside Him for eternity. He, not us, is the only one who can do this.

We've taken the scripture Paul wrote about our bodies being God's temples and let Satan twist that into another place of shame instead of exalting the beauty that it is. We've treated ourselves the way we'd never treat anyone else then expected *people* to come in and fill the void we've left with a different response than we have. We expect others to treat us better than we treat ourselves. Then we wonder why God doesn't love us and make us feel better about ourselves. We aren't starting from a place of identity. That's what Job did that we'd all do well to implement.

I know this might seem like an odd follow up to the conclusion of the last chapter that said we all need to get over ourselves, but stick with me for a minute. The reality is that we cannot elevate ourselves beyond what our original design was because it is in doing so that we lose our value. It's like painting over a priceless piece of art. It's like tearing down the Taj Mahal and building a production house. Or damming up Niagara Falls and putting in a little water fountain where it once roared over the rocks. That's what we don't realize we're doing when we make so much of ourselves and demanding God do so as well. We are looking at *us* all wrong. We are taking magnificence and making it microscopic which is exactly what Satan wants.

If you read Job, you see on repeat how Satan's goal was to get rid of Job's integrity. The one thing Job had in spades. The one thing God exalted. Job maintaining his integrity required continual sacrifice, continual connection to an identity that could be found only in God. It is what equipped him for the incredible good works he was doing that he lists out for his friends during one of his long talks. Job got it and he submitted his entire life to being God's physical vessel here on earth that demonstrated Him to the world.

It wasn't that Job was so great in and of himself. It was that *GOD* was so great through Job.

It's been said that integrity is doing the right thing when no one is looking. That was the story of Job. That's how he knew that his friends were wrong. He understood his own heart and his reverence for God. He knew that he was more concerned about being in a wrong place with God and ending up right where he found himself – surrounded by tragedy and leveled by devastation – as a result. The fact that he was there yet his heart really was one of surrendered service to God told him that this destruction and loss *wasn't* his doing at all. It was God's.

I could be wrong, but I think that's why it was to God that Job assigned the troubles that had come upon him. He knew that God had the ability to prevent them, to create prosperity and allow disaster. Although he didn't know that Satan was behind the attacks, he wasn't wrong in assigning God some responsibility for his condition. God did bring Job to Satan's attention not just once but twice and asked Satan if he'd considered Job. It wasn't a passing mention, but an intentional conversation. He didn't *cause* Satan to attack Job, He just allowed it to happen – within the limits He set that to us don't seem much like limits. It seems more like a grand, sweeping permission slip that's wholly unjust as we understand justice especially towards a person as righteous as Job. Historians have debated whether Job was even a Jew, so he may not have even been one of "God's chosen people" yet here he was creating history itself because of his reverence for God.

I think we underestimate the value God places on us being vessels and that's why we try to exalt ourselves. Job might not have been spending his life trying to make himself mean more than he should have, but he did get a lesson in being a vessel in a new way during his period of immense suffering. At no point in the entire story do we hear that Job compromised his integrity nor that he sinned. In fact, the book tells us that Job didn't sin at all in what he said at the beginning.

When God finally comes on the scene both to talk to Job and then to tell Job's friends they'd spoken incorrectly of Him unlike Job, it seems safe to draw the conclusion that throughout the entire situation, Job never fell prey to sin. Yet, what was Job's response? Repentance. He literally said to God, "My ears had heard of you but now my eyes have seen you. Therefore I despise myself and repent in dust and ashes." Job *repented*. Why? If he'd done nothing wrong, if God endorsed him at the beginning, endorsed him at the end, and Job did not sin, what required repentance? It makes no sense, at least not from an earthly perspective.

As I write this, today is Ash Wednesday. It's a day when people go to church or Mass and have ashes drawn on their foreheads as a symbol and reminder of the journey that surrendering our lives is intended to be. The one Jesus exampled.

"While we were still sinners, Christ died for us."
(Romans 5:8)

For the first time that I can recall in my lifetime, Ash Wednesday happens to coincide with Valentines Day. While I agree that Valentines is a commercialized holiday, I think there is a message here that we can choose to take away. Ashes and love mingled together can easily be translated as,

"There is no greater love than this: that a person would lay down his life for the sake of his friends."
(John 15:13, Aramaic Bible in Plain English)

It's interesting to me how many times in scripture we see people who aren't actively or, as far as we know, even passively sinning against God put on sackcloth and ashes. They fast. Some weep. All seek the Lord. They act in intercession and ask for His intervention. They look for His involvement. They mourn over sins they may have not personally committed but ones that nevertheless affect the body of believers. Their desire isn't that just *one* of us be right with God, but that *all* of us are. They long for unity.

That's what God required of Job – to intercede for his friends, to be the go between to restore right relationship with them and God, to lay down his life (that for all intents and purposes looked like it had already been destroyed) – for his friends. That's when the surrender of Job's life occurred by him willingly *choosing* to give it over *despite* his friends' sins against God and against him. That's what it means to be a priest, an intercessor, a prophet, a leader, a friend. A co-believer in the Body and Bride of Christ.

When we try to change that identity into something else, something *we* think it should be, we miss its magnificence. Only God can make something magnificent. Only God is big enough to make something mortal have eternal value. Only God can make the lowly things of the world shame the wise because only God works in the currency of eternity. That's why we need Him. Otherwise, our lives have absolutely no meaning, no point, no value other than the immediate gratification we can find to satisfy the flesh. Not all those things are bad. Many are wonderful gifts. They just don't last.

I've wrestled with how to approach this Ash Wednesday. Although I usually celebrate neither Ash Wednesday nor Valentines Day, I think there is a reason they are specifically combined this year of all years. I'm in that follow up season. The one *after* the worst of disaster has occurred, the one *after* God has met with me, the one where it's not that God has personally asked me to stand in the gap for other people but where He's asking me,

> *"Will you lay down the rest of your life intentionally? Will you allow unity to be the call on your days, regardless of how unfair, unjust, or brutal life or people seem? Will you, like my servants past, allow yourself to become an intercessor, one who mourns not for yourself but for all my people, who surrenders your vessel to be my vessel in ways you never wanted to conceive? Will you grieve as my heart grieves – not for your own loss, but for the rest of humanity?"*

That's what Ash Wednesday and Valentines Day this year represent to me. Love and death intermingled into something so much more than me. I've stopped believing in coincidence so suffice it to say that it's also divine timing that Easter falls the very day after my birthday and Good Friday the day before it this year. Appropriately, I feel like I am living out Holy Saturday in 2024. Like I am mired in the day between death and life, the now and the not yet. The "tension" as a friend of ours so often likes to call it.

There is something about willingly giving yourself up to death, which is exactly what Jesus did, that's different than the destruction that comes on you and forces you to sit in ashes not of your own choosing like Job initially did. Twice we see him sit in ashes but each occurrence was for a different reason. The first time wasn't about repentance. It was grief. It was loss and sorrow and a deep abiding anguish that, as boils spread across his body, made the ash heap the only place he could be comforted.

The second time was repentance. But not for sin. For perspective. For understanding. For a knowledge of God that as Job said, was "too wonderful for me to know." Tragedy *never* feels wonderful. Grief never makes you joyful. Not in the immediate. These things *feel* in our humanity like they are going to bury us and render us helpless for all the rest of our days. That's what a limited, *human* perspective of God leaves us with, no matter how surrendered and service-oriented we are.

I don't think Job had to go through all of this in order to live out his days as a dedicated servant of God's. I think he likely would have continued to do that no matter what because that's how strong his reverence for God was. But I think tragedy changed his perspective and his understanding of who God really is in ways that were worth everything he endured.

I think, like me, Job would tell you that if that is what you get to know of God, you'd do it all again. Even though you'd never wish it on your worst enemy. Even though it is the absolute worst thing you've ever experienced. Even though you feel while you're in it like you are stuck in a Holy Saturday that has no end, that Easter will never come and the resurrected you will never exist. Even though hope itself feels like it has been conquered and that the sting of death does in fact win.

There is something about getting to a place of grief and yet intentional surrender that changes absolutely everything. If you've seen the series *The Chosen*, the last episode in Season 3 shows a frustrated Simon Peter.[72] The writers paint a picture that isn't in scripture but isn't intended to be. Its purpose is to show us humanity in contrast to Jesus. To help us engage with the wrestling of Simon Peter (and his wife) that we all go through in some capacity if we really want to know and be with Jesus. Simon is grieving. Deeply. He's also angry. Things have not gone the way he expected and he feels leveled by reality. Especially the one where he knows Jesus *could* have spared him and his family this pain and suffering but He didn't.

There is a sense of injustice that happens when we expect God to do things for us because we are in relationship with Him. There is a closeness that we begin to foster in His presence that makes us feel as if we are protected. I imagine Job felt that. Satan knew it existed. We *are* protected. The things that God never allows to pass through His hands that *would* affect us had He said yes is probably so long that we have no idea what tragedy we have been spared.

Yet, the things He does allow are the places where we wrestle. We want to know why He says yes to healing some people, some diseases, some situations, and others He doesn't. We want to understand how we can be in places that He has quite literally, like Simon Peter, called us to be and yet still we end up suffering. It makes no earthly sense. I don't think it ever will. It shouldn't. We are made for Eden – the one where no serpent can get in, where no temptation can seize us, where no deception ever gets a chance. Where the curse does not exist.

People have hurt me in this season in ways that I've felt some days like I simply cannot bear. Maybe you too have been there. It would be so easy for all of us to identify what sound like really justifiable reasons to walk away, to leave, to tout the mantra of things we hear out there – church hurt, toxic family members, trauma, hurt people hurting people, boundaries, etc. It's not that those things don't have their place. It's just that the most important narrative is remembering that to choose *only* those things would be to leave before Ash Wednesday. To stop before Job's story ends. To hear God's answer, then walk away.

That's not complete surrender. That's not reconciliation. That's ending the story in process, in the middle of it before the most important parts occur. It's leaving the house swept clean but empty, exposed to danger. It's exalting myself to being the kind of vessel *I* want to be instead of the one God created me to be. The one that *He* fills. The one that empties itself so that it is with *Him* that I am made able to do things I could not on my own possibly bear. Things that would break my own strength in an instant. To make *myself* the author of my story (and others') instead of Him.

Do I think I'll get this right in a day or even a season, maybe a few years? No. I think it's intended to be a lifelong journey. That's what relationship is. That's how reconciliation works. If I want to enchant myself with the God He really is, I need to disenchant myself with the version of me that I have manufactured. If I want to reconcile my disenchantment with the God I deemed Him to be, I have to surrender to the One that actually exists. The God that truly lives bids me to worship, to honor Him, to represent Him – not in my own strength, but out of my lack and with His abundance.

On days when I feel abandoned, lost, and overlooked, I have a choice. I can look to the people that used to be my companions in expectation that all be easily fixed or I can worship the God who was and is and is to come, the One who makes a way in the wilderness and streams in the desert, and I can believe that this isn't the end of our story either. No matter how it all goes here, the day of resurrection is coming. Redemption is occurring. Unity in eternity is literally being built by Jesus Himself in our Father's house. Who am I to say no to that because life here is dredged in grief and mired in sorrow in more seasons than I want to count?

Tragedy has its place. Grief has its purpose. Loss carries with it value. Sorrow brings lament. All these things were intended and necessary in an upside-down kingdom. Suffering leads the way to being the likeness of God, the image-bearers He always meant. It's the way we'd never choose. We make so much of ourselves. Yet we are so much less than we think and at once so much more than we ever imagined.

It is not always from sin that we must repent, turn, and walk in a different direction. Sometimes it is out of love that we choose the repentance of deeper submission, eternal perspective, and unity not just with God ourselves but between God and *all* people. Sometimes what we give up aren't the things that distract us but the reliance we have on our own understanding of who God is, how He moves, and our identity.

Sometimes what we fast from during our own wilderness treks aren't the things we indulge in but rather the things that make us believe we are less than, not enough, and unworthy. Because sometimes what we are intended to replace them with is an enchantment with a holy God that is so majestic, so powerful, so all-knowing, so sacrificial, and so loving that we cannot help but stand in humble awe of Him and desire to reflect *that* God to the world. A God so dangerous *and* so good that He does allow tragedy because tragedy isn't what will kill us. It's the absence of *Him*, of His Presence. This is what should linger long and make us ponder much. Sometimes it is in being less than we thought that we discover we are more than we ever imagined.

Vessels. Made for the Almighty.

Chapter Twenty Four: Perseverance

"It always seems impossible until it's done."

~Nelson Mandela[73]

I was born in the middle of a blizzard in Michigan where snow piles higher than fenceposts. During my lifetime, I've experienced some powerful storms. Hurricanes in Alabama, floods in Texas, tornadoes in both, ice that shut down the state and absolute downpours that forced me to stop on the side of the road in Arkansas because I couldn't see two inches in front of me. I've witnessed incredible electrical storms in the summer skies of eastern Pennsylvania along with some heavy winter snowstorms.

As I write this chapter, we are under a tornado watch. Pretty common for Texas this time of year. Here, spring especially brings some powerful thunderstorms. New life, new growth occurring against the backdrop of potential destruction and death. In Texas, lightning stretches across the sky wider than the eye can see. Thunder echoes so loudly at times you jump out of your seat. Some storms are so dangerous that we take shelter in the bathtub. After the clouds clear, some of us drive around to assess the damage. There is something about witnessing the aftermath of brutal storms that brings a sense of awe.

I wondered for the longest time why God came to Job in a whirlwind. At first glance it seems so callous and uncaring. Everything had just fallen apart and Job was being mercilessly attacked from every direction. To ask him to hold on to his integrity at this juncture seemed downright unjust. Then, instead of extending comfort and doling out a tender gentleness, storm clouds started stirring up dust and the wind began whipping around Job's feverish, boil-stricken body. A storm was how God finally showed up.

In scripture, there are two primary reasons whirlwinds occurred. One was a demonstration of God's power and might, the other His righteous anger. When God showed up inside the whirlwind to talk to Job, I think most of us would question what He was doing. Why not come in a calmer manner? Job had been through enough. Even if it was necessary that He come with some intensity, why not more like He did with Moses? How did a whirlwind make His top choice?

It wasn't until I experienced my own modern day versions of Job's story that I began to understand why God showed up in a storm. There is something about going through extreme situations that acquaint us with need differently. Sometimes it's the point where despair begins to overtake our perspective and grief itself isn't even the worst thing we have to bear. I've been through enough pain in deep enough measure for me to know that there is no way to intellectualize our way out of everything. There may be people who tell you otherwise, but to do so is to do the same thing as Adam and Eve. It is to walk past the tree of life, pluck the fruit of the tree of knowledge, trade in dependency for death, and leave a cavernous hole in our understanding.

I think one of the reasons we experience pain and suffering at such intense levels is because we need to know that knowledge was never the answer. Knowing things was never going to save us. Knowledge doesn't have that kind of power. If it did, Jesus wouldn't have needed to go to the cross. He knew the answers to all our questions. He had the solutions for all of our problems. He understood the very things that hold our cells together and our original design was completely clear to Him. He wasn't confused like us and He didn't need the knowledge we chase after every day. He had all of that in spades. Neverthless, He died, suffered, and was separated from the Father – for our rescue.

The answer was never knowledge. That's just what we convinced ourselves it was. When Eve looked at the fruit, she determined in her own heart that it was good for wisdom. God never said that. Even the serpent never said, "you will be wise." When he spoke to Eve, he told her she would know good and evil. (Genesis 3:4) Of course, he left out the part about how she'd gain knowledge but not comprehension, knowledge but not understanding, knowledge but not clarity, knowledge but not power. She would know things she couldn't handle, things she couldn't make sense of, things she couldn't comprehend. That knowledge might be *of* things – *of* good and evil – but it wouldn't mean that she would be any wiser. She *wasn't* going to be like God. That was the deception. She would never be like God in the sense she expected because wisdom belongs to Him alone and it cannot be plucked from a tree.

Growing up primarily in Texas, I've come to appreciate storms. Many people here put on tin roofs just so they can sit on the porch and hear the rain fall. Storms are an experience in Texas, not just something that happens outside to water the lawn. Storms aren't things that we stay indoors and away from. When the rain starts to fall, especially after a dry season, you'll find most of us Texans outdoors soaking it up, sitting on the porch in rocking chairs and talking about how it feels so good. In Texas, storms are something you feel coming in your bones, just like autumn arrives in New England in the fall.

Physical suffering will do things to a person that losing anything else does not, and physical pain can come as a result of emotional loss. Losing someone who mattered more to you than anyone else can truly break your heart. It can physically manifest in ways we don't often grant enough consideration for. I know because it happened to me last year. It was more than I could bear. God was merciful in that the actual circumstances of certain things lasted 40 days on the dot. That's not a coincidence. Like Jesus in the wilderness, I think the timing was divine and providential – both spiritually and physically. I don't know how I would have physically survived if those specific things had lasted much longer. There were moments during that time when I needed God to be so near. To be gentle, to be tender, to extend to me the ability to pour out my deep wounding and experience His deep comfort in return.

Then there were times during that same 40 day period when, like Job, I needed God in a whirlwind. One who was bigger than everything I was enduring. One who saw what I couldn't. One who revealed Himself to me. One who was powerful beyond measure. One who spoke with an authority that pulled me out of my despair. His goodness was never going to do that. The advice I was given by people during that period – to focus on God's goodness - was well-intended but misguided. I was in the middle of spiritual warfare. So was Job. Goodness wasn't the piece (or peace) either of us needed. Both of us were in need of something greater.

That's what we don't realize God can offer. Where we might think we need tenderness and goodness, sometimes what we actually need is power. Not a power of our own, but rather an awareness of someone else's power, someone bigger than us upon which we can rely. Someone who will fight our unseen enemy. Someone who is so safe and so dangerous all in one that we can trust Him to do for us what we cannot do for ourselves.

If 2019 had not played out as it did in my life followed a few years later by 2023, I don't know if I would have understood God's response in the way I do now. I don't know that I would have developed an appreciation for it where I actually have gratitude now for Him showing up in a whirlwind rather than it being calm. There's something about experiencing things that are so out of control, so outrageous, so incredibly not okay at all that makes you *need* a God bigger than it all. That's what I didn't know. It isn't just about knowing that the God of Heaven and Earth exists. It's about experiencing Him in His fullness.

There comes a point in both grief and in battle when we need to know that someone other than us is in charge. Someone we can trust. There comes a time when despair can feel so deep and death so near that, like Job, you *do* wish you'd never been born. It feels in that moment that having never even experienced joy would be worth not having to experience this. I don't think God gets upset with us for feeling things so deeply because He does too. Over and over in scripture we see how He not only longs for us but also is deeply grieved at ever having made humanity. He aches over what it has done to itself, how it has marred its own glory, and the slavery to which it has ensnared itself. He too wrestles with the emotions caused by a world gone wrong.

The book of Job is often viewed as a long discourse on pain. That's certainly how I viewed it the many dozens of times I read it. Then I really began to experience the depths of it in my own life and my perspective changed. That's when I realized that pain is a major part of the storyline, but it isn't the focus. The real landscape of the book of Job is found in the heavenly realms. If we want to understand its ending, we have to go back to its beginning. If we want to grasp God's response, we need to understand His viewpoint.

When the book of Job opens, Job is prosperous. He's protected by God. His protection, however, is made up of only one thing: God's word. That's all it took. God spoke and it simply was. Just like He'd spoken creation into existence. Job did nothing himself to make sure that he was protected by God. He couldn't. Job just did what he understood God wanted of him so he could be in right relationship with God. Job sought to be righteous and holy before God. But protection was out of his hands. That's something God gave Job when and how He chose.

I think it's important for us to take a moment to understand that what applied to Job likewise applies to us. Job couldn't create or ensure his own protection – and neither can we. Job sought relationship and rightness before God. That was his main life purpose. The same is true for us. We aren't needy creatures because we're somehow broken.

Need is inherent to our being.

It is our design, our DNA, our destiny. Need isn't what makes us less than. It isn't the result of sin. It's what we were intended for all along. Need is our way back to Eden. It is our only hope, and dependency, our saving grace.

The reason I think it's so critical for us to grasp and hold onto this truth is because what God did next, what happened to Job, is exactly what's going to happen to us. God's word protected Job. Then He spoke again. This time, He changed His approach. The angels came to present themselves to God which is apparently their custom and this time Satan came too. Satan didn't ask God about Job. God brought Job up. *God's own words* removed Job's hedge of protection and provision. If Proverbs is correct that our words hold the power of life and death,[74] we have to remember the original source of them. God is the Author of all things in existence, including language.

When God changes direction, which usually comes with some serious disruption to our life's circumstances, it is important for us to remember that He hasn't changed His purposes. He just shifted how we are going to experience them. We are the ones who feel like we're on shifting sand and to a degree we are. Circumstances are always a moving target and things we were never intended to build our lives upon. What made the Garden of Eden safe in any measure was never Adam and Eve's circumstances. Things were still in process there. Serpents who could tempt mankind got in and, at some point, even with purpose and capability and a job to do that Adam wholly fulfilled on his own, God Himself said it wasn't good. Our circumstances – even right within the very Eden God has created for us to live – can be bad.

Safety is found in a Person, not a place, and *that's* what we don't want to have to accept or allow to be true. We want to be independent. The farther into western culture especially that you get, the more apparent this is. I live in Texas. If there is one thing just about every Texan will tell you, it is that they are independent. We fly the state flag at the same height as the national one because we can. It's not arrogance – we did earn the right. Yet, it's been transposed into a form of independence that defies our true reality.

We cannot actually live independent. Maybe of the federal government (with a whole lot of effort) but certainly not as individual people. God will never let that happen. It's not how He made us and if He's really always working for our good, then He's never going to let us become anything except dependent. As I said before, He'll walk us right to the gates of hell offering an invitation to dependency but it's not something He'll force us to choose. The choice is always ours. From God's perspective, when He brought up Job and when He brings up us, it's not because "we need a lesson" or are always "living in sin." Job and Jesus were neither yet both suffered in immense measure.

**God allows our circumstances to change course
because He's issuing an invitation to war.**

That's really how the book of Job begins. It starts with authority in dispute. In certain translations of Job, rather than being called Satan, he's titled as the Adversary. Adversary means one who opposes, attacks, contests, fights against determinedly, relentlessly, and often in a hostile manner.[75] Adversary here is also one who defies authority of. The contrast between Satan and Job is clear. Satan knows God on a level Job doesn't and still Job serves God and shuns evil. Satan however doesn't. That's really the point. Spiritual warfare. Ending the war in the heavenly realms so that good, good as it actually is not our conjured up human definition, conquers evil forever.

I know it sounds like a fairytale, yet, one of the greatest theologians of our time, C.S. Lewis, wrote, *"Some day you will be old enough to start reading fairytales again."*[76] Some day you may suffer enough to believe in them too. That's the thing about pain. It beckons us to go deeper. It calls us to seek more. It forces us into places and realms we might otherwise never travel. As much as we like to look at the surface of Adam and Eve's story and assume that they just did something wrong and now we're all stuck, the plot is so much bigger. An eternal God would never reduce Himself down to our limited understanding.

Another important piece for us to recognize is that the invitation to story is also an invitation to war. It is making the invisible visible and we are the place where all that occurs. All of us know this on some inherent level, but we can deny its truth if we wish. However, suffering is a crucible of sorts that, when experienced, forces us to acknowledge that things we cannot see do affect us. Thoughts, emotions, germs, wind, gravity, the list goes on and on. It's not really all that far-fetched to believe that the spiritual realm does the same thing. The hard part is believing that it is a truer reality than everything we touch and see.

Revelation tells us all this will disappear and be replaced with new things. We should be celebrating because how grand of a story and experience that will be. All our dreams and all this hard work we put in will actually one day come true. And it will be *better*. Better than all we could ever ask or imagine as Paul says. Instead, because things are so hard and pain so difficult and suffering so immense in the here and now, we find it near impossible to endure much less believe in something that *feels* so unrealistic. We need a big God for a big situation and I think that's why God came in a whirlwind.

The point at which Job found himself was near despair. His friends were useless, serving at this point to only increase his misery not comfort him in it. His wife had been handed her own life-altering set of circumstances with nowhere better than Job to take it. His community had completely turned their backs on him and now were mocking him to his face. Even children were bold enough to come spit on him.

Job's health wasn't getting any better. If anything, it was worsening. He'd been ravaged to the point that he was emaciated. Gaunt. A shell of the man he once was, unrecognizable to himself and his friends. They were already there to grieve with him but seeing him, witnessing his condition, pained them even more. He wasn't at all the Job they knew. His body and circumstances had more than betrayed him. Again, this is the point at which we'd all expect someone more like Mother Teresa to show up than we would a God who comes at you in a whirlwind.

If we are to persevere, if we are to endure long and much, if we are to be like Jesus, we are not going to be able at times to rely on our own strength. Some seasons, maybe even some lifetimes, we are going to find ourselves in modern day versions of Job's shoes more times than we can count. It is in these instances when our one and only rescue will come in whirlwind. We *need* a God so powerful.

Last year, the last thing I needed was something gentle.

Something tender. Something that sounded like it would soothe my aching, battered soul. I needed a God bigger and more in control than the people around me. I needed a God who didn't try to tell me that His goodness was great. I didn't need sense made of my surroundings. There was no hope of them making sense.

Deceit isn't sensible and spiritual warfare isn't founded on earthly logic.

I needed the very same thing I said Job did at the beginning of this book. I needed an audience with a God who I now knew had not relinquished His throne. Because for all intents and purposes, that is exactly how 2023 *felt*. It *felt* and in many ways *looked* like He had given it all up. Like He had given over the reins of control to people and places that had no business holding them.

People I trusted to be God-honoring, truth-telling people weren't doing battle with me. Some were actively working against me in fact. It was confusing. The very places community was supposed to hold me most were the places where, just like Job's situation, they disappeared or worse – told me the same things Job's friends told Job. It wasn't at all helpful. It wasn't at all good. Telling me God was good, telling me love was how scripture defines it, telling me I'd be okay when I was exactly the opposite wasn't at all what I needed.

When you find yourself in the middle of a spiritual war between God and Satan, you must expect that many people around you won't understand. Unless they're going through it too, more often than not they probably won't understand your experience. Even if they are enduring in large part what you are too as Job's wife was, that doesn't mean they'll share your response or see things from your point of view. Sometimes it really is just you and God and this is what I think we have to prepare ourselves for. Some seasons as you walk through the valley of the shadow of death, it is His rod that protects you, His staff that comforts you. Not words, not hugs, not tenderness. Just truth.

Sometimes we need a powerful God. One bigger than all we can fathom because the battle on our horizons, the one inside our homes, sometimes the one that attacks our physical bodies – it is a spiritual one, and that enemy is so much bigger than us. He is more powerful and crafty than we realize. If he could get to Adam and Eve in the most safe place in all existence, if he could get to Jesus in the wilderness, if he could get to Job the most righteous man on the planet, then he can and *will* get to us. Sometimes God will let him.

That is what we have to prepare ourselves for. Instead of assuming that God isn't good and that He owes us, we have to start viewing our lives from the lens God had at the beginning of Job so we can have the response Job did at the end.

M y life in great measure has been an experiment in perseverance. There are those who, when you say something like that, respond with how you're just making yourself a victim. I don't think that's the case. Job actually was a victim but his laments weren't with a victim mindset. They were built on pain and he was commended in James for perseverance because he didn't surrender his faith. I've lived long enough now to know faith is where I will return time and time again. No matter how far I run or how deep the pain, God is always bigger. That's not some realization I have or some intellectual acknowledgement to which I force myself to assent. God being bigger for me has been an experience. But it's one I have to come back to time and time again.

I think it was the same for Job. Whirlwinds are an experience. They aren't something someone tells you about and you understand. It has been the power of experiencing an undertow during an incoming hurricane that has taught me how strong the ocean is. It is being in a place that mere minutes earlier was just a puddle and now could sweep me with rushing water straight to my death that has shown me how dangerous floods can be. It is standing under icicles that have frozen and are cascading down the side of a rocky mountain that I've realized how tiny I am. It has been having the electricity go out, the winds howl around the house in high pitched screams, and sitting in the bathroom with a battery powered radio and a flashlight that has acquainted me with just how little protection a house really offers us.

Yet, the most powerful thing of all has been witnessing the aftermath. It is driving around a neighborhood, sometimes unable to even get through all the debris that you realize just how terrible the storm was and sometimes how much worse it could have been. Sometimes it is the worst it could have been. I think that was Job's story. I'm not God so I won't say that with certainty, but I think there is an extremity to Job's story that most of us never experience. Although my life isn't done, I'm glad to say that that hasn't thus far been me. I am grateful for that degree of God's mercy towards me.

Nevertheless, what I have experienced *has* leveled me. It has made it impossible some days to breathe. It has nearly conquered me. To this, I think both Jesus and Job relate. You don't start sweating like droplets of blood when you're doing okay. Jesus didn't go into His arrest, flogging, and crucifixion being okay. He wasn't okay or He wouldn't have asked for prayer. He wasn't at peace or He wouldn't have begged the Father for another way. That's just not how suffering works. Suffering *should* render us speechless, it *should* make us incapable, it *should* have an effect.

Suffering is intended to be experienced.

That's why suffering has to be met with perseverance. It is the only way. You aren't going to escape suffering. You can medicate it. You can numb it. You can run from it. You can even choose to end your life and land face to face with Jesus. That doesn't mean that you escaped. You wouldn't be there if you hadn't endured suffering to some degree. If it had no effect. Suffering always has an effect. It always has a purpose and there is no amount of "getting your life right" or "making all the right decisions" or even "mustering through and soldiering on" that is going to change this.

One of the things I've had to reconcile with about suffering is that it only matters in small measure whether or not its at our own hands. Suffering is part of the human experience and it doesn't matter how good or bad you are. It simply is. It is because the one thing that was true when Adam and Eve got here that remains true today and was true for Job and Jesus is we are all born into war.

A spiritual battlefield in the heavenly places is the backdrop of all our days.

There is no amount of self-improvement or "taking your power back" that is going to rid you of this story. You were born to spiritual warfare, so like Job, you have to choose how to live your days. James, the same one that commended Job for persevering, also wrote,

> "*Consider it pure joy, my brothers and sisters, whenever you face trials of many kinds, because you know that the testing of your faith produces perseverance. Let perseverance finish its work so that you may be mature and complete, not lacking anything.*" (James 1:2-4)

This may be one of the most overquoted yet misapplied scriptures. In our independent-minded culture, we see this as a call for us to do something. To conjure up courage and force ourselves to believe "the pain is worth the gain." Yet, that's not what I see Jesus and Job do. They did what James prescribes instead. They *let* perseverance finish its work. Just as God has allowed so much pain, suffering, and spiritual warfare to occur, we also have something we have to *let* serve a purpose. Perseverance.

Perseverance is a finishing work. It isn't where we start. It's where we end. It is the part that keeps us holding on when we're at the end of our ropes, hanging by a single thread. Perseverance is the hardest part for the hardest period and it often looks nothing like we think it will. Perseverance is a steadfastness, a "continued steady belief or efforts, withstanding discouragement or difficulty," and "implies resolute and unyielding holding on in following a course of action."[77] It is "not giving up. It is persistence and tenacity, the effort required to do something and keep doing it till the end, even if it's hard."[78] Sometimes perseverance looks like, against all odds, simply continuing to breathe.

This is what I mean when I say we have to set our minds before our circumstances happen. I know that isn't always possible because some of us, many of us, are born into things that we have no clue how to view until they've already deeply shaped our perspective. In many ways, all human beings are born as victims. That's why we have to choose our mindset. We have to *choose* renewal and regeneration like Romans 12:1-3 (AMPC) reminds us. Perseverance isn't a requirement because maturity is always optional. Aging may occur naturally, but maturity is an investment not everyone chooses to make no matter how old they get.

What James tells us when he says to consider it pure joy isn't that we look upon our trials as enjoyable experiences. Jesus didn't do that. Neither did Job. They recognized them as storms, as painful endurances, as things neither one of them wanted to go through. God Himself says this of His own perseverance with mankind over and over in the Bible. Perseverance isn't enjoyable for anyone, God included. Yet, it is necessary for everyone.

God's perseverance doesn't have the same effect as ours. He doesn't need the maturity we do. He isn't lacking anything. However, He knows that we do. He does want to make things complete. He says over and over how He is unifying things, bringing them together, how He is *finishing* what He set out to do. His work is not complete though its effects echo throughout all the annals of history. So, for our sakes and His own, he is doing battle with Satan. He is making all things new. He is ending this order of things so that a better one can reign. That requires conquering evil and ending its day.

Perseverance is what ensures that as many as are willing to join His family do. He is willing to suffer long and much to rescue as many as possible. Just as He gave Adam and Eve a choice, He does the same for you and me. He will never stop doing so until the time of history is complete. Our trials will be many. They will vary in size and kind. James assures us of this fact. Our faith, the one thing we need to make it through, is guaranteed to be tested. Testing makes it stronger and its strength in turn matures us, makes us complete, fills those voids so that there is nothing we lack.

That was always God's purpose. The one in Eden, where we were intended to live in peace? That hasn't changed. Our circumstances have. But His goal of being *with* us, of living out His name? That too is the same. If He has to allow things, so do we. If Job had to allow suffering to inform his understanding, so will we. If Jesus had to endure injustice and pain, we will too. It is reconciling ourselves to the fact that this isn't a *bad* thing that is the hard piece. Our God is a good One. Greater than all we can fathom. But He is also mighty, dangerous, and without limit. He is the one we need.

As much as the whirlwind was a demonstration of God's power and might to Job, I believe it was also a display of His anger to Satan. If we view the end of the book in light of its beginning, we see that this entire book is a roadmap to spiritual warfare. The story isn't about Job although it most certainly affected him and he is commended for and blessed as a result of his persevering. This book is about God. It is about God reminding Satan that his day is limited, his power restrained, his effects restricted. It is God's unspoken invitation to us to trust Him as we join Him in things invisible. Things, like Job, we are not privy to.

We have to recall that God issued Satan an invitation to war and Satan took Him up on it. Not once but twice. All of heaven and a good portion of earth witnessing its effects in one way or another. God doesn't want to see His creation suffering. He doesn't enjoy our pain. He's not a masochist though He understands better than all of us that this is the only way. That's why He limits things – not just for us, but for Himself too. He cares that Satan is as evil as he is and He has no intention of letting that permanently go. Even now there are limits. Just like we witness the aftermath of some storms and recognize just how much worse they could have been.

When God came to Job in the whirlwind, I think in large measure it was a relief. It assured Job that when all *felt* lost, when hope *seemed* gone, when despair *appeared* to have won, God was still on the throne. His strength was apparent and His anger revealed in both earthly and heavenly realms. I think it is a reassurance to our soul to know that God is bigger than what we know.

This world seeks after knowledge like it is gold. The same knowledge that we traded eternal life for in Eden is the same knowledge we chase after today. Yet, God tells us that our *faith* is the gold – that it's even more precious.[79] We act like if we just know more, we'll be saved. We'll have life again. It'll be as if we hadn't chosen between eternal life and the fruit of knowing good and evil. Yet, that's never the case.

No matter how much knowledge we gain, we never become God. In fact, the wisest – not just most knowledgeable but *wisest* – man to ever live, Solomon, clarified for us that this wasn't the answer. He said:

> *"When I applied my mind to know wisdom and to observe man's labor on earth – his eyes not seeing sleep day or night – then I saw all that God has done. No one can comprehend what goes on under the sun. Despite all his efforts to search it out, man cannot discover its meaning. Even if a wise man claims he knows, he cannot really comprehend it."* (Ecclesiastes 8:16-17)

Knowledge will never have the same effect as faith. It can't. Faith is a form of dependency – the very way in which we were created. The very thing we need most. That's why chasing a life that enchants us isn't ever going to satisfy us in this place. That will always be chasing a fantasy.

If there is one thing we have to reconcile with more than anything, it is the God He really is. The One warring for our rescue in the heavenlies. One establishing everything under His Son's feet. One preparing a new place for us to live. One making a way in the wilderness and streams in the wasteland. Disenchantment is a healthy thing so long as the object with which we disenchant ourselves is a version of God and a version of life that we conjured up. We may long for it, eternity being set in our hearts by God Himself, but the one we need can only be seen with an eternal perspective. One that requires dependency. One that relies on faith.

Our faith is our most precious commodity because it is what bridges the gap between here and there, now and not yet, the Eden that was and the Eden to come, heaven and earth. Dolly Parton is quoted as saying, "Storms make trees take deeper roots."[80] The tree of the knowledge of good and evil served its purpose and no longer exists, but the Tree of Life did exactly as she said. No longer planted merely in the Garden of Eden, whose gates are closed to us, the Tree of Life has multiplied and grown. Revelation tells us it now stands on *each* side of the river of the water of life in eternity. It still has fruit, but its purpose now is even greater: "The leaves of the tree are for the healing of the nations." (Revelation 22:2, NIV)

If there is one way I don't want to end this book, it is by wrapping it up in a bow. Life is not going to be okay, and I think it's important we reconcile ourselves to that. It is our very expectation that it will be that gets us into so much trouble. Life is quite often like the beginning of creation – the part where "darkness was over the surface of the deep." (Genesis 1:2, NIV) There's a chaos that exists when things are incomplete, when the Spirit of God is hovering, when our lives are yet to be fully formed, while they're still in certain measure empty.

I think it is when we see it from this place – the one where things are not as they should be, but they are *in process* of being made complete – that we can rest. I think this is how faith works. It teaches us to do what we were always designed to. It teaches us the dependency on God that Adam and Eve knew. They had no idea about Satan or about spiritual warfare. They didn't need to. Same as Job. These things weren't necessary for them, or for us, to know. What was most important is what God revealed to Job. What He reveals to us. That He is on the throne. That He can be trusted. That our circumstances are not our truest reality. That faith, dependency, is key.

Faith is supposed to be the lens through which we choose to see our circumstances instead of our circumstances being the lens through which we view our faith.

Faith is what turns the upside down kingdom right side up.

We're all suffering from the vertigo of being off balance. Faith rights the ship and levels our viewpoint. It changes our horizon and equips us for living the present even though the present isn't permanent. That's the place I think we have to get to if we are going to make it. The one Job reached. The one that reminded Satan he isn't going to win the war in the heavenlies. God loves us too much to allow this to be the full story.

Faith is our invitation to join Him in the story that makes our stories carry weight. If we are going to let perseverance do its work to make us complete, to mature us, to ensure we really do lack nothing, then we have to accept that we don't need a God who is safe. We don't need Eden this side of the grave. We can traverse a cursed earth and war-torn place and still be safe. It's us who believe we can't. It's God who comes in a whirlwind to tell us we can. Not by telling us how great we are, but by revealing how immense He is.

Storms change things. In one fell swoop, they can level an entire landscape. They can also give us faith. They can take our pain and put it in perspective. They can invite us into a war in the spiritual realms that, rather than destroying us, rather than pitting us against each other, makes us both humble and brave. Job was both by the end. It takes humility to pray for your friends and stand like Jesus, as priest and intermediary between God and men. Especially ones who have hurt you. Ones who completely misrepresent God but are certain the entire time they haven't.

It also takes humility to rebuild. Job lived to see his great-great grandchildren. He lived to see his herds double in size. He lived to witness a life he himself didn't create and could, again, be ripped away in an instant. God gave Job absolutely no guarantees. Rather, He gave the gift of perseverance – twice. First it was through suffering and pain in extreme doses and extreme ways. Second was the rebuild.

It takes a long time to wait on animals to be born, to raise each of them, for every herd and flock to increase slowly. Thousands upon thousands of animals don't just appear. It takes a while. Ten more babies weren't born at once. Job and his wife had raised their kids. They were on the horizon of grandkids when all of theirs died. I don't know how old they were when they had to start having kids again, but my guess is at least my age. I'm 46. If I had ten more kids right now, I'd probably be about 66 when the last one was born. Nearly 86 when they were all finally raised.

All along the way, I'd have to go through the process of re-accomplishing what I'd already done. Of laying in bed at night equally grateful that God had given me another one to love and cherish while acutely aware at once of the graves in the backyard that each new baby somehow didn't replace. Even in my gratitude at being given another opportunity, I know it wouldn't be easy. Life comes with burden and frustration either way.

Letting perseverance have its way can be at times the hardest cure for the hardest pain. It makes no earthly sense. It wasn't ever intended to. That's the purpose of faith. It sees what our eyes have no vision for. Perseverance is an opportunity. One we don't want to choose yet desperately need. Whether or not we allow it to do its work just as God allows tragedy to reshape His creation while He repurposes it for good is entirely our decision. It is not an easy one and I don't want to gloss over that. I don't want to act like any of this is easy. If I've learned anything, it is that, no matter how many times I've been through this, I will wrestle with it again. This battle is not once and done.

Satan is coming back, just like he did with Job. When one thing doesn't work, he tries another form of attack. We have been commissioned into war and there is no other way out than through. I've wrestled so much, especially in the last year, with how hard all of this is to live out. I understand the intellectual reality of it but it's the living of it that brings me to my knees. My capacity to comprehend does not equate to my ability to endure. Maybe that's where you find yourself. Maybe you, like me, thought perseverance wouldn't be something you were called to so many times over. Maybe you also feel weary. Maybe you've experienced things that feel impossible to endure and, in the human perspective, actually are without some type of divine intercession.

Sometimes I think we unconsciously believe that persevering has a limit, a stop sign, a plateau point where we arrive. Yet, over and over we find ourselves weaving our way right to left, left to right, through switchback after switchback, making less progress up the mountainside than we are trudging side to side. Down can eventually start to seem like a better choice, or at least a faster one. It can feel so exhausting navigating hills and valleys, jungles and deserts, rivers and wastelands, pits and hunger, and we wonder when it all will be over. What the point will have been when we're done.

I think Job felt some of this desperation. Even in his faith that he could trust God or his willful declaration that he would despite all it cost him, he was still human. He still experienced the effects of war. The spiritual battle didn't escape him and the invisible combat occurring in the heavenly realms was made visible through Job's earthly circumstances. That's what Satan's counting on – that we'll give more heed to our temporary conditions than our eternal ones. It's

242

why God tells us faith is our greatest need, dependency the life support on which we all need to put ourselves.

Trouble is never going to *feel* like scripture says it actually is, like "treasures of darkness, riches stored in secret places," (Isaiah 45:3) but then feelings are never absolute truth. Sometimes they're the things that deceive us the most. This is why we have to see through eyes of faith, a faith that is tested so it produces in us, like it did in Job, the ability to persevere. Perseverance is where we get to reap the pure joy James talks about. Not in its midst, but like Job, on its back end. The one where we are made complete, where our lack is filled. Where, like Job eventually did, we find our stories rewritten and our history redeemed.

We reconcile our disenchantment with the God who allowed tragedy by being enchanted with the God that Job found in the storm.

One big enough to make tragedy not Satan's way of conquering us but our way of partnering with God in conquering him. Evil has a limited day. Goodness doesn't. That's the beauty of it.

My friends weren't wrong that God's goodness is worthy of focusing on. It is. Absolutely. It's just that, in order to experience that, sometimes we need the God who is an Overcomer. The One who does battle in heavenly places for earthly reasons. The One who allows earthly conflict to accomplish heavenly purposes. The One who is Eternal and redeems all things. The One with whom an audience causes disenchantment to flee.

All of us Modern Day Jobs have a place to take these things. A God big enough to handle them. A God dangerous enough to hold us while we wrestle and rail like Job with our reality. He is our one sufficiency. Our only hope. Emmanuel. God with us.

The God we most need.

"This is what the LORD says –
your Redeemer, who formed you in the womb:

I am the LORD,
who has made all things,
who alone stretched out the heavens,
who spread out the earth by myself...

I will give you the treasures of darkness,
riches stored in secret places,
so that you may know that I am the LORD,
the God of Israel, who summons you by name...

I am the LORD, and there is no other;
apart from me there is no God.
I will strengthen you,
though you have not acknowledged me,
so that from the rising of the sun
to the place of its setting
men may know there is none besides me.
I am the LORD, and there is no other."

~Isaiah 44:24, 45:3, 5-6

Author's Note

I never intended to write this book and a number of people have asked me how it came to be. I can say with all honesty, it wasn't me. I don't know that I ever would have set out to write a book, much less this one. Instead, I think the story has written me. It's been in the writing that I've realized God was always the one authoring it and I'm just living the experience of it. And that's really what we were created for anyway.

There is so much more to say. There always is. God is always bigger than we will know and understanding Him broader than life itself. I didn't set out to tackle the life of Job and I know I have barely begun to cover some drops in the bucket. This is life, really my own, as it was handed to me. I still don't know what I don't know and I think I will continue to study the life of Job for the rest of my days. There is so much left into which to tap. So much I wrote that isn't even included on these pages.

I think in part God shared with us the story of Job because He wants us to share our pain. I think representing Him, being His ambassadors in this world, is the same thing as I saw but didn't at all understand when I was a little girl. We live in a world full of people in pain. The cure isn't ridding the earth of pain. It isn't to eliminate suffering. We are called to bring light to dark places and that's really the thing that I hope we all take away. As much as God has shed light on our dark space, He wants us to do the same.

As I said at the beginning, trench dwelling is one of the places God has enabled me to traverse well. I can't fix your pain and I can't eradicate your suffering. What I can do is hold space. Where I am unable to be physically present with you, know that I have prayed. Over every life, every person, every one that is touched in any way through the words God's allowed me to put on these pages. I'd love to hear your stories. I'd love to know how you too have learned to traverse pain. How your disenchantment with God led you down roads unexpected. If that is a road you are still traveling, one where you feel the horizon never ending, or like me – one you've been on and now find yourself on yet again, you are not alone. Feel free to reach out. I'd love to connect.

Acknowledgements

First and foremost, to Emmanuel, the God who is With Me. It's You. It's always been You. You are the beginning and the end of my story, the One who sees me, who never runs away. Without you, there would be no story, no words worth sharing, no encouragement for people in the trenches. You have brought purpose out of my pain, birthed meaning to my days, and showed me the tangible reality of how You weave goodness into shattered dreams. It is because of You that I now know - trouble was always part of the journey, the doorway to the path home. Thank you for the courage to speak bold truth, to not give weight to opinions stated, and to allow my life's tragedies to show me what it really means to get dirty just like You. It's always been grace upon grace.

Dad - I know you couldn't be here today, but there wasn't one page of this book that you weren't present in while I was writing. Every page holds a piece of you. This story and these words are as much yours as my own. I hope that when I get to heaven to see you, you'll hug me tight and say, "Precious daughter, this was always the plan all along and it was worth every bit of the journey. Now you know – it was for us both." I may cry now and I may cry then, but in large measure because of you, I know what it means to persevere. I am so grateful for your example and your dedication to this. It has made an incredible difference and not just for me but for so many people. Thank you.

To my kids (and the ones our family keeps growing to include too) – If Grandpa hadn't died, we wouldn't know what it means to design our own story of faith. He paved us the way and now it's our turn to carry the torch. It was always going to be that way, we just didn't know it. If life hadn't fallen apart not just once, but twice, I'd never know just how deep your love, commitment, and wisdom lie. Y'all are some of my most favorite humans on earth and I love you all more than words can ever convey. So much of this journey is yours as well as my own. We are all better people for not only having known and been loved by Grandpa and each other, but also for having our own experiences of suffering that force us into the trenches of change. There will never be a day that I don't pray for you and wish not only goodness for you but also enough shattered dreams that we all come to understand exactly what Grandpa did. That somehow God's best for our lives always includes both. May you want Him and seek Him more than you ever do anything else.

To Ben – God put you on this planet to bring so much life to places. Places that I thought wouldn't ever be held again once my Dad died. Places that bring people you'd never expect together. Like us. In one year, there was so much life and death, not just once but twice, and you were present in both. You hug like God and pray with such gratitude that I can't help but be left each time with peace. I know you never imagined this would be your story. I didn't imagine it being mine either. Yet, here we are, "your hand in my hand, that eye-to-eye reflection, all the fights, the mad, the good, the bad, the way love hurts and heals." Maybe the hurt really is the healing. Thank you for letting your story become our story, lives torn apart and rewoven together into something both hard and beautiful. The two things we each do best. You are my favorite random adventure partner, my favorite person to laugh with, and my favorite arms to be held inside. No matter how many days we get together, I will always want so many more. I love you.

To Scott Monk – You have so unexpectedly championed this book and, in turn, me before ever having read a word. You have no idea how many times that has kept me going. I appreciate you and love sharing our Enneagram 4ness. What I have come to value perhaps most of all is your pause. You pause to think, pause to pray, pause to collect your thoughts. You pause to allow God to show up in a moment and it invites an indwelling power to truly be present "on earth as it is in heaven." Thank you for reading, commenting, encouraging, and most of all – for being you.

To Michelle Hurst – Somehow life really does come full circle and sometimes in the most beautifully unexpected ways. Thank you for taking on this project in a very busy season and for giving me not only honest feedback but what feels like a part of you. I am grateful for your willingness not just to write a synopsis, but also to allow what is written here to impact you. Your words ground me in a way I still don't have my own words to describe and I am so grateful to have the opportunity to do this part of life with you. A writer's life isn't one we can really explain but it means so much to share it with someone else on the same road. Thank you, thank you, thank you.

To Kyle Colborn, Corbitt, and Colborn Audio Recording Studio – When I saw a recording studio pop up here in little College Station, Texas, I thought how crazy it was that this was life. Then I read your bio and thought, "Wow. God really does appoint everything a time and place and season. Nothing is an accident." For believing in this vision just by hearing my idea, for taking a chance on me, for working with me week after week and teaching me how to do something I'd never in a million years have even thought of, thank you. You really do help people steward their creative abilities and I am so glad that this is your journey too. https://colbornaudiorecording.com/

To Sara, Krista, and Clarissa – You were the first ones to remind me that love sees you. The first to send a note, over 2,000 miles away, that said our hearts hurt because yours does too. Thank you for over 4 decades of never letting go, always showing up, always being true. Life has taken us on roads we never imagined. It's been terrible and it's been beautiful and I can't imagine having done it with anyone else but you. I had no idea this would be our destiny but here we are and I'm grateful for us learning even now, more than 40 years later, how to be more real together. Sometimes it is the family you choose that binds your wounds more than anyone else.

To our Downtown Bryan Peeps – Y'all have left an impact on my life that I can say is unique to you. You have been light and love, joy and support, tears and hugs, wisdom and acceptance, creativity and fun in ways the world needs so much more of. You've shown me that community doesn't always have to have everything in common. We can be so different and yet all have something to offer. It's been an unexpected connection and one I'm so very grateful for. You've taught me a lot about being true. Extra big hugs to you guys, Schaefer and JT. Your presence said everything I needed to know on one of my very worst days and I love you both so much.

To Justin and Alyson Swiderski – Y'all showed up in the most random place (Sacul, TX) and grew some stuff and none of us knew you were planting love and friendship too. I might've never told you but meeting y'all that day – on the heels of a deep season of loss of community and fear of what tomorrow held – showed me that God had gone before me into every one of my days and yours too. Y'all and we were exactly where we all were supposed to be. It's rare to meet people and instantly know they're your people, but that is true with you. Thanks for being an unexpected reminder that love is real and hope is true.

To Will Harris – Thank you for saying hard things in hard spaces. Thank you for pursuing the Lord with all you are and constantly giving over your heart. Thank you for challenge and wisdom, for truth a world doesn't want but needs to hear, for a love so deep and compassionate that it beckons us to draw near. Thank you for wrestling and being courageous enough to share it. To go first more often than most of us dare and to seek out a knowledge of God and His ways that changes how the rest of us know Him and live. And To Your Precious Wife, Marissa – you exemplify love, support, and care at a level not many people do. Your prayers change things. Your heart is evident and I know it's a lot to do all you do, so know that every single moment matters. The hard ones, the good ones, the ones that seem entirely overlooked – not one is background noise. Every single one is building life that would not and could not exist without you. You are seen and your presence matters.

To Blake Chilton – There is a clinging to truth that resides in you that has not only challenged and changed my life but also many others' too. I know it's anything but easy to show up week after week and do what you do, much less to uproot your life, plant a church, and constantly nurture not only it but your own growth too. You never preach as if arrival or perfection in this life are the goal. Instead, you make faithfulness possible. I appreciate your heart, dedication, and continual pursuit of the Lord and His people. Thank you for being you.

To Mom – Thank you for the many discussions, for the hours devoted to reading and commenting, and for exploring subjects so hard for both of us to relive. You've been a sounding board in many ways and your supportive encouragement has made a big difference. You've made me think more and understand God better. You poured into a God-instilled love for words in me when I was first on this planet and now again decades later. I am so very grateful for this gift.

To Ashley L. – This is a book you may never read. For all of our differences, there is so much we share and you have been a light for me on some really dark days. A reminder that life doesn't always look at all the way we imagined and that's ok. Your picture hangs on my fridge and I see it daily. I doubt I will ever take it down. I love you. You matter. It is a gift to call you friend.

Granny – Your steadfastness, your joy, your pursuit of a life that was led by discipline yet marked by joy has shown me that hard is possible. Life doesn't have to be a constant chore. We can be what makes the difference. That's what you and Grandpa were for me. Thank you for taking so very many notes, for pursuing God so much that the Bibles you left behind are filled to the brim with the story of your pursuit. You said it like it was too – it wasn't just fluff, meant to "suffice." You wrote truth and I appreciate your legacy along with Grandpa's and Dad's of staying true. Of doing the hard things, day in and day out, and renewing your mind and attitude so that instead of the hard side of the coin being your greatest truth, it was the joy of the Lord being your strength. May I be more like you.

Job – Not that many people have set out to tackle your life in a book and I'm not sure my attempt here is really sufficient. A whole lot of us have related and that's perhaps more where I have landed. I know you probably didn't see and at the time may not have cared if your experience was going to reach billions, but it has. And I'm so grateful to be one of them. When I get to heaven, I look forward to hearing your perspective, not just the one I think you had. There's so much I'm sure I've missed. I'm likely one that you'd have had to pray for too. My hope is that my life, like yours, doesn't end just old and full of loss but also old and full of years.

Jesus, always You are the beginning and the end. None of this would be possible without You. I cannot seem to escape this. You really are better than all we can ask or imagine, and You're greater than all that we must endure. I'll never understand a love so extravagant and the beautiful thing is that I don't have to. Being more than I can even comprehend is what makes you so safe, so dangerous, so wholly worth entrusting myself to. When I am afraid, You are there. When I am wandering, You are there. When I am enraged and frustrated and overwhelmed with this world, You understand. There is no place I can go, no emotion I can experience that you don't get. Every time I'm hit with another flaming arrow of the enemy and I forget all these things that are true amidst all the pain, You help me find my way back to You, to Truth, again. Thank you for taking on skin. For doing things none of us humans ever would. I don't know what it will be like to see You face to face but I can imagine my words will only fall short. I look forward to that day more than anything. May I never get so wrapped up on this earth in things so good that I forget they are the result of You being so holy. May I continue to work out this gift of salvation in ways that make me realize I constantly need You. Give me a right perspective of myself and a right perspective of You. May they always end up in the right order. Thank You for doing the absolutely unexpected and inviting us into a story so terrible, so tragic, so wonderful, so magnificent, so *much* that it renders us, like Job, speechless and in awe of You. May we never stop seeking that. Keep changing us into Your likeness. May it not be once our lives are over that it mattered that *we* lived, but that You lived in us and that *You* are the one the world witnessed. May our lives be Your gift. I love you.

About the Author

Alanna Matcek is a writer and freelance professional whose personal journey through loss, grief, change, and growth have shaped her passion for helping others navigate real-life challenges. With over 20 years in the legal industry and a Master's Degree in Counseling and Life Coaching, Alanna has walked with thousands of people through some of life's darkest moments. She brings a unique perspective to the concepts of resiliency and suffering, offering others guidance, support, and practical tools for growth. Alanna lives in Texas with her husband, three dogs, and an ever-growing family of adult children, stepchildren, and grandchildren. Her favorite activities besides reading, writing, and good conversation involve Jeeps, Harleys, live music, and photographing nature. *Modern Day Job* is her first published book.

Contact Alanna via e-mail:

alannamatcek@yahoo.com

Follow Alanna on various social media platforms:

Instagram (alanna.matcek)

Facebook (Alanna Matcek)

Notes

Chapter One: Trouble

[1] *Oxford English Dictionary*, s.v. "disenchantment (*n.*)," July 2023, https://doi.org/10.1093/OED/1509306048
[2] Lewis, C.S. and Pauline Baynes. 1970. *The Lion, The Witch and The Wardrobe: A Story for Children*. New York, NY: Collier Books.

Chapter Two: The Way Through

[3] Lewis, C.S. 1967. *Letters to an American Lady*. Grand Rapids: Wm. B. Eerdmans Publishing Co. This was written on June 17, 1963 to Mary Willis Shelburne.
[4] July 18, 2016, Verily Magazine, O., The Oprah Magazine. See also: Winfrey, Oprah. *"What I Know For Sure."* New York, NY: Macmillan.
[5] The Twelve Steps | Alcoholics Anonymous (aa.org). https://www.aa.org/the-twelve-steps

Chapter Three: Character on Trial

[6] McKee, Robert. 1997. *Story: Substance, Structure, Style, and the Principles of Screenwriting*. New York, NY: Harper Collins Publishers, Inc.
[7] Martin, Civilla D. "His Eye Is on the Sparrow." 1905. Written by songwriter Civilla D. Martin and composed by composer Charles H. Gabriel. His Eye Is On The Sparrow « HymnPod. https://hymnpod.com/2009/03/07/his-eye-is-on-the-sparrow/ See also: Vincent D. Homan (2013). *A Foot in Two Worlds: A Pastor's Journey From Grief to Hope*. WestBow Press. p. 112.

Chapter Four: When Hope Takes a Back Seat

[8] Original author unknown. https://www.inspirationalstories.com/proverbs/italian-hope-is-the-last-thing-ever-lost/
[9] Brown, Brené. 2015. *Rising Strong*. London, England: Vermilion.

Chapter Five: Knowing

[10] Tim Burton, Danny Elfman, Jonathan Sheffer, Steve Bartek, and Bruce Fowler. *BATMAN RETURNS*. USA/UK, 1992.

Chapter Six: Pain

[11] Romans 8:24, KJV & Philippians 3:7, TLB, emphasis mine
[12] Jalāl al-Dīn Rūmī (Maulana), Jelaluddin Rumi, Kabir Helminski, Andrew Harvey. 2005. *"The Rumi Collection: An Anthology of Translations of Mevlâna Jalâluddin Rumi"*, p.7, Shambhala Publications.
[13] Lewis, C.S. 2001. *The Problem of Pain*. New York, NY: HarperOne.
[14] *"Jim Morrison: Ten Years Gone"*. "Creem Magazine" Interview with Lizzie James, 1981.

Chapter Seven: The Driver Named Trust

[15] Maya Ying Lin, Michael Brenson. 1998. *"Maya Lin"*, Elemond-Electa.

Chapter Eight: The Wilderness Isn't Home

[16] Tolkien, J. R. R. 1991. *The Fellowship of the Ring*. The Lord of the Rings 1. London, England: HarperCollins.
[17] Henley, William E. 1888. *Book of Verses*. London: D. Nutt. (The title "Invictus" was added by Arthur Quiller-Couch when the poem was printed in the *Oxford Book of English Verse. See* Arthur Thomas Quiller-Couch, ed. (1902). *The Oxford Book of English Verse, 1250–1900* (1st (6th impression) ed.). Oxford: Clarendon Press. p. 1019.)

Chapter Nine: Longing

[18] https://www.goodreads.com/quotes/675472-longing-is-the-agony-of-the-nearness-of-the-distant. Although I cannot locate the original source, this quote is regularly attributed to Martin Heidegger, thus I have done so here as well based on all information I could find.

Chapter Ten: Faith and The Injustice of It All

[19] Bukowski, Charles. 1982. *Ham on Rye*. Santa Barbara: Black Sparrow.
[20] Spafford, Horatio G. "It Is Well with My Soul." 1873. It Is Well with My Soul > Lyrics | Horatio G. Spafford (timelesstruths.org)

Chapter Eleven: For the Joy

[21] Majors, Katie Davis. Grief. *Facebook*. February 2, 2023.
[22] Nouwen, Henri. 1994. *Here and Now: Living in the Spirit*. New York, NY: The Crossroad Publishing Company, Kindle.

Chapter Twelve: Waiting

[23] Elliot, Elisabeth. 1984. *Passion and Purity: Learning to Bring Your Love Life Under Christ's Control.* Old Tappan, N.J.: Revell.

The Interlude

[24] Tozer, A.W. 1948. *The Pursuit of God: The Human Thirst for the Divine.* See also: https://www.standardebooks.org/ebooks/a-w-tozer/the-pursuit-of-god.
[25] "Interlude." *Merriam-Webster.com.* 2024. https://www.merriam-webster.com (2 April 2024). https://www.merriam-webster.com/dictionary/interlude.
[26] *Oxford English Dictionary,* s.v. "providence (*n.*)," November 2022, https://doi.org/10.1093/OED/4224794687.
[27] "Grace." Collins English Dictionary – Complete and Unabridged, 12th Edition 2014 © HarperCollins Publishers 1991, 1994, 1998, 2000, 2003, 2006, 2007, 2009, 2011, 2014.
[28] Genesis 3:4 and 3:7.

Chapter Thirteen – Eternal Perspective

[29] https://www.goodreads.com/quotes/360384-if-we-are-the-sheep-of-his-pasture-remember-that Note: Although this quote is readily available and continually attributed to Jim Elliot online, I cannot locate with certainty the original source. My guess is it might be in his journals, all of which I have not yet read. Thus, my attribution here is granted to him based on all information I could locate.
[30] Lemmel, Helen H. "Turn Your Eyes Upon Jesus." 1922. Turn Your Eyes upon Jesus > Lyrics | Helen H. Lemmel (timelesstruths.org)

Chapter Fourteen: Desire

[31] Rowling, J.K. and Mary, GrandPré. 1999. *Harry Potter and the Chamber of Secrets.* New York, NY: Arthur A. Levine Books, an imprint of Scholastic Press.
[32] McConaughey, Matthew. 2020. *Greenlights.* New York, NY: Crown.
[33] Job 1:8, Job 2:3, Job 42:7-8
[34] "Integrity." American Heritage® Dictionary of the English Language, Fifth Edition. Copyright © 2016 by Houghton Mifflin Harcourt Publishing Company. Published by Houghton Mifflin Harcourt Publishing Company. All rights reserved.
[35] Giglio, Louie. 2021. *Don't Give the Enemy a Seat at Your Table.* Nashville, TN: Passion Publishing, W Publishing Group, an imprint of Thomas Nelson.

Chapter Fifteen: Whose Story Is This Anyway?

[36] Nazarian, Vera. 2010. *The Perpetual Calendar of Inspiration.*

Highgate Center, VT: Spirit, an imprint of Norilana Books.
[37] Dobkin, David, Director. *Fred Claus*. Warner Bros. 2007.

Chapter Sixteen: On Being Wounded People

[38] Nouwen, Henri. 1972. *The Wounded Healer*. New York: NY. Image Doubleday.
[39] Angelou, Maya. 2009. *I Know Why the Caged Bird Sings* (1st ed.). New York, NY: Ballantine Books.
[40] Crowe, Cameron. 1996. *Jerry Maguire*. United States: TriStar Pictures.
[41] Psalm 139
[42] Freeman, Emilie. "194: Being Human with Kate Bowler." The Next Right Thing. September 28, 2021. https://emilypfreeman.com/podcast/194/.
[43] Bowler, Kate. 2021. *No Cure for Being Human: (And Other Truths I Need to Hear)*. New York, NY: Random House.

Chapter Seventeen: Managing Expectations

[44] Thomas, Gary. 2019. *When to Walk Away: Finding Freedom from Toxic People*. Grand Rapids, MI: Zondervan.
[45] Brown, Brené. 2021. *Atlas of the Heart: Mapping Meaningful Connection and the Language of Human Experience*. New York, NY: Random House.
[46] *Id.*
[47] Rowe, Mike. "304: The Shadow on the Wall is You with Scott Strode." The Way I Heard It with Mike Rowe. March 7, 2023. https://podcasts.apple.com/us/podcast/304-the-shadow-on-the-wall-is-you-with-scott-strode/id1087110764?i=1000603130391.

Chapter Eighteen: Sanctuary on a Desert Road

[49] Date unknown but believed to be during a sermon Martin Luther King, Jr. gave in August 1958.
[49] "Sanctuary" (n.) © Cambridge University Press & Assessment 2024.
[50] Freeman, Emilie. "212: How to Walk Out of a Room." The Next Right Thing. February 2022. https://emilypfreeman.com/podcast/212/.
[51] *Where I Belong* by Building 429. Songwriters Jason Ingram and Jason Roy. Essential Records. 2011.
[52] Parsons, John. *Sanctuary of the Heart: Further thoughts on Parashat Terumah*. Publication date unknown. Accessed 2024. https://hebrew4christians.com/Scripture/Parashah/Summaries/Terumah/Sanctuary/sanctuary.html.
[53] *Id.*
[54] I wrote this quote on a sticky note more than 10 years ago. I believe

it may have been stated or written by Linda Dillow in connection with her book *Calm My Anxious Heart* but I have been unable to verify that with certainty. I recall writing it down after reading her book and meeting her many years later at a women's event where she spoke. It could be a paraphrase though too many years have passed now for me to recall.

Chapter Nineteen: The Redemption Piece

[55] I cannot locate the original source of when Elisabeth Elliot stated this. However, it is consistently attributed to her, therefore I have done so here. https://www.azquotes.com/quote/823706.

[56] Crockett, David. 1835. Tennessee. https://www.tsl.texas.gov/treasures/republic/alamo/crockett-01.html.

[57] Lewis, C.S. 1980. *The Weight of Glory and Other Addresses, Revised and Expanded Edition.* New York, NY: Macmillan.

[58] *Run To The Father* by Cody Carnes and Kari Jobe. Songwriters Matt Maher, Ran Jackson, and Cody Carnes. Capitol Christian Music Group. 2019.

[59] Furtick, Holly. "Waiting on an Answer." September 15, 2023. 20:20 https://www.youtube.com/watch?v=Q4naaU4fRMk

[60] *Id.* 21:43

Chapter Twenty: Grief

[61] Tozer, A.W. 2015. *The Root of the Righteous.* Chicago, IL: Moody Publishers. (Originally written in 1955 and published by Christian Publications, Inc. © 1995, 1986 by Lowell Tozer.)

[62] Newkirk, Drew. "Enneagram type 4. Epic Overview." May 23, 2022. 45:25. https://www.youtube.com/watch?v=p-LCB7El7m8&list=PLtkCVeJvlLO2vOjIZ539VLqMlSwvynlwk&index=14.

[63] Tozer, A.W. 1948. *The Pursuit of God: The Human Thirst for the Divine.* See also: https://www.standardebooks.org/ebooks/a-w-tozer/the-pursuit-of-god.

Chapter Twenty One: Agency

[64] TerKeurst, Lysa. 2020. *Forgiving What You Can't Forget.* Nashville, TN: Thomas Nelson.

[65] Spafford, Horatio G. "It Is Well with My Soul." 1873. It Is Well with My Soul > Lyrics | Horatio G. Spafford (timelesstruths.org)

[66] Elliot, Jim. October 28, 1949. https://www.kevinhalloran.net/jim-elliot-quote-he-is-no-fool/. See also: Henry, Matthew. 1855. "He is no fool who parts with that which he cannot keep, when he is sure to be recompensed with that which he cannot lose." *(The Complete Works of*

the Rev. Matthew Henry [his unfinished commentary being excepted], London: A. Fullarton & Co., 1855 [reprinted Grand Rapids: Baker Book House, 1979], vol. II, p. 634)

Chapter Twenty Two: Bearing Witness

[67] Perry, Jackie Hill. "Hagar: The Suffering Servant (Genesis 16)." November 28, 2023. 55:39. https://www.youtube.com/watch?v=Xn2nc78Dftg.
[68] Acts 1:15-26

Chapter Twenty Three: Vessels

[69] Chambers, Oswald. 2014. *The Quotable Oswald Chambers*. Reprint Edition. Grand Rapids, MI: Our Daily Bread Publishing.
[70] The Ed Clay Show. "The Power of Family, Faith and Music: Drake White's Inspirational Story." February 2, 2024. https://youtu.be/SrknplxpDTg. Clip mentioned here was posted by Drake White on February 7, 2024 on his Instagram page: DrakeWhiteStomp.
[71] Lewis, C.S. 1952. *Mere Christianity*. United Kingdom: Geoffrey Bles. "Imagine yourself as a living house. God comes in to rebuild that house. At first, perhaps, you can understand what He is doing. He is getting the drains right and stopping the leaks in the roof and so on; you knew that those jobs needed doing and so you are not surprised. But presently He starts knocking the house about in a way that hurts abominably and does not seem to make any sense. What on earth is He up to? The explanation is that He is building quite a different house from the one you thought of - throwing out a new wing here, putting on an extra floor there, running up towers, making courtyards. You thought you were being made into a decent little cottage: but He is building a palace. He intends to come and live in it Himself."
[72] https://watch.thechosen.tv

Chapter Twenty Four: Perseverance

[73] Quote believed to be from Nelson Mandela. I am not the first to try to discover its origins. This is the closest I could locate: https://quoteinvestigator.com/2016/01/05/done/.
[74] Proverbs 18:21
[75] "Adversary." Abused, Confused, & Misused Words by Mary Embree. Copyright © 2007, 2013 by Mary Embree. https://www.thefreedictionary.com/adversary.
[76] Lewis, C.S. and Pauline Baynes. 1970. *The Lion, The Witch and The Wardrobe: A Story for Children*. New York, NY: Collier Books.

[77] "Perseverance." Collins COBUILD Advanced Learner's Dictionary. Copyright © HarperCollins Publishers. 2024.

[78] *Vocabulary.com Dictionary*, s.v. "perseverance," accessed April 11, 2024. https://www.vocabulary.com/dictionary/perseverance.

[79] 1 Peter 1:7

[80] https://www.southernliving.com/culture/dolly-parton-quotes. Although I cannot locate the original source for this quote, it is repeatedly attributed to Dolly Parton. Thus, I've done likewise here.

www.ingramcontent.com/pod-product-compliance
Lightning Source LLC
Chambersburg PA
CBHW062154080426
42734CB00010B/1684